AT HOME
with the WORD
2 0 0 7

Sunday Scriptures and
Scripture Insights

James Weaver
Anne Elizabeth Sweet, OSCO
Mary Ellen Hynes
Jennifer Willems

ALSO AVAILABLE IN A LARGE PRINT EDITION

LTP
LITURGY
TRAINING
PUBLICATIONS

Acknowledgments

All scripture excerpts used in this work are taken from the *Lectionary for Mass for Use in the Dioceses of the United States of America, second typical edition, Volume 1* copyright © 1970, 1997, 1998 Confraternity of Christian Doctrine, Washington, D.C. All rights reserved. No part of this work may be reproduced or transmitted in any form or by any means, electronic or mechanical, including photocopying, recording, or by any information storage retrieval system, without permission in writing from the copyright owner.

Seasonal prayers, Prayers before Reading the Word and Prayers after Reading the Word are from: *Prayers for Sundays and Seasons, Year C* by Peter Scagnelli, Chicago: Liturgy Training Publications, 1997.

AT HOME WITH THE WORD 2007 © 2006 Archdiocese of Chicago: Liturgy Training Publications, 1800 North Hermitage Avenue, Chicago IL 60622; 1-800-933-1800; fax 1-800-933-7094; orders@ltp.org; www.LTP.org. All rights reserved.

Visit our website at www.LTP.org.

The cover art for this year's *At Home with the Word* is by Jeanne Troxel. The interior art is by Kathy Ann Sullivan. The book was edited by Mary Fox and Lorie Simmons. Mary Fox was the production editor. The design is by Anne Fritzinger. Kari Nicholls typeset the book in Matrix and Minion.

Printed in the United States of America.

ISBN-10: 1-56854-566-5
ISBN-13: 978-1-56854-566-0

AHW07

Welcome to At Home with the Word 2007

SCRIPTURE READINGS

For each Sunday you will find full texts of the three readings, as well as (on most Sundays) the psalm from the *Lectionary for Mass* proclaimed in Roman Catholic churches in the United States.

SCRIPTURE INSIGHTS

Two scripture scholars share the fruits of their studies and reflection on scripture. James L. Weaver holds degrees from Yale University and the University of Chicago in history, divinity, and New Testament and Early Christian Literature. He is pursuing a doctorate in the Department of New Testament and Early Christian Literature at the University of Chicago. He has been a catechist with the Rite of Christian Initiation of Adults at a parish in Chicago and taught Christology for the Archdiocese of Chicago. His main research interest is biblical interpretation in the early Church. James has written Scripture Insights for Advent, Christmas, Lent, and Easter seasons, as well as for the solemnities of the Most Holy Trinity and the Body and Blood of Christ. Sister Anne Elizabeth Sweet has an MA in theology from Catholic Theological Union and a Ph.D. in New Testament and Early Church History from the University of Notre Dame. She has lived the monastic life for thirty-five years, the first twenty-five as a Benedictine working in religious education. For the past ten years she has been a Trappestine sister at Our Lady of the Mississippi Abbey, teaching at various abbeys and writing for *Homily Service, Celebration, The Bible Today, Cistercian Studies Quarterly,* and the Seasons of Faith religious education series. She also arranges publicity for the abbey's candy business. Sister Anne Elizabeth has written Scripture Insights for Ordinary Time.

PRACTICE OF PRAYER

Here, on most Sundays, you will find at least a part of the responsorial psalm. Seasonal prayers for beginning and ending your scripture study are provided at the opening of each season of the year.

PRACTICE OF VIRTUE (FAITH, HOPE, OR CHARITY)

Two writers focus on these most essential human virtues. Mary Ellen Hynes holds master's degrees in pastoral studies and religious education from Loyola University Chicago. She is a theology teacher and a freelance writer. Mary Ellen has written the practices for Advent, Lent, Easter, Pentecost, the Ascension of the Lord, the solemnities of the Most Holy Trinity and the Body and Blood of Christ, and the Sixth and Seventh Sundays in Ordinary Time.

Jennifer Willems is the assistant editor of the Catholic Post, Peoria, Illinois, and has freelanced for religious publications. She has been a pastoral associate and the director of the Rite of Christian Initiation of Adults process. Jennifer has written the practices for Christmas, Easter, most of Ordinary Time, and the solemnity of Christ the King.

WEEKDAY READINGS

For those who want to read more scripture, see the opening of each season for a list of scripture texts read at Mass on weekdays and on feasts falling on weekdays.

ART FOR THE YEAR OF LUKE

For the cover, Jeanne Troxel shows an inviting corner to study Scripture. Just as God keeps calling us to listen to his word, so does this scene. The crucifix is a representation of the San Damiano cross. It was at that cross that Saint Francis heard God call him to repair the church. Jeanne, a Chicago resident, works in oils and pastels. She earned a bachelor of arts degree in visual communications at Indiana University, Bloomington, and studied painting and drawing at the Art Institute of Chicago.

Kathy Ann Sullivan continues the contemplative mood with the interior designs. Her scratchboard technique draws viewers to meditate on the liturgical seasons. From the images of our ancestors in faith on the Jesse tree to the oil lamps in the Ordinary Time/Fall depiction, the symbols pull us into phases of the church year. Kathy Ann designed the biblical water scenes in the baptismal font at Saint Mary's Cathedral, Colorado Springs.

Table of Contents

The Season of Lent

The Paschal Triduum

The Easter Season

Summer Ordinary Time

Autumn Ordinary Time

The Lectionary

by Martin F. Connell

WHAT IS A LECTIONARY?

A lectionary is an ordered selection of readings, chosen from both testaments of the Bible, for proclamation in the assembly gathered for worship. Lectionaries have been used for Christian worship since the fourth century. Before the invention of the printing press in the fifteenth century, the selection and order of the readings differed somewhat from church to church, often reflecting the issues that were important to the local communities of the time.

For the four centuries between the Council of Trent (1545–1563) and the Second Vatican Council (1963–1965), the readings in most Catholic churches varied little from year to year and were proclaimed in Latin, a language that many Catholics no longer understood. Vatican II brought dramatic changes. It allowed the language of the people to be used in the liturgy and initiated a revision of the Lectionary. The Bible became far more accessible to Catholics and once again a vibrant source of our faith and tradition.

THE THREE-YEAR LECTIONARY CYCLE

The new Lectionary that appeared in 1970 introduced a three-year plan that allowed a fuller selection of readings from the Bible. During year A, the Gospel readings for Ordinary Time are taken from Matthew, for Year B from Mark, and for year C from Luke. This liturgical year 2007 begins on the First Sunday of Advent, December 3, 2006, and ends with the celebration of Christ the King, November 25, 2007. It is Year C, the year of Luke.

YEAR C: THE GOSPEL OF LUKE

Most of the Gospel readings proclaimed in your Sunday assembly this year and printed in *At Home with the Word 2007* are from the Gospel of Luke. The introduction to this gospel on pages 8–9 and the Scripture Insights for each week will help you recognize and appreciate the contribution this Gospel makes to our faith.

THE GOSPEL OF JOHN

You might ask: What about the Fourth Gospel? The Gospel of John is not assigned a year of its own because it constitutes so much of our reading during certain seasons and times of the year.

The readings from Year A on the third, fourth, and fifth Sundays of Lent are from the Gospel of John, and they are proclaimed every year in parishes celebrating the Rite of Christian Initiation of Adults (RCIA) when the elect are present. These three wonderful stories from the Gospel of John — the woman at the well (on the third Sunday), the man born blind (on the fourth Sunday), and the raising of Lazarus (on the fifth Sunday) — accompany the celebration of the scrutinies in the process of Christian initiation. During Years B and C, you will find two sets of readings on these Sundays in *At Home with the Word:* one set for Sunday Masses at which the scrutinies of the RCIA are celebrated and another set for masses at which they are not celebrated.

The Gospel of John also appears for the Mass of the Lord's Supper on Holy Thursday and for the long Passion reading on Good Friday. And on most of the Sundays of Easter—during the fifty days from Easter Sunday until Pentecost—the Gospel of John is proclaimed at the liturgy.

THE DIFFERENCE BETWEEN THE BIBLE AND THE LECTIONARY

Because the Lectionary uses selections from the Bible arranged according to the seasons and feasts of the church year, the assembly often hears a mixture of appropriate texts "out of order" from their position in the Bible. However the overall shape of the Lectionary comes from the ancient church practice of *lectio continua*, a Latin term that describes the successive reading through books of the Bible from Sunday to Sunday.

You can see *lectio continua* in practice if you consider the Gospel texts for the Eleventh Sunday in Ordinary Time, June 17, up to the solemnity of Christ the King, November 25. Though not every verse is included, the Lectionary moves from chapter 7 in Luke through chapter 23.

Although Christians hold the Gospels in particular reverence, the first two readings provide strong teaching as well and make up nearly two–thirds of the material in the Lectionary. The first reading often echoes some image or idea in the Gospel, as is the Church's intention. The second reading often stands on its own and comes from a letter of Paul or some other letter of the New Testament. Notice, for example, that the second readings from late June through November take us through Galatians, Ephesians, Hebrews, Romans, and 1 Corinthians. The stretch of Ordinary Time in Summer and Autumn provides a perfect opportunity for sustained attention to one or a few sections of the Bible.

UNITY WITH OTHER CHRISTIAN CHURCHES IN THE WORD OF GOD

The basic plan of the Lectionary for Catholics is universal. The readings proclaimed in your church on a particular Sunday are the same as those proclaimed in Catholic churches all over the globe. The Lectionary is one of the main things that makes our liturgy so "catholic," or universal.

The revision of the Roman Catholic Lectionary has been so well received that other Christian churches have begun to follow its three-year cycle. So Catholics and their neighbors who attend other Christian churches often hear the same word of God proclaimed and preached in their Sunday gatherings. We may not talk about the Sunday readings with neighbors and therefore don't realize that the readers read the same scripture passages and the preachers preach on the same scriptural texts. This is really a remarkable change when we consider how very far apart Catholic and Protestant churches were before the Second Vatican Council.

Although Roman Catholics always hear the New American Bible translation in their liturgy, and that is what you will find in this book, the Church has approved other translations for study, such as the New Revised Standard Version (NRSV) and the New Jerusalem Bible. When preparing to hear the readings on Sunday, it is helpful to read more than one translation, and also to read more than the Lectionary passage so that you understand the context in which it occurs in the Bible. Consulting various Bibles, and perhaps a few Bible study tools will enrich your preparation. (See Studying and Praying Scripture, which begins on page 10.)

May your celebration of the liturgy in your parish be deepened by the preparations you make with this book. And may your work with scripture during the liturgical year help you feel ever more "at home with the Word" of God.

YOUR RESPONSES INVITED

The LTP staff appreciates your feedback. E-mail: ahw@ltp.org.

An Introduction to the Gospel of Luke

by Michael Cameron

Luke's gospel, together with its sequel, the Acts of the Apostles, presents a breathtaking narrative of early Christianity, from Gabriel announcing the birth of John the Baptist in Jerusalem to the apostle Paul announcing the gospel of Jesus in Rome. This majestically conceived, magnificently crafted epic makes up about a quarter of the New Testament.

Luke was a second-generation Christian who may have been a Gentile admirer of Judaism before his conversion. He was well educated, traveled widely, wrote excellent Greek, and was influenced by contemporary modes of writing history. He echoes the atmosphere, the language, and at times even the style of the Old Testament. Luke tells us directly that he is handing on what contemporaries of Jesus have reported (1:1–4). Writing about fifty years after Jesus' time, he incorporates many stories and sayings from Mark and Matthew. Nevertheless, he shapes the traditions according to his own rich perspective.

Luke is a theologian with a historical bent, possessing a strong sense of the salvation story's development through three phases of time. *The time of Israel* is the period of "the law and the prophets" (16:16) from the creation to the appearance of John the Baptist. The entire Old Testament portrayed Israel growing in the knowledge of God and awaiting the future "redemption of Jerusalem" (2:38). Luke's gospel represents this time poetically through the infancy narrative (chapters 1 and 2), with its unforgettable characters who represent Old Testament piety at its best. *The time of Jesus* extends from his baptism to his ascension (chapters 3 to 24), when salvation is definitively accomplished in the words and works of the Messiah, especially his death and resurrection in Jerusalem (24:44–47). Luke accentuates the dramatic immediacy of salvation by a strategic use of the word "today" (fulfillment "today," 4:21; salvation "today," 19:9; paradise "today," 23:43). *The time of the church* stretches from Pentecost until Jesus returns. Anticipated in 24:48, this period begins to unfold in the 28 chapters of the Acts of the Apostles.

Luke's work has a distinctive, sweet air, a beautiful mildness. His naturally humane outlook finds deep resonance with Jesus' concern for people's healing and salvation. In contrast to Mark's rough prophet, Matthew's wise teacher, and John's mystical divine, Luke's Jesus is the herald of healing peace. From the early scene announcing "liberty to captives" (4:17–19) to the last healing of the high priest's slave who arrested him (22:50–51), Luke's Jesus is the good and gentle Savior. At the same time, Luke is blunt about Jesus' severe demands on those who become his disciples (14:25–33; 17:7–10), who must take up their cross daily (9:23) and leave *everything* to follow him (a favorite idea, 5:11, 28; 14:33).

Luke is an exquisite storyteller, with a keen eye for deep characters, pungent story lines, poignant ironies, and heartwarming endings. As with all such masters, his pen's slightest stroke speaks volumes, as when Jesus agonizes while the disciples sleep "from grief" (22:45), or Peter denies Jesus a third time and "the Lord turned and looked at Peter" (22:61). Luke's arresting vignettes anticipate the stained glass storytelling of the great medieval cathedrals. It is not accidental that artists have often rendered Luke as a portrait painter, or that the church has made Luke the patron saint of artists.

Luke contains certain features that the other gospels omit or mention only in passing. Joy is a distinct emphasis (1:14, 47; 2:10; 10:17, 21; 15:7, 10; 19:37; 24:41), as are prayer (3:21; 6:12; 11:5–8; 18:1–8; 23:44), the Holy Spirit (1:15, 41, 67; 2:27; 4:18; 10:21; 11:13), Jesus' friendships with women (7:36–50; 8:2–3; 10:38–42; 23:27–31; 23:55), and his teaching on hospitality (9:49–50; 10:25–37; 14:12–14; 15:4) and right attitude about wealth (6:24–25; 12:13–21; 16:19–31). If Luke's gospel had somehow not survived, our loss would be incalculable.

Luke alone gives us the *stories* of his infancy narrative, including the birth of John the Baptist, the angel Gabriel's Annunciation to Mary (1:26–38), and her Visitation to Elizabeth (1:39–45); the liturgical songs of Mary (1:46–55, the Magnificat) and Zechariah (1:67–79, the Benedictus); he draws images of the crowded inn at Bethlehem, Jesus lying in the manger, shepherds frightened by angels singing "Peace on Earth" (2:1–20), hoary Simeon exclaiming his praise (2:28–32, the Nunc Dimittis), old Anna prophesying redemption, (2:36–38), the young Jesus cross-examining the scholars (2:46), and Mary keeping in her heart the mysteries about her son (2:19, 51).

Luke's memorable *characters* include the judgmental Pharisee Simon (7:39–47), the hungry learner Mary (10:39), the repentant taxman Zacchaeus (19:1–10), and the distraught disciple Cleopas (24:18–24). Special *dramas* abound:

Jesus raised up a widow's only son at his funeral, then "gave him to his mother" (7:11–17), healed the woman bent double for eighteen years (13:10–17), and cured ten lepers among whom the Samaritan alone returned to say thanks (17:11–19). He painted a host of affecting scenes: Jesus reading in his home synagogue (4:16–20), Peter repenting at Jesus' knees (5:8), the woman bathing Jesus' feet with her tears (7:38), Jesus praying with sweat "like drops of blood" (22:44).

Further, Luke transmitted many unique *sayings* of Jesus. "One's life does not consist of possessions" (12:15). "Do not be afraid any longer, little flock" (12:32). "The kingdom of God is among you" (17:21). "Father, forgive them, they know not what they do" (23:34). "Today you will be with me in Paradise" (23:43). And many well-known *parables* are found only in Luke: the Good Samaritan (10:25–37), the Woman's Lost Coin (15:8–10), the Prodigal Son (15:11–32), the Rich Man and Lazarus (16:19–29), the Widow and the Unjust Judge (18:1–8), the Pharisee and the Tax Collector (18:9–14).

Luke's first sentences in the prologue (1:1–4) address an otherwise unknown figure named Theophilus (the name means "God's friend"), who symbolizes any Christian seeking a deeper understanding of Jesus. For each reader who takes up his "orderly sequence" with serious intent, Luke has a single stirring aim. Literally translated, it reads, "that you may come to know a deep assurance about the teachings you have received."

Studying and Praying Scripture

by Michael Cameron

A recent study claimed that only 22% of American Catholics read the Bible regularly, and just 8% are involved in scripture groups. Not many know how profoundly biblical the Roman Catholic church has been from its very roots, steeped in the words and spirit of the Old and New Testaments, "always venerating the divine scriptures as she venerates the Body of the Lord" (Vatican II). How may Catholics learn to read scripture? What follows briefly sketches a path for seekers.

PREPARING TO READ

Become an apprentice to the Bible. Ordinary people can reach a good level of understanding, but it costs: The Bible yields its riches to those who dedicate themselves to the search for understanding. Start by reading daily, even if only for a few minutes. Join a group that reads and discusses scripture together.

You will need tools. Think of yourself as a prospector for the Bible's gold. Nuggets on the ground are easily picked up, but the really rich veins lie beneath the surface. Digging requires study, commitment, and skills.

Invest in tools that reap the harvest of others' labors. Buy a study Bible with introductions, explanatory notes, and maps. Use another translation for devotional reading and comparison. Get access to a Bible dictionary with detailed information on biblical books, concepts, geography, customs, and other topics. Bible concordances will help you find all occurrences of particular words. A dictionary of biblical theology will give guidance on major theological ideas. A Bible atlas will give a sense of the locations and movements in the biblical stories. Recent church documents on the Bible offer rich instruction to seekers.

READING FOR KNOWLEDGE

Get to know historical contexts suggested by a passage. Learn all you can about the Bible's basic story line, salvation history, beginning with Israel and continuing in the church. Salvation by God's grace, obedience to God's will, and judgment on sin are basic to both Old and New Testaments. Learn particularly about the covenants with Abraham and David that emphasize God's grace. The covenant with Moses presumes God's grace and emphasizes obedience. Both covenant traditions re-emerge and are fulfilled in the new covenant in Jesus, who pours out his life to save all people (grace) but is extremely demanding of his disciples (obedience).

Read entire books of the Bible in order to gain a sense of the whole from which the snippets of the Sunday lectionary are cut. Try to imagine what the books meant for their original authors and audiences. Ask how and why a book was put together: What is its structure, outline, main themes, literary forms, overall purpose?

Get to know the Old Testament narratives and the psalms, but learn the gospels especially. The lectionary's yearly focus on Matthew, Mark, or Luke offers an opportunity to learn each one. John is the focus during the church's special seasons.

READING FOR WISDOM

Read as one who seeks God, like the writer of Psalm 119. Ask what the text is asking you to believe, do, or hope for. Jesus' powerful proclamation in Mark 1:15 gives a strong framework: "This is the time of fulfillment" (now is the time to be attentive and ready to act); "the kingdom of God is at hand" (God is about to speak and act); "repent" (be willing to change your mind and move in a fresh direction); "believe in the gospel" (embrace the grace that has already embraced you).

Read books straight through, a self-contained section at a time, carefully, slowly, and meditatively. Stop where natural breaks occur at the end of stories or sequences of thought.

Beware of the sense that you already know what a text is going to say. Read attentively, asking what God is teaching you through this text at this minute about your life or about your communities—family, church, work, neighborhood, nation. Trust the Spirit to guide you to what you need.

READING FOR WORSHIP

The goal of reading the Bible is not learning new facts or getting merely private inspiration for living, but entering communion with God. Allow the Bible to teach you to pray by giving you the words to use in prayer. The psalms are especially apt for this, but any part of the Bible may be prayed. This practice dating back more than fifteen hundred years is called lectio divina, Latin for "sacred reading."

Read scripture in relation to the Eucharist. The Bible both prepares for Jesus' real presence and explains it to the understanding. The same Jesus who healed the lepers, stilled the storm and embraced the children is present to us in the word and in the sacrament.

The Bible is a library of untold spiritual riches. The church intends that this treasury be "wide open to the Christian faithful" (Vatican II).

RESOURCES

Brown, Raymond E., SS. *Responses to 101 Questions on the Bible*. Paulist Press, 1990.

Casey, Michael. *Sacred Reading: The Ancient Art of Lectio Divina*. Triumph, 1996.

Magrassi, Mariano. *Praying the Bible*. Liturgical Press, 1998.

Martin, George. *Reading Scripture as the Word of God*. 4th ed. Servant, 1998.

McKenzie, John L., SJ. *Dictionary of the Bible*. MacMillan, 1965.

Paprocki, Joe. *God's Library: Introducing Catholics to the Bible*. Twenty-Third, 1999.

The Bible Documents: A Parish Resource. Liturgy Training Publications, 2001.

The Bible Today. Periodical for general readers.

The Catholic Study Bible. General editor, Donald Senior, cp. Oxford, 1990.

The Collegeville Bible Commentary. Eds. Dianne Bergant and Robert J. Karris. Liturgical Press, 1990.

The Collegevile Pastoral Dictionary of Biblical Theology. Ed. Carroll Stuhlmueller, cp. Liturgical Press, 1996.

Prayer before Reading the Word

In this and every year,
in this and every place,
O God everlasting,
your word resounds in the wilderness of Advent,
calling us to stand upon the height
and to behold the splendor of your beauty.

Fill in the valleys of our neglect;
bring low our mountains of self-centeredness
Prepare in our hearts
your way of righteousness and peace.
Let our love become a harvest of goodness,
which you will bring to completion
for the day of Christ Jesus,
who was, who is and who is to come,
your Son who lives and reigns with you
in the unity of the Holy Spirit,
God for ever and ever. Amen.

Prayer after Reading the Word

God of holiness,
whose promises stand through all generations,
fulfill the longings of a humanity
weighed down by confusion and burdened
        with fear.

Raise up our heads and strengthen our hearts,
that we may proclaim to all people
the good news of your presence in our midst.
May we delight to share with them
your peace, which surpasses all understanding.

We ask this through our Lord Jesus Christ,
        your Son,
who lives and reigns with you
in the unity of the Holy Spirit,
God for ever and ever. Amen.

Weekday Readings

December 4: *Isaiah 2:1–5; Matthew 8:5–11*
December 5: *Isaiah 11:1–10; Luke 10:21–24*
December 6: *Isaiah 25:6–10a; Matthew 15:29–37;*
December 7: *Isaiah 26:1–6; Matthew 7:21, 24–27*
**December 8: Solemnity of the Immaculate Conception of
the Blessed Virgin Mary**
Genesis 3:9–15, 20; Ephesians 1:3–6, 11–12; Luke 1:26–38

December 9: *Isaiah 30:19–21, 23–26; Matthew 9:35–10:1,
5a, 6–8*
December 11: *Isaiah 35:1–10; Luke 5:17–26*
December 12: Feast of Our Lady of Guadalupe
Zechariah 2:14–17; Luke 1:26–38
December 13: *Isaiah 40:25–31; Matthew 11:28–30*
December 14: *Isaiah 41:13–20; Matthew 11:11–15*
December 15: *Sirach 48:17–19, 9-11; Matthew 11:16–19*
December 16: *Sirach 48: 1–4, 9–11; Matthew 17:9a, 10–13*

December 18: *Jeremiah 23:5–8; Matthew 1:18–25*
December 19: *Judges 13:2–7, 24–25a; Luke 1:5–25*
December 20: *Isaiah 7:10–14; Luke 1:26–38*
December 21: *Song of Songs 2:8–14; Luke 1:39–45*
December 22: *1 Samuel 1:24–28; Luke 1:46 to 56*
December 23: *Malachi 3:1–4, 23–24; Luke 1:57–66*

December 3, 2006

READING I *Jeremiah 33:14—16*

The days are coming, says the LORD, when I will fulfill the promise I made to the house of Israel and Judah. In those days, in that time, I will raise up for David a just shoot; he shall do what is right and just in the land. In those days Judah shall be safe and Jerusalem shall dwell secure; this is what they shall call her: "The LORD our justice."

READING II *1 Thessalonians 3:12—4:2*

Brothers and sisters: May the Lord make you increase and abound in love for one another and for all, just as we have for you, so as to strengthen your hearts, to be blameless in holiness before our God and Father at the coming of our Lord Jesus with all his holy ones. Amen.

Finally, brothers and sisters, we earnestly ask and exhort you in the Lord Jesus that, as you received from us how you should conduct yourselves to please God —and as you are conducting yourselves— you do so even more. For you know what instructions we gave you through the Lord Jesus.

GOSPEL *Luke 21:25—28, 34—36*

Jesus said to his disciples: "There will be signs in the sun, the moon and the stars, and on earth nations will be in dismay, perplexed by the roaring of the sea and the waves. People will die of fright in anticipation of what is coming upon the world, for the powers of the heavens will be shaken. And then they will see the Son of Man coming in a cloud with power and great glory. But when these signs begin to happen, stand erect and raise your heads because your redemption is at hand.

"Beware that your hearts do not become drowsy from carousing and drunkenness and the anxieties of daily life, and that day catch you by surprise like a trap. For that day will assault everyone who lives on the face of the earth. Be vigilant at all times and pray that you have the strength to escape the tribulations that are imminent and to stand before the Son of Man."

Practice of Prayer

Psalm 25:4 — 5, 8 — 9, 10, 14 (1b)

R. To you, O Lord, I lift my soul.

Your ways, O LORD, make known to me;
    teach me your paths.
Guide me in your truth and teach me,
    for you are God my savior,
    and for you I wait all the day. R.

Good and upright is the LORD,
    thus he shows sinners the way.
He guides the humble to justice and
    teaches the humble his way. R.

All the paths of the LORD are kindness and
      constancy
    toward those who keep his covenant
      and his decrees.
The friendship of the LORD is with those who
      fear him,
    and his covenant for their instruction. R.

Practice of Hope

It is said that all ventures that bear good fruit begin with reflection. As we begin a new liturgical year, creating a Jesse tree invites reflection. The Jesse tree is a centuries-old tradition with relevance today. Start by recalling with your family or community the scriptures recounting stories of Jesus' ancestors. Then fashion symbols for them from clay, paper, or cloth. Hang your artworks from a sturdy branch weighted with sand or tones in a large container. The Jesse tree recalls for us the longing experienced by the generations of faithful Israelites who waited for a savior. It reminds us, too, of our deepest longings—for the time when Christ's work on earth will be complete, when God will be all in all, when justice and peace will reign. As you prepare this Advent tree of life, ask what situations, from personal to global, need healing today.

Scripture Insights

The season of Advent is a time of joyful expectation for Catholic Christians. The lighting of the four candles of the Advent wreath anticipates the celebration of the birth of Jesus.

But there is also a sober dimension to Advent as we prepare to receive the Savior. Penance, fasting, and almsgiving are a traditional part of that preparation. How do joy and sober preparation coexist in this season?

In the Gospel, Jesus commands his disciples to be "vigilant at all times." He warns, "Beware that your hearts do not become drowsy."

Why is vigilance an aspect of Advent? And how do signs in the sky, roaring seas, and death by fright kick off a season having to do with joyful expectation? Remember that Jesus' coming is a two-fold event in the Gospel of Luke. The birth of Jesus anticipates the second advent of his return at the end of time.

If Advent is a season pregnant with the possibility of a new beginning, it is also a time of reflection on the purpose of Christian life and our shared destiny as people of God. Paul makes this clear in his encouraging words to the Thessalonian Church. He warmly describes their faithful lives, but he also is aware that "the coming of our Lord Jesus" will be a time of judgment.

Advent must be more than wreaths and crèches. It also must be about how we use the time we have been given. Whether we choose to live in drowsiness or vigilance is up to us.

♦ Is there a correlation between acting justly and redemption?

♦ In what way are Paul's words helpful for your preparation work?

♦ When have you been disturbed by contradictions in your life? What aspects of your faith helped you through these?

READING I *Baruch 5:1—9*

Jerusalem, take off your robe of mourning
> and misery;
>> put on the splendor of glory from
>> God forever:
Wrapped in the cloak of justice from God,
> bear on your head the mitre
> that displays the glory of the eternal name.
For God will show all the earth your splendor:
> you will be named by God forever
> the peace of justice, the glory of
> God's worship.

Up, Jerusalem! stand upon the heights;
> look to the east and see your children
gathered from the east and the west
> at the word of the Holy One,
> rejoicing that they are remembered by God.
Led away on foot by their enemies they left you:
> but God will bring them back to you
> borne aloft in glory as on royal thrones.
For God has commanded
> that every lofty mountain be made low,
and that the age-old depths and gorges
> be filled to level ground,
> that Israel may advance secure
> in the glory of God.
The forests and every fragrant kind of tree
> have overshadowed Israel
> at God's command;
for God is leading Israel in joy
> by the light of his glory,
> with his mercy and justice for company.

READING II *Philippians 1:4—6, 8—11*

Brothers and sisters: I pray always with joy in my every prayer for all of you, because of your partnership for the gospel from the first day until now. I am confident of this, that the one who began a good work in you will continue to complete it until the day of Christ Jesus. God is my witness, how I long for all of you with the affection of Christ Jesus. And this is my prayer: that your love may increase ever more and more in knowledge and every kind of perception, to discern what is of value, so that you may be pure and blameless for the day of Christ, filled with the fruit of righteousness that comes through Jesus Christ for the glory and praise of God.

GOSPEL *Luke 3:1—6*

In the fifteenth year of the reign of Tiberius Caesar, when Pontius Pilate was governor of Judea, and Herod was tetrarch of Galilee, and his brother Philip tetrarch of the region of Ituraea and Trachonitis, and Lysanias was tetrarch of Abilene, during the high priesthood of Annas and Caiaphas, the word of God came to John the son of Zechariah in the desert. John went throughout the whole region of the Jordan, proclaiming a baptism of repentance for the forgiveness of sins, as it is written in the book of the words of the prophet Isaiah:
A voice of one crying out in the desert:/

"Prepare the way of the Lord,/ make straight his paths./Every valley shall be filled/and every mountain and hill shall be made low./The winding roads shall be made straight,/ and the rough ways made smooth,/ and all flesh shall see the salvation of God."

Practice of Prayer

R. The Lord has done great things for us; we are
filled with joy.

When the LORD brought back the captives of Zion,
we were like men dreaming.
Then our mouth was filled with laughter,
and our tongue with rejoicing. R.

Then they said among the nations,
"The LORD has done great things for them."
The LORD has done great things for us;
we are glad indeed. R.

Restore our fortunes, O LORD,
like the torrents in the southern desert.
Those who sow in tears
shall reap rejoicing. R.

Although they go forth weeping,
carrying the seed to be sown,
they shall come back rejoicing,
carrying their sheaves. R.

Practice of Faith

Misa, musa, and mesa—Mass, song, and feasting—
will all be in evidence Tuesday in Hispanic communities to honor *La Morenita del Tepayac,* also
known as Our Lady of Guadalupe. Mariachi
trumpets will serenade her before dawn, calling
everyone to the celebration. Often little boys are
dressed as Saint Juan Diego (the Aztec Indian who
encountered the Lady), and little girls are dressed
as Indian women of that time. The beloved story
is read or reenacted. After Mass, in many parishes,
breakfast treats will be served in the parish hall.
Later, people may come to the Guadalupe image
with a flower and serenade the Blessed Mother.
They rejoice because *La Guadalupana* manifested
compassion, healing, and help to an oppressed
people. Her image, left on Juan Diego's *tilma*
(cloak), is still vibrant more than four centuries
later. Peace treaties have been signed in the basilica
where the tilma is displayed.

Scripture Insights

This week's readings provide geography and history lessons. Luke, in particular, tries to orient his
readers in space and world history.

Starting with a wide-angle lens encompassing
the empire, he sharpens his focus on the eastern
Roman Empire and a few of its regions and leaders. (A Bible atlas can help locate these places.)
Saint Paul writes to the church at Philippi in
Macedonia(northern Greece), a church with whom
he had an especially warm relationship. His writing from a jail cell lends special poignancy to his
words, "how I long for all of you with the affection of Christ Jesus." Separated by both distance
and prison walls, Saint Paul overcomes imposed
limitations through letter-writing. The Prophet
Baruch and John the Baptist in the Gospel also
refer to a sort of imprisonment—the forced
removal of Jerusalem's population to Babylon
after the fall of the kingdom of Judah in the early
sixth century B.C. The cause of Baruch's joy is the
prediction that the people of Jerusalem will return
one day to the city from which they were stolen.
The prophetic words that come to John the Baptist
as he begins his ministry are from Isaiah 40. These
verses celebrate Cyrus of Persia's defeat of Babylon
and the end of Israel's exile from its holy city.

Everyone knows the pain of separation as well
as the joy of reunion. These readings use history
to describe a future spiritual event—a reunion
with God.

• What is the significance of Baruch and John's
(quoting Isaiah) words about the lowering of
mountains and the raising of valleys?

• How might Saint Paul's prayer (toward the end
of the passage) be relevant to your life?

• When did you feel furthest from your loved
ones? What reunions, human and spiritual, do
you look forward to?

December 17, 2006

THIRD SUNDAY OF ADVENT

READING I   *Zephaniah 3:14—18a*

Shout for joy, O daughter Zion!
  Sing joyfully, O Israel!
Be glad and exult with all your heart,
  O daughter Jerusalem!
The LORD has removed the judgment
      against you,
  he has turned away your enemies;
the King of Israel, the LORD, is in your midst,
  you have no further misfortune to fear.
On that day, it shall be said to Jerusalem:
  Fear not, O Zion, be not discouraged!
The LORD, your God, is in your midst,
  a mighty savior;
he will rejoice over you with gladness,
  and renew you in his love,
he will sing joyfully because of you,
  as one sings at festivals.

READING II   *Philippians 4:4—7*

Brothers and sisters: Rejoice in the Lord always. I shall say it again: rejoice! Your kindness should be known to all. The Lord is near. Have no anxiety at all, but in everything, by prayer and petition, with thanksgiving, make your requests known to God. Then the peace of God that surpasses all understanding will guard your hearts and minds in Christ Jesus.

GOSPEL   *Luke 3:10—18*

The crowds asked John the Baptist, "What should we do?" He said to them in reply, "Whoever has two cloaks should share with the person who has none. And whoever has food should do likewise." Even tax collectors came to be baptized and they said to him, "Teacher, what should we do?" He answered them, "Stop collecting more than what is prescribed." Soldiers also asked him, "And what is it that we should do?" He told them, "Do not practice extortion, do not falsely accuse anyone, and be satisfied with your wages."

Now the people were filled with expectation, and all were asking in their hearts whether John might be the Christ. John answered them all, saying, "I am baptizing you with water, but one mightier than I is coming. I am not worthy to loosen the thongs of his sandals. He will baptize you with the Holy Spirit and fire. His winnowing fan is in his hand to clear his threshing floor and to gather the wheat into his barn, but the chaff he will burn with unquenchable fire." Exhorting them in many other ways, he preached good news to the people.

Practice of Prayer

Psalm 12:2 — 3, 4, 5 — 6(6)

R. Cry out with joy and gladness,
    for among you is the great and
        Holy One of Israel.

God indeed is my savior;
    I am confident and unafraid.
My strength and my courage is the LORD,
    and he has been my savior.
With joy you will draw water
    at the fountain of salvation.   R.

Give thanks to the LORD, acclaim his name;
    among the nations make known his deeds,
    proclaim how exalted is his name.   R.

Sing praise to the LORD for his
        glorious achievement;
    let this be known throughout all the earth.
Shout with exultation, O city of Zion,
    for great in your midst
        is the Holy One of Israel!   R.

Practice of Charity

In 2004, Catholic Relief Services joined with local organizations in eastern Democratic Republic of Congo to support the restoration of roughly 300 miles of railroad track destroyed by civil war. People living along the route spent months making these rough ways smooth—battling overgrown brush, trees, and hundreds of deadly snakes by hand. Before the tracks were restored, residents had no choice but to walk great distances along the railroad bed carrying food and all other vital supplies. That July, cheers greeted a national Peace Train as it made its first trip across the war-torn country. Now farmers would be able to transport their crops to market, medicines would become available in rural areas, and people could travel again. All this would have been impossible without the help of CRS. To learn more about Catholic Relief Services' work around the world, visit www.catholicrelief.org.

Scripture Insights

Those who have experienced insomnia know the irritation of watching the clock as the possibility of sleep flits away. In these moments, anxiety sometimes gets the full run of your mind, posing a worst-case scenario for the future. You wrack your mind, trying to come up with solutions, but often it seems there is nothing to do except get out of bed and keep busy until sleep comes.

In today's epistle, the jailed apostle Saint Paul instructs the Philippians to "Have no anxiety." He immediately follows with practical advice, "but in everything, by prayer and petition, with thanksgiving, make your requests known to God." Incarcerated and facing an uncertain future, Saint Paul has direct experience of what he's writing. Don't entertain anxiety, he says. Do something about it. But prayer is not Saint Paul's only practical advice. "Your kindness," he commands, "should be known to all." Likewise, when the crowds, tax collectors, and soldiers ask John the Baptist what they should do, he recommends specific courses of action for each. He urges the crowds to share their abundance. He tells the tax collectors and soldiers to stop their abuses. For those of us who wonder, like the crowds who flocked to John the Baptist, "What should we do?" today's Gospel supplies a simple and straightforward answer. We are to pray, help those in need, and avoid doing harm. Then, we are more likely to be free of anxiety and able to rejoice at the advent of "a mighty savior" in our midst.

◆ In the reading from Zephaniah, who is being addressed? What reasons are given for rejoicing?

◆ Why do the circumstances of Saint Paul's incarceration make his encouragement to rejoice more or less persuasive to you?

◆ When have you assumed a certain thorny problem required a complicated answer but found a solution in a simple spiritual insight?

December 24, 2006

READING I   *Micah 5:1—4a*

Thus says the LORD:
You, Bethlehem-Ephrathah
    too small to be among the clans
      of Judah,
from you shall come forth for me
    one who is to be ruler in Israel;
whose origin is from of old,
    from ancient times.
Therefore the Lord will give them up,
      until the time
    when she who is to give birth has borne,
and the rest of his kindred shall return
    to the children of Israel.
He shall stand firm and shepherd his flock
    by the strength of the LORD,
    in the majestic name of the LORD,
    his God;
and they shall remain, for now his greatness
    shall reach to the ends of the earth;
    he shall be peace.

READING II   *Hebrews 10:5—10*

Brothers and sisters: When Christ came into the world, he said: "Sacrifice and offering you did not desire, but a body you prepared for me; in holocausts and sin offerings you took no delight. Then I said, 'As is written of me in the scroll, behold, I come to do your will, O God.'"

First he says, "Sacrifices and offerings, holocausts and sin offerings, you neither desired nor delighted in." These are offered according to the law. Then he says, "Behold, I come to do your will." He takes away the first to establish the second. By this "will," we have been consecrated through the offering of the body of Jesus Christ once for all.

GOSPEL   *Luke 1:39—45*

Mary set out and traveled to the hill country in haste to a town of Judah, where she entered the house of Zechariah and greeted Elizabeth. When Elizabeth heard Mary's greeting, the infant leaped in her womb, and Elizabeth, filled with the Holy Spirit, cried out in a loud voice and said, "Blessed are you among women, and blessed is the fruit of your womb. And how does this happen to me, that the mother of my Lord should come to me? For at the moment the sound of your greeting reached my ears, the infant in my womb leaped for joy. Blessed are you who believed that what was spoken to you by the Lord would be fulfilled."

Practice of Prayer

Psalm 80:2—3, 15—16, 18—19 (4)

R. Lord, make us turn to you; let us see your face
    and we shall be saved.
O shepherd of Israel, hearken,
    from your throne upon the cherubim,
        shine forth.
Rouse your power,
    and come to save us. R.

Once again, O LORD of hosts,
    look down from heaven, and see;
take care of this vine,
    and protect what your right hand
        has planted,
    the son of man whom you yourself
        made strong. R.

May your help be with the man of your
        right hand,
    with the son of man whom you yourself
        made strong.
Then we will no more withdraw from you;
    give us new life, and we will call
        upon your name. R.

Practice of Hope

Today's first reading presents a paradox: the majestic ruler who is also a shepherd—the humblest of rural occupations. It is an image of reconciliation. The Gospel continues the theme, demonstrating how, even before his birth, Christ's presence fosters community in the shared joy of Mary and Elizabeth. As you assemble the figures of your crèche, recall how Christ's saving action of death and resurrection restores all creation to wholeness. The cluster of barnyard animals huddled around the manger reflects the peace of the reign of the kingdom of God. Adding flowers and plants to poke up from the straw will hint at the newness to creation. Suspend some glittering stars overhead. Make your crèche a thing of great beauty! Many families begin the journey of the Magi by placing them today in a room far from the crèche and moving them a little closer each day until they arrive at the crèche on the feast of the Epiphany.

Scripture Insights

One of the traditional terms for the interpretation of the Bible is "exegesis." The word is Greek in origin and means something similar to "drawing out." An exegete studies the scriptures in an attempt to discover, or draw out, meaning. You need not think of exegesis as some kind of mystical or esoteric activity. By reading today's passages and trying to make sense of them, you are engaged in the act of exegesis, one of Christianity's most ancient traditions. In the first few centuries after Jesus, the early Church took great pains to show that its faith was nothing novel or recent. They wanted to show that Jesus' life, death, and resurrection had been prophesied in the scriptures. Today's first reading from Micah allows us to read as the early Christians did. Nowhere in the prophet's words do we see the name of Jesus or Mary. Indeed, the prophet Micah lived centuries before either of them. To his earliest readers, Micah was likely understood to have prophesied the rise of an Israelite king from the ancestral line of David, whose roots lay partly in Bethlehem (southern Israel). But it is scarcely possible for Catholic Christians to read this prophecy of "a ruler in Israel," who comes forth from Bethlehem, one who "shall stand firm and shepherd his flock by the strength of the Lord," without thinking of the birth and ministry of Jesus. And what Catholic can read "she who is to give birth" to this ruler and not think of Mary?

• What other women in the Bible besides Elizabeth became pregnant despite believing that they could not? How was Mary different?

• How do you allow the person of Jesus to guide you through Scripture?

• When you say the "Hail Mary," what meaning do the words, "Blessed are you among women" have?

Christmas

Prayer before Reading the Word

By the light of a star, O God of the universe,
You guided the nations to the Light of the world.

Until this Redeemer comes again in glory,
We, with the Magi, seek the face of the Savior.
Summon us with all those who thirst now
To the banquet of love.
May our hunger be filled and our thirst
        be quenched
With your word of truth.

We ask this through our Lord Jesus Christ,
        your Son,
Who lives and reigns with you
In the unity of the Holy Spirit,
God for ever and ever. Amen.

Prayer after Reading the Word

In the beginning, O God, was your Word,
And now in time your Word becomes flesh,
The light that shines unconquered
Through the darkness of the ages
And has made his dwelling place among us
Transforming earth's gloom into heaven's glory.

As we behold upon the mountains
the messenger who announces your peace,
Touch our lips as well that we may lift up
        our voices
As bearers of good news and heralds of salvation.
We ask this through our Lord Jesus Christ,
Emmanuel, God with us,
Your Son who lives and reigns with you
In the unity of the Holy Spirit,
God for ever and ever. Amen.

Weekday Readings

December 25: Solemnity of the Nativity of the Lord
 Day: *Isaiah 52:7–10; Hebrews 1:1–6; John 1:1–18*
December 26: Feast of Saint Stephen
 Acts 6:8–10; 7:54-59; Matthew 10:17–22
December 27: Feast of Saint John
 1 John 1:1–4; John 20:1a, 2–8
December 28: Feast of the Holy Innocents
 1 John 1:5–2:2; Matthew 2:13–18;
December 29: Fifth Day in the Octave of Christmas
 1 John 2:3–11; Luke 2:22–35
December 30: *Sixth Day in the Octave of Christmas*
 1 John 2:12–17; Luke 2:36–40

January 1: Solemnity of the Blessed Virgin Mary,
 The Mother of God
 Numbers 6:22–27; Galatians 4:4–7; Luke 2:16–21
January 2: *1 John 2:22–28; John 1:19–28*
January 3: *1 John 2:29–3:6; John 1:29–34*
January 4: *1 John 3:7–10; John 1:35–42*
January 5: *1 John 3:11–21; John 1:43–51*
January 6: *1 John 5:5–13; Mark 1:7–11*

January 8: Feast of the Baptism of the Lord
 Isaiah 42:1–4, 6–7; Luke 3:15–16
January 9: *Hebrews 2:5–12; Mark 1:21–28*
January 10: *Hebrews 2:14–18 ; Mark 1:29–30*
January 11: *Hebrews 3:7–14; Mark 1:40–45;*
January 12: *Hebrews 4:1–5, 11; Mark 2:1–12*
January 13: *Hebrews 4:12–16; Mark 2:13–17*

December 25, 2006

READING I   *Isaiah 9:1—6*

The people who walked in darkness
    have seen a great light;
upon those who dwelt in the land of gloom
    a light has shone.
You have brought them abundant joy
    and great rejoicing,
as they rejoice before you as at the harvest,
    as people make merry when
        dividing spoils.
For the yoke that burdened them,
    the pole on their shoulder,
and the rod of their taskmaster
    you have smashed, as on the day
        of Midian.
For every boot that tramped in battle,
    every cloak rolled in blood,
    will be burned as fuel for flames.
For a child is born to us, a son is given us;
    upon his shoulder dominion rests.
They name him Wonder-Counselor,
    God-Hero,
    Father-Forever, Prince of Peace.
His dominion is vast
    and forever peaceful,
from David's throne, and over his kingdom,
    which he confirms and sustains
by judgment and justice,
    both now and forever.
The zeal of the LORD of hosts will do this!

READING II   *Titus 2:11—14*

Beloved: The grace of God has appeared, saving all and training us to reject godless ways and worldly desires and to live temperately, justly, and devoutly in this age, as we await the blessed hope, the appearance of the glory of our great God and savior Jesus Christ, who gave himself for us to deliver us from all lawlessness and to cleanse for himself a people as his own, eager to do what is good.

GOSPEL   *Luke 2:1—14*

In those days a decree went out from Caesar Augustus that the whole world should be enrolled. This was the first enrollment, when Quirinius was governor of Syria. So all went to be enrolled, each to his own town. And Joseph too went up from Galilee from the town of Nazareth to Judea, to the city of David that is called Bethlehem, because he was of the house and family of David, to be enrolled with Mary, his betrothed, who was with child. While they were there, the time came for her to have her child, and she gave birth to her first-born son. She wrapped him in swaddling clothes and laid him in a manger, because there was no room for them in the inn.

Now there were shepherds in that region living in the fields and keeping the night watch over their flock. The angel of the Lord appeared to them and the glory of the Lord shone around them, and they were struck with great fear. The angel said to them, "Do not be afraid; for behold, I proclaim to you good news of great joy that will be for all the people. For today in the city of David a savior has been born for you who is Christ and Lord. And this will be a sign for you: you will find an infant wrapped in swaddling clothes and lying in a manger." And suddenly there was a multitude of the heavenly host with the angel, praising God and saying:

    "Glory to God in the highest
        and on earth peace to those
            on whom his favor rests."

Practice of Prayer

Psalm 96:1—2, 2—3, 11—12, 13 (Luke 2:11)

R. Today is born our Savior, Christ the Lord.

Sing to the Lord a new song;
    sing to the LORD, all you lands.
Sing to the LORD; bless his name. R.

Announce his salvation, day after day.
    Tell his glory among the nations;
    among all peoples, his wondrous deeds. R.

Let the heavens be glad and the earth rejoice;
    let the sea and what fills it resound;
    let the plains be joyful and all that is in them!
Then shall all the trees of the forest exult. R.

They shall exult before the LORD, for he comes;
    for he comes to rule the earth.
He shall rule the world with justice
    and the peoples with his constancy. R.

Practice of Charity

Phil Calabrese won't be getting much sleep tonight. He'll be up at 5 a.m. on Christmas, rushing to open the doors of the Dominican Priory in River Forest, Illinois. Soon a fleet of 400 others will join him. They'll slice ham, assemble plates, and head out in all directions to deliver food, books, and toys. This rather vast undertaking began after Phil made a Cursillo retreat in 1970. Moved to do service, he learned that the local Meals on Wheels didn't operate on Christmas Day, and offered to help fill in the gap. Soon a local pastor invited Phil to speak to his parish. Volunteers poured in, as did names of families in need. Today, Christmascheer.org serves about 7,500 people in forty-five communities. Phil and his fellow volunteers would love to assist individuals or parishes who want to replicate their feat. Contact them at their website. (Contributions are also welcome.)

Scripture Insights

Nativity scenes and crèches are central to Christmas for many people. Figurines of sheep, perhaps of a donkey or a goat, shepherds, wise men, Joseph, Mary and, of course, the infant Jesus are crowded into the manger scene. A star often is suspended over all. We may be excused if we forget that the Gospels of Matthew and Luke give different accounts of the birth of Jesus. The star and the wise men are Matthew's, and we encounter them at the feast of the Epiphany. The manger, the shepherds, their flocks, and the angels are Luke's.

Imagine meeting a Martian studying family life on our planet. What would he make of a crèche? He might see the admiring shepherds, the adoring Magi, and attentive parents kneeling over their infant as an artistic rendering of how humans act around babies. Perhaps our Martian would have some questions about the rustic setting, the wise men's attire, and the star, but he might conclude the scene to be unremarkable. Paradox is at the heart of the Christian religion. The ancient world provided few more potent symbols of defeat and despair than the cross, a symbol of victory and hope for Christians. The raw power of the crèche is its radiation of paradox. What is more ordinary than a cluster of adults smiling and cooing over a crib, but more extraordinary than the doctrine of the Incarnation, which teaches that Jesus of Nazareth was both fully human and divine?

• Titus refers to "blessed hope" and "the appearance of the glory of our great God and savior Jesus Christ." Are his eyes on the past or the future?

• Does your family have a Christmastime tradition that reflects "just living"?

◆ What burden is lifted from you with the coming of Christ?

December 31, 2006

THE SOLEMNITY OF THE HOLY FAMILY OF JESUS, MARY, AND JOSEPH

READING I *1 Samuel 1:20—22, 24—28*

In those days Hannah conceived, and at the end of her term bore a son whom she called Samuel, since she had asked the LORD for him. The next time her husband Elkanah was going up with the rest of his household to offer the customary sacrifice to the LORD and to fulfill his vows, Hannah did not go, explaining to her husband, "Once the child is weaned, I will take him to appear before the LORD and to remain there forever; I will offer him as a perpetual nazirite."

Once Samuel was weaned, Hannah brought him up with her, along with a three-year-old bull, an ephah of flour, and a skin of wine, and presented him at the temple of the LORD in Shiloh. After the boy's father had sacrificed the young bull, Hannah, his mother, approached Eli and said: "Pardon, my lord! As you live, my lord, I am the woman who stood near you here, praying to the LORD. I prayed for this child, and the Lord granted my request. Now I, in turn, give him to the LORD; as long as he lives, he shall be dedicated to the LORD." Hannah left Samuel there.

[Alternate reading: Sirach 5:2—6, 12—14]

READING II *1 John 3:1—2, 21—24*

Beloved: See what love the Father has bestowed on us that we may be called the children of God. And so we are. The reason the world does not know us is that it did not know him. Beloved, we are God's children now; what we shall be has not yet been revealed. We do know that when it is revealed we shall be like him, for we shall see him as he is.

Beloved, if our hearts do not condemn us, we have confidence in God and receive from him whatever we ask, because we keep his commandments and do what pleases him. And his commandment is this: we should believe in the name of his Son, Jesus Christ, and love one another just as he commanded us. Those who keep his commandments remain in him, and he in them, and the way we know that he remains in us is from the Spirit he gave us.

[Colossians 3:12—21 or 3:12—17]

GOSPEL *Luke 2:41—52*

Each year Jesus' parents went to Jerusalem for the feast of Passover, and when he was twelve years old, they went up according to festival custom. After they had completed its days, as they were returning, the boy Jesus remained behind in Jerusalem, but his parents did not know it. Thinking that he was in the caravan, they journeyed for a day and looked for him among their relatives and acquaintances, but not finding him, they returned to Jerusalem to look for him. After three days they found him in the temple, sitting in the midst of the teachers, listening to them and asking them questions, and all who heard him were astounded at his understanding and his answers. When his parents saw him, they were astonished, and his mother said to him, "Son, why have you done this to us? Your father and I have been looking for you with great anxiety." And he said to them, "Why were you looking for me? Did you not know that I must be in my Father's house?" But they did not understand what he said to them. He went down with them and came to Nazareth, and was obedient to them; and his mother kept all these things in her heart. And Jesus advanced in wisdom and age and favor before God and man.

Practice of Prayer

Psalm 84:2 – 3, 5 – 6, 9 – 10 (see 5a)

R. Blessed are they who dwell in your house,
　　O Lord.

How lovely is your dwelling place, O LORD
　　of hosts!
　　My soul yearns and pines for the courts
　　of the LORD.
My heart and my flesh cry out for the
　　living God.　R.

Happy they who dwell in your house!
　　Continually they praise you.
Happy the men whose strength you are!
　　Their hearts are set upon the pilgrimage.　R.

O LORD of hosts, hear our prayer;
　　hearken, O God of Jacob!
O God, behold our shield,
　　and look upon the face of your anointed.　R.

Practice of Hope

"If you want peace, work for justice" were the famous words of Pope Paul VI. In 1970, a young married couple in St. Louis took this wise guidance seriously. Kathy and Jim McGinnis founded the Institute for Peace and Justice, still going strong more than thirty-five years later. The goal of the Institute is "helping people find learnable and doable alternatives that incorporate justice and peace into an active quest for peace in their lives." To this end, a Family Pledge of Nonviolence is available free on the Institute's website. The pledge covers areas of respect, communication, listening, forgiveness, respect for nature, creative play, and courage to confront violence in all its forms. It also provides a commitment for a family check-in once a month for the next 12 months, to reaffirm the new behaviors family members are learning. Find the Pledge at www.ipj-ppj.org/pledge.html.

Scripture Insights

Curtis Flood, an African American pioneer of integration in major league baseball, remembered the reaction of a hostile opposing team and its supporting fans. Decades after the event, he still spoke with shock at the way he, the sole black man on either team, had been treated to swarms of insults. "They called me everything but a child of God."

Who is a child of God? The author of the first letter of John states that what makes people into God's children is the love God gives to them. In this reading we also learn that "God is love." Love is not only what God expresses to the world by designating certain individuals, such as Samuel and Jesus Christ, to bear witness to it. Love is what God is.

This is an extraordinary and distinctively Christian claim. Although all-powerful, God is not power. Although the source of reason and wisdom, God is not mind. God is love. If we are God's children, then we are children of love.

How, then, shall we be children of love who express our true identity? We might begin by leaving aside the divisions and injustices plaguing our human family and by bearing witness against them whenever they arise. We are the children of a loving Creator. When the crowds called Curtis Flood everything but a child of God, they called him every name except the one that perhaps best described him. And themselves as well.

◆ What do you think motivated Hannah to leave the son she so desperately wanted at the Shiloh sanctuary?

◆ What do you think the author of First John means when he says "what we shall be has not yet been revealed"?

◆ When have you heard religion used to justify unfair treatment of someone on the grounds that they were Catholic?

READING I   *Isaiah 60:1—6*

Rise up in splendor, Jerusalem!
> Your light has come,
>> the glory of the LORD shines upon you.

See, darkness covers the earth,
>> and thick clouds cover the peoples;

but upon you the LORD shines,
>> and over you appears his glory.

Nations shall walk by your light,
>> and kings by your shining radiance.

Raise your eyes and look about;
>> they all gather and come to you:

your sons come from afar,
>> and your daughters in the arms of
>>> their nurses.

Then you shall be radiant at what you see,
>> your heart shall throb and overflow,

for the riches of the sea shall be emptied out
>>> before you,
>> the wealth of nations shall be brought
>>> to you.

Caravans of camels shall fill you,
>> dromedaries from Midian and Ephah;

all from Sheba shall come
>> bearing gold and frankincense,
>> and proclaiming the praises of the LORD.

READING II   *Ephesians 3:2—3a, 5—6*

Brothers and sisters: You have heard of the stewardship of God's grace that was given to me for your benefit, namely, that the mystery was made known to me by revelation. It was not made known to people in other generations as it has now been revealed to his holy apostles and prophets by the Spirit: that the Gentiles are coheirs, members of the same body, and copartners in the promise in Christ Jesus through the gospel.

GOSPEL   *Matthew 2:1—12*

When Jesus was born in Bethlehem of Judea, in the days of King Herod, behold, magi from the east arrived in Jerusalem, saying, "Where is the newborn king of the Jews? We saw his star at its rising and have come to do him homage." When King Herod heard this, he was greatly troubled, and all Jerusalem with him. Assembling all the chief priests and the scribes of the people, he inquired of them where the Christ was to be born. They said to him, "In Bethlehem of Judea, for thus it has been written through the prophet:

> *And you, Bethlehem, land of Judah,/are by no means least among the rulers of Judah;/since from you shall come a ruler,/who is to shepherd my people Israel."*

Then Herod called the magi secretly and ascertained from them the time of the star's appearance. He sent them to Bethlehem and said, "Go and search diligently for the child. When you have found him, bring me word, that I too may go and do him homage." After their audience with the king they set out. And behold, the star that they had seen at its rising preceded them, until it came and stopped over the place where the child was. They were overjoyed at seeing the star, and on entering the house they saw the child with Mary his mother. They prostrated themselves and did him homage. Then they opened their treasures and offered him gifts of gold, frankincense, and myrrh. And having been warned in a dream not to return to Herod, they departed for their country by another way.

Practice of Prayer

Psalm 72:1—2, 7—8, 10—11, 12—13 (see 11)

R. Lord, every nation on earth will adore you.

O God, with your judgment endow the king,
    and with your justice the king's son;
he shall govern your people with justice
    and your afflicted ones with judgment. R.

Justice shall flower in his days,
    and profound peace, till the moon be
        no more.
May he rule from sea to sea,
    and from the River to the ends
        of the earth. R.

The kings of Tarshish and the Islands shall
      offer gifts;
    the kings of Arabia and Seba shall
      bring tribute.
All kings shall pay him homage,
    all nations shall serve him. R.

For he shall rescue the poor when he cries out,
    and the afflicted when he has
      no one to help him.
He shall have pity for the lowly and the poor;
    the lives of the poor he shall save. R.

Practice of Faith

We don't know how many Magi there were. Scripture doesn't say. People have gotten the idea there were Three Wise Men from the fact that three gifts are named—gold, frankincense, and myrrh. However, three was a powerful symbolic number for early Christians, because they knew of three races and three continents—Africa, Europe, and Asia. Medieval paintings show the Magi as an African, an Asian, and a European. Often they are traveling on a camel, an elephant, and a horse. This proclaimed in a graphic way the message of Epiphany: Christ came for all. Tradition has given names to the three: Caspar, Melchior, and Balthasar. Your family can proclaim the message of Christ by tracing their initials in chalk over your front door today. 20 + C + M + B + 07

marks your commitment to Christian hospitality for the coming year. It says: All are welcome.

Scripture Insights

The word "epiphany" comes to us directly from Greek *(epiphaneia)*, the language in which our New Testament texts were composed. The ancient Greek definition of the word is "appearance" or "visible manifestation" and frequently describes the appearance of a divinity or a god to a human being. This is quite different from the word's colloquial English meaning in which an epiphany is a sudden realization or a bright idea that seemingly comes from nowhere. The appearance of the infant Jesus to the magi, who have been led from the east by a star, is an epiphany in the ancient sense of the world.

Today's Gospel is a story of two kings. One is Herod, who ruled over the Roman imperial province of Judea for more than thirty years as a friend of both Mark Antony and Augustus Caesar. The second is Jesus, the child born in a stable the magi have traveled far to see.

Imagine that we know nothing of Jesus Christ or Christianity. To which of these two, Herod or the baby in the stable, would we expect the magi to pay homage? Against all reasonable expectation they bow before the child in the stable, arousing the anxiety of the ruthless worldly king. Christianity often runs contrary to expectations. Our king, Jesus Christ, entered the world in humble circumstances. His rule was confirmed, complete with crown and royal purple robe, during his Passion, when he was nailed to a cross and left to die. The epiphany of the Lord shows us God disclosed in the most unlikely people and circumstances.

• What is the "mystery" in the passage from Ephesians?

• How do you celebrate Epiphany in your home? How is God manifest in your life, family, home, work place, or school?

• Tell of a time that you were surprised that someone helped you see God.

Winter Ordinary Time

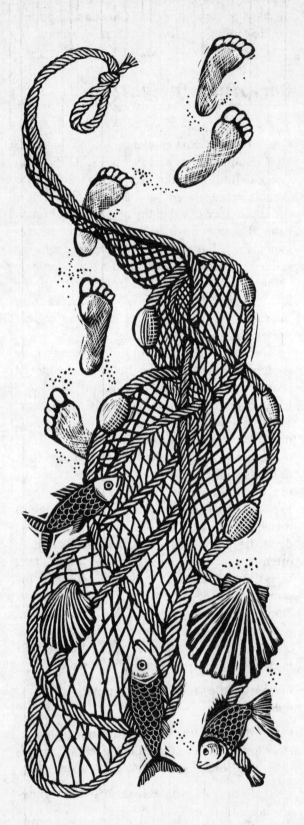

Prayer before Reading the Word

In you, O Lord our God,
we find our joy,
for through your law and your prophets
you formed a people in mercy and freedom,
in justice and righteousness.

You call us with your voice of flame.
Give us ears to hear,
Lives to respond,
And voices to proclaim the good news
      of salvation,
Which we know in our Savior Jesus Christ,
Who lives and reigns with you and the
      Holy Spirit,
One God, now and forever. Amen.

Prayer after Reading the Word

In your word, Lord God,
you reveal your power to heal and save us.

Let this good news echo throughout the world,
in every tongue and in every culture,
so that people everywhere may gladly embrace
the salvation and life you offer to all.

We ask this through our Lord Jesus Christ,
      your Son,
who lives and reigns with you
in the unity of the Holy Spirit,
God for ever and ever. Amen.

Weekday Readings

January 15: *Hebrews 5:1–10; Mark 2:18–22*
January 16: *Hebrews 6:10–20; Mark 2:23–28*
January 17: *Hebrews 7:1–3, 15–17; Mark 3:1–6*
January 18: *Hebrews 7:25–8:6; Mark 3:7–12*
January 19: *Hebrews 8:6–13; Mark 3:13–19*
January 20: *Hebrews 9:2–3, 11–14; Mark 3:20–21*

January 22: *Hebrews 9:15, 24–28; Mark 3:22–30*
January 23: *Hebrews 10:1–10; Mark 3:31–35*
January 24: *Hebrews 10:11–18; Mark 4:1–20;*
January 25: Feast of the Conversion of Saint Paul
   Acts 22:3–16; Mark 16:15–18
January 26: *2 Timothy 1:1–8; Mark 4:26–34*
January 27: *Hebrews 11:1–2, 8–19; Mark 4:35–41*

January 29: *Hebrews 11:32–40; Mark 5:1–20*
January 30: *Hebrews 12:1–4; Mark 5:21–43*
January 31: *Hebrews 12:4–7, 11–15; Mark 6:1–6*
February 1: *Hebrews 12:18–19, 21–24; Mark 6:7–13*

February 2: Feast of the Presentation of the Lord
   Malachi 3:1–4; Hebrews 2:14–18; Luke 2:22–40
February 3: *Hebrews 13:15–17, 20–21; Mark 6:30–34*

February 5: *Genesis 1:1–19; Mark 6:53–56*
February 6: *Genesis 1:20–2:4a; Mark 7:1–13*
February 7: *Genesis 2:4b–9, 15–17; Mark 7:14–23*
February 8: *Genesis 2:18–25; Mark 7:24–30*
February 9: *Genesis 3:1–8; Mark 7:31–37*
February 10: *Genesis 3:9–24; Mark 8: 1–10*

February 12: *Genesis 4:1–15, 25; Mark 8:11–13*
February 13: *Genesis 6:5–8; 7:1–5, 10; Mark 8:14–21*
February 14: *Genesis 8:6–13; 20–22; Mark 8:22–26*
February 15: *Genesis 9:1–13; Mark 8:27–33*
February 16: *Genesis 11:1–9; Mark 8:34–9:1*
February 17: *Hebrews 11:1–7; Mark 9:2–13;*

February 19: *Sirach 1:1–10; Mark 9:14–29*
February 20: *Sirach 2: 1–11: Mark 9:30–37*

READING I *Isaiah 62:1–5*

For Zion's sake I will not be silent,
for Jerusalem's sake I will not be quiet,
until her vindication shines forth like
the dawn
and her victory like a burning torch.

Nations shall behold your vindication,
and all the kings your glory;
you shall be called by a new name
pronounced by the mouth of the LORD.
You shall be a glorious crown in the hand of
the LORD,
a royal diadem held by your God.
No more shall people call you "Forsaken,"
or your land "Desolate,"
but you shall be called "My Delight,"
and your land "Espoused."
For the LORD delights in you
and makes your land his spouse.
As a young man marries a virgin,
your Builder shall marry you;
and as a bridegroom rejoices in his bride
so shall your God rejoice in you.

READING II *1 Corinthians 12:4–11*

Brothers and sisters: There are different kinds of spiritual gifts but the same Spirit; there are different forms of service but the same Lord; there are different workings but the same God who produces all of them in everyone. To each individual the manifestation of the Spirit is given for some benefit. To one is given through the Spirit the expression of wisdom; to another, the expression of knowledge according to the same Spirit; to another, faith by the same Spirit; to another, gifts of healing by the one Spirit; to another, mighty deeds; to another, prophecy; to another, discernment of spirits; to another, varieties of tongues; to another, interpretation of tongues. But one and the same Spirit produces all of these, distributing them individually to each person as he wishes.

GOSPEL *John 2:1–11*

There was a wedding at Cana in Galilee, and the mother of Jesus was there. Jesus and his disciples were also invited to the wedding. When the wine ran short, the mother of Jesus said to him, "They have no wine." And Jesus said to her, "Woman, how does your concern affect me? My hour has not yet come." His mother said to the servers, "Do whatever he tells you." Now there were six stone water jars there for Jewish ceremonial washings, each holding twenty to thirty gallons. Jesus told them, "Fill the jars with water." So they filled them to the brim. Then he told them, "Draw some out now and take it to the headwaiter." So they took it. And when the headwaiter tasted the water that had become wine, without knowing where it came from—although the servers who had drawn the water knew—, the headwaiter called the bridegroom and said to him, "Everyone serves good wine first, and then when people have drunk freely, an inferior one; but you have kept the good wine until now." Jesus did this as the beginning of his signs at Cana in Galilee and so revealed his glory, and his disciples began to believe in him.

Practice of Prayer

R. Proclaim his marvelous deeds to all the nations.

Sing to the LORD a new song;
  sing to the LORD, all you lands.
Sing to the LORD; bless his name. R.

Announce his salvation, day after day.
Tell his glory among the nations;
  among all peoples, his wondrous deeds. R.

Give to the LORD, you families of nations,
  give to the LORD glory and praise;
  give to the LORD the glory due his name! R.

Worship the LORD in holy attire.
  Tremble before him, all the earth;
say among the nations: The LORD is king.
  He governs the peoples with equity. R.

Practice of Faith

With last week's celebration of the Baptism of the Lord, we officially wrapped up the season of gift giving. Today we are reminded that some gifts are never out of season. These gifts are meant to be given away freely, for the benefit of all. Some call this "stewardship." While we've heard about the need to share our time, talent, and treasure, Saint Nicholas of Myra Parish in Hays, Kansas, has taken this to a new level by tithing as a parish. Each month a different community service organization receives a portion of what has been collected at weekend Masses so it can continue its vital work. The parish didn't start at ten percent of its income but is working in that direction slowly but surely. This is a good time to consider how we're sharing our gifts with others. Even a little effort can make a big difference.

Scripture Insights

The joy of a wedding feast—what a fitting note on which to begin this season of Ordinary Time, having just ended our Christmas celebration of the Incarnation of the Son of God. In today's first reading, Isaiah proclaims God's love. He says, "For the Lord delights in you and makes your land his spouse. . . . your Builder shall marry you; and as a bridegroom rejoices in his bride so shall your God rejoice in you."

The early Christians understood this prophecy—and others like it as fulfilled in Jesus. Each of the Gospels refer to Jesus as a bridegroom. Similarly, the book of Revelation portrays the joy of the age to come as the wedding feast of the Lamb of God.

How fitting that the Fourth Gospel situates the first of Jesus' miracles at a wedding feast. John calls these miracles "signs," as they disclose Jesus' identity. Through them, Jesus "revealed his glory and his disciples began to believe in him."

At issue is the lack of wine—an indispensable part of the wedding celebration. In providing wine, Jesus did more than alleviate the plight of an embarrassed host. In both the Old Testament and Jewish non-biblical writings, an abundance of wine was a sign of the Messianic Age. In the passage immediately preceding today's Gospel text, Jesus is acclaimed as Messiah. While the association of wine and the messianic age may not occur to contemporary readers, it would have been one early Christians readily made. May we, with them, see and believe—and rejoice in the presence of the heavenly Bridegroom who has made us his own.

• How are the promises of today's first reading fulfilled in Jesus?

• How could you daily live out the "joy" of Jesus' wedding feast?

• How did you come to know the gifts the Holy Spirit gave you?

January 21, 2007

READING I   Nehemiah 8:2 — 4a, 5 — 6, 8 — 10

Ezra the priest brought the law before the assembly, which consisted of men, women, and those children old enough to understand. Standing at one end of the open place that was before the Water Gate, he read out of the book from daybreak till midday, in the presence of the men, the women, and those children old enough to understand; and all the people listened attentively to the book of the law. Ezra the scribe stood on a wooden platform that had been made for the occasion. He opened the scroll so that all the people might see it —for he was standing higher up than any of the people—; and, as he opened it, all the people rose. Ezra blessed the LORD, the great God, and all the people, their hands raised high, answered, "Amen, amen!" Then they bowed down and prostrated themselves before the LORD, their faces to the ground. Ezra read plainly from the book of the law of God, interpreting it so that all could understand what was read. Then Nehemiah, that is, His Excellency, and Ezra the priest-scribe and the Levites who were instructing the people said to all the people: "Today is holy to the LORD your God. Do not be sad, and do not weep"—for all the people were weeping as they heard the words of the law. He said further: "Go, eat rich foods and drink sweet drinks, and allot portions to those who had nothing prepared; for today is holy to our LORD. Do not be saddened this day, for rejoicing in the LORD must be your strength!"

READING II   1 Corinthians 12:12 — 14, 27

Longer: 1 Corinthians 12:12 – 30

Brothers and sisters: As a body is one though it has many parts, and all the parts of the body, though many, are one body, so also Christ. For in one Spirit we were all baptized into one body, whether Jews or Greeks, slaves or free persons, and we were all given to drink of one Spirit. Now the body is not a single part, but many. You are Christ's body, and individually parts of it.

GOSPEL   Luke 1:1 — 4; 4:14 — 21

Since many have undertaken to compile a narrative of the events that have been fulfilled among us, just as those who were eyewitnesses from the beginning and ministers of the word have handed them down to us, I too have decided, after investigating everything accurately anew, to write it down in an orderly sequence for you, most excellent Theophilus, so that you may realize the certainty of the teachings you have received.

Jesus returned to Galilee in the power of the Spirit, and news of him spread throughout the whole region. He taught in their synagogues and was praised by all.

He came to Nazareth, where he had grown up, and went according to his custom into the synagogue on the sabbath day. He stood up to read and was handed a scroll of the prophet Isaiah. He unrolled the scroll and found the passage where it was written:

The Spirit of the Lord is upon me, /because he has anointed me /to bring glad tidings to the poor. / He has sent me to proclaim liberty to captives /and recovery of sight to the blind, /to let the oppressed go free, /and to proclaim a year acceptable to the Lord.

Rolling up the scroll, he handed it back to the attendant and sat down, and the eyes of all in the synagogue looked intently at him. He said to them, "Today this Scripture passage is fulfilled in your hearing."

Practice of Prayer

Psalm 19:8, 9, 10, 15 (see John 6:63c)

R. Your words, Lord, are Spirit and life.

The law of the LORD is perfect,
    refreshing the soul;
the decree of the LORD is trustworthy,
    giving wisdom to the simple. R.

The precepts of the LORD are right,
    rejoicing the heart;
the command of the Lord is clear,
    enlightening the eye. R.

The fear of the LORD is pure,
    enduring forever;
the ordinances of the Lord are true,
    all of them just. R.

Let the words of my mouth
    and the thought of my heart
    find favor before you,
O LORD, my rock and my redeemer. R.

Practice of Hope

This Sunday we hear much about law. We have to consider where the law leads us. Does it point us to a greater love and appreciation of God and God's people or to a greater love of the law? In revealing his mission, Jesus gives us the answer— and a clue about our own mission. If we are to bring glad tidings to the poor, we must find reliable ways to stay informed about who they are. If we are to proclaim liberty to captives, we must know the ways they are held bound. The Claretian Missionaries offer a way to monitor social injustices across the globe at its website, http//salt.claretian pubs.org. On the site, too, will be the United States Conference of Catholic Bishops' response to conflicts, natural disaster and legislation.

Scripture Insights

Personal testimony in the Bible, as in Luke today, is powerful. The evangelist tells us that, although not one of the first disciples, he investigated the "word" passed on to his generation. In his second volume, the Acts of the Apostles, Luke summarizes that his subject is "all that Jesus did and taught until the day he was taken up" into heaven. He writes that Theophilus might know the "certainty" or truth concerning the "word" of the teaching he has received. Luke's conviction is evident.

Two similar testimonies are found in the Gospel of John. In the first, as in Luke, the author expresses his hope that his account will lead others to faith. The second stresses the truth of what has been recorded since it comes from the hand of one of these first disciples. Saint Paul testifies to his experience of the Risen Jesus (Galatians 1:11–24, note the reference to truth in verse 20), but also to the testimony he "received" from the Lord through the Church (1 Corinthians 11:23–25; 15:3–8). The depth of his experience and conviction is evident. Indeed, one can assert that the author of every book in the Christian Scriptures writes from a depth of personal conviction and experience—and from the desire to share that with others. How easy it is to overlook that. Today's Lectionary, setting before us accounts of two proclamations of God's Word, calls us to be more open to that Word, for they are trustworthy words, words of Spirit and of life.

◆ What responses to the proclamation of God's Word are evident in today's Scriptures?

◆ Have you ever tried to read the weekday scriptures? How would that benefit you?

◆ Have you ever felt connected to a crowd of strangers? Did you understand the strangers as members of the Body of Christ?

January 28, 2007

READING I *Jeremiah 1:4—5, 17—19*

The word of the LORD came to me, saying:
> Before I formed you in the womb
>> I knew you,
>> before you were born I dedicated you,
>> a prophet to the nations I appointed you.

> But do you gird your loins;
>> stand up and tell them
>> all that I command you.
> Be not crushed on their account,
>> as though I would leave you crushed
>>> before them;
> for it is I this day
>> who have made you a fortified city,
> a pillar of iron, a wall of brass,
>> against the whole land:
> against Judah's kings and princes,
>> against its priests and people.
> They will fight against you
>> but not prevail over you,
> for I am with you to deliver you,
>> says the LORD.

READING II *1 Corinthians 12:31—13:13*

Shorter: 1 Corinthians 13:4–13

Brothers and sisters: Strive eagerly for the greatest spiritual gifts. But I shall show you a still more excellent way.

If I speak in human and angelic tongues, but do not have love, I am a resounding gong or a clashing cymbal. And if I have the gift of prophecy, and comprehend all mysteries and all knowledge; if I have all faith so as to move mountains, but do not have love, I am nothing. If I give away everything I own, and if I hand my body over so that I may boast, but do not have love, I gain nothing.

Love is patient, love is kind. It is not jealous, it is not pompous, it is not inflated, it is not rude, it does not seek its own interests, it is not quick-tempered, it does not brood over injury, it does not rejoice over wrongdoing but rejoices with the truth. It bears all things, believes all things, hopes all things, endures all things.

Love never fails. If there are prophecies, they will be brought to nothing; if tongues, they will cease; if knowledge, it will be brought to nothing. For we know partially and we prophesy partially, but when the perfect comes, the partial will pass away. When I was a child, I used to talk as a child, think as a child, reason as a child; when I became a man, I put aside childish things. At present we see indistinctly, as in a mirror, but then face to face. At present I know partially; then I shall know fully, as I am fully known. So faith, hope, love remain, these three; but the greatest of these is love.

GOSPEL *Luke 4:21—30*

Jesus began speaking in the synagogue, saying: "Today this Scripture passage is fulfilled in your hearing." And all spoke highly of him and were amazed at the gracious words that came from his mouth. They also asked, "Isn't this the son of Joseph?" He said to them, "Surely you will quote me this proverb, 'Physician, cure yourself,' and say, 'Do here in your native place the things that we heard were done in Capernaum.'" And he said, "Amen, I say to you, no prophet is accepted in his own native place. Indeed, I tell you, there were many widows in Israel in the days of Elijah when the sky was closed for three and a half years and a severe famine spread over the entire land. It was to none of these that Elijah was sent, but only to a widow in Zarephath in the land of Sidon. Again, there were many lepers in Israel during the time of Elisha the prophet; yet not one of them was cleansed, but only Naaman the Syrian." When the people in the synagogue heard this, they were all filled with fury. They rose up, drove him out of the town, and led him to the brow of the hill on which their town had been built, to hurl him down headlong. But Jesus passed through the midst of them and went away.

Practice of Prayer

Psalm 71:1—2, 3—4, 5—6, 15—17

R. I will sing of your salvation.

In you, O LORD, I take refuge;
  let me never be put to shame.
In your justice rescue me, and deliver me;
  incline your ear to me, and save me. R.

Be my rock of refuge,
  a stronghold to give me safety,
  for you are my rock and my fortress.
O my God, rescue me from the hand
    of the wicked. R.

For you are my hope, O LORD;
  my trust, O God, from my youth.
On you I depend from birth;
  from my mother's womb
    you are my strength. R.

My mouth shall declare your justice,
  day by day your salvation.
O God, you have taught me from my youth,
  and till the present I proclaim your
    wondrous deeds. R.

Practice of Faith

In these weeks between the Christmas and Lenten seasons, we are encouraged to claim our gifts and use them selflessly. As disciples joined to Jesus' mission, we are bound to proclaim his good news. The Paulist Fathers know that people need to make the gospel part of their lives before taking it out to others. They developed Disciples in Mission to help church communities renew their faith. With varied methods, this process focuses parishioners on the Lenten Sunday readings. Activities aid families in understanding their faith. Other resources provide for both teen and adult groups. Through prayer and discussion, participants come to know the church's mission. By Easter, there is new energy to spread the faith. The Paulist National Catholic Evangelization Association sponsors Disciples in Mission. You can find more information at www.disciplesinmission.org.

Scripture Insights

". . . Stand up and tell them/all that I command you./Be not crushed on their account,/as though I would leave you crushed before them./ . . . They will fight against you/but not prevail over you,/for I am with you to deliver you, says the LORD."

God's words to the prophet Jeremiah can be applied to Jesus. No doubt, Jesus often reflected on such biblical texts when pondering his vocation. Luke depicts one such example in the texts heard in last Sunday's Gospel. Today's Gospel repeats verse 21 and resumes the story, focusing on the reactions Jesus receives.

How quickly, how radically these reactions shift. Luke records that "all spoke highly of him and were amazed. . . ." But he also cited a dubious attitude. People asked, for instance, "Isn't this the son of Joseph?" The inflection can be surmised from Jesus' response. It was as if they said, "he can't be anybody special. . . . we know who he is. . . . who does he think he is?"

Jesus *knew* who he was. As was the case with the prophet Jeremiah in today's first reading, God ordained his mission even before he was born. As with Jeremiah, whose prophetic vocation entailed intense suffering, Jesus met resistance and rejection from the very beginning. The people in the synagogue cast Jesus out of the city, intending to kill him. This time, he walked away. Later, he would not be able to. Even at his death, no human prevailed over him. God was with him and delivered him, bringing salvation to all who receive him.

◆ What light do the Scriptures referred to in today's Gospel shed on Jesus' mission?

◆ Why are my reactions to "prophets" sometimes like those of the people in the synagogue?

◆ Has there been anyone in your lifetime that you would call a prophet?

READING I   *Isaiah 6:1—2a, 3—8*

In the year King Uzziah died, I saw the LORD seated on a high and lofty throne, with the train of his garment filling the temple. Seraphim were stationed above.

They cried one to the other, "Holy, holy, holy is the LORD of hosts! All the earth is filled with his glory!" At the sound of that cry, the frame of the door shook and the house was filled with smoke.

Then I said, "Woe is me, I am doomed! For I am a man of unclean lips, living among a people of unclean lips; yet my eyes have seen the King, the LORD of hosts!" Then one of the seraphim flew to me, holding an ember that he had taken with tongs from the altar.

He touched my mouth with it, and said, "See, now that this has touched your lips, your wickedness is removed, your sin purged."

Then I heard the voice of the Lord saying, "Whom shall I send? Who will go for us?" "Here I am," I said; "send me!"

READING II   *1 Corinthians 15:1—11*

Shorter: 1 Corinthians 15:3—8, 11

I am reminding you, brothers and sisters, of the gospel I preached to you, which you indeed received and in which you also stand. Through it you are also being saved, if you hold fast to the word I preached to you, unless you believed in vain. For I handed on to you as of first importance what I also received: that Christ died for our sins in accordance with the Scriptures; that he was buried; that he was raised on the third day in accordance with the Scriptures; that he appeared to Cephas, then to the Twelve. After that, he appeared to more than five hundred brothers at once, most of whom are still living, though some have fallen asleep. After that he appeared to James, then to all the apostles. Last of all, as to one born abnormally, he appeared to me. For I am the least of the apostles, not fit to be called an apostle, because I persecuted the church of God. But by the grace of God I am what I am, and his grace to me has not been ineffective. Indeed, I have toiled harder than all of them; not I, however, but the grace of God that is with me. Therefore, whether it be I or they, so we preach and so you believed.

GOSPEL   *Luke 5:1—11*

While the crowd was pressing in on Jesus and listening to the word of God, he was standing by the Lake of Gennesaret. He saw two boats there alongside the lake; the fishermen had disembarked and were washing their nets. Getting into one of the boats, the one belonging to Simon, he asked him to put out a short distance from the shore. Then he sat down and taught the crowds from the boat. After he had finished speaking, he said to Simon, "Put out into deep water and lower your nets for a catch." Simon said in reply, "Master, we have worked hard all night and have caught nothing, but at your command I will lower the nets." When they had done this, they caught a great number of fish and their nets were tearing. They signaled to their partners in the other boat to come to help them. They came and filled both boats so that the boats were in danger of sinking. When Simon Peter saw this, he fell at the knees of Jesus and said, "Depart from me, Lord, for I am a sinful man." For astonishment at the catch of fish they had made seized him and all those with him, and likewise James and John, the sons of Zebedee, who were partners of Simon. Jesus said to Simon, "Do not be afraid; from now on you will be catching men." When they brought their boats to the shore, they left everything and followed him.

Practice of Prayer

Psalm 138:1—2, 2—3, 4—5, 7—8 (1c)

R. In the sight of the angels I will sing your
    praises, Lord.

I will give thanks to you, O LORD, with all
    my heart,
    for you have heard the words of my mouth;

in the presence of the angels
  I will sing your praise;
I will worship at your holy temple
  and give thanks to your name. R.

Because of your kindness and your truth;
  for you have made great above all things
  your name and your promise.
When I called, you answered me;
  you built up strength within me. R.

All the kings of the earth shall give thanks to
   you, O LORD,
  when they hear the words of your mouth;
and they shall sing of the ways of the LORD:
  "Great is the glory of the LORD." R.

Your right hand saves me.
  The LORD will complete what he has done
   for me;
  your kindness, O LORD, endures forever;
  forsake not the work of your hands. R.

Practice of Charity

Jennah, Megan, and Elizabeth eagerly responded to the call to go to Cologne, Germany, for World Youth Day 2005. Though the trip would take them far from their central Illinois home, they knew it would be the chance of a lifetime. They anticipated sharing their faith with other youth and deepening their relationship with Jesus. But they weren't the only ones who responded. Others were taken by the teen's trust in God. Their small community rallied, with Catholics and non-Catholics alike, supporting them financially and spiritually. That mutual giving allowed for dialogue and faith-sharing with friends, neighbors, and strangers before the girls left U.S. soil. The teens returned every good deed with prayer. These young people demonstrated powerfully that leaving everything in God's hands didn't leave them empty-handed at all. Are we brave enough to do the same?

Scripture Insights

"Depart from me, Lord, for I am a sinful man." "Woe is me . . . . For I am a man of unclean lips . . . ." Such heartfelt cries of awareness of sinfulness may be uncommon in our day. So much so, that some thirty years ago, psychiatrist Karl Menninger wrote the book *Whatever Became of Sin?* The awareness of personal sinfulness that comes to the fore in today's Scriptures stems from the experience of the holiness and magnanimity of God. Clearly, such experiences are not one's doing, and Isaiah and Simon were taken by surprise. But if we read the text closely, we detect evidence of things that ready one for such experiences. Isaiah is in the Jerusalem temple, where elements of the liturgy provide the setting of his experience. Simon Peter, even while engaged in fisherman's tasks, is among those listening to the Word of God that Jesus proclaimed. What profound experiences of God and self were opened up listening to the Word and participating in the liturgy! Isaiah and Simon came to know something about who God is. They also experienced the purifying and transforming power of God in the face of their sinfulness. While there is nothing one can do to "make" such experiences happen, predisposing oneself to them through attentiveness to word and liturgy helps. Also needed is an openness to the experience of God's presence and power. Life was not the same for Isaiah and Simon after their experiences, nor will it be for us. There is no need to fear. The God who calls is faithful.

◆ What similarities are there between Saint Paul's experience of the Lord recounted in today's second reading and the experiences of Isaiah and Saint Peter?

◆ How do you meet the living God in Word and worship?

◆ Do you find it hard to blend spiritual experiences with daily life?

READING I   *Jeremiah 17:5—8*

Thus says the LORD:
Cursed is the one who trusts in
      human beings,
    who seeks his strength in flesh,
    whose heart turns away from the LORD.
He is like a barren bush in the desert
    that enjoys no change of season,
but stands in a lava waste,
    a salt and empty earth.
Blessed is the one who trusts in the LORD,
    whose hope is the LORD.
He is like a tree planted beside the waters
    that stretches out its roots to the stream:
It fears not the heat when it comes;
    its leaves stay green;
in the year of drought it shows no distress,
    but still bears fruit.

READING II   *1 Corinthians 15:12, 16—20*

Brothers and sisters: If Christ is preached as raised from the dead, how can some among you say there is no resurrection of the dead? If the dead are not raised, neither has Christ been raised, and if Christ has not been raised, your faith is vain; you are still in your sins. Then those who have fallen asleep in Christ have perished. If for this life only we have hoped in Christ, we are the most pitiable people of all.

But now Christ has been raised from the dead, the firstfruits of those who have fallen asleep.

GOSPEL   *Luke 6:17, 20—26*

Jesus came down with the Twelve and stood on a stretch of level ground with a great crowd of his disciples and a large number of the people from all Judea and Jerusalem and the coastal region of Tyre and Sidon. And raising his eyes toward his disciples he said:
    "Blessed are you who are poor,
      for the kingdom of God is yours.
    Blessed are you who are now hungry,
      for you will be satisfied.
    Blessed are you who are now weeping,
      for you will laugh.
    Blessed are you when people hate you,
      and when they exclude and insult you,
      and denounce your name as evil
      on account of the Son of Man.
Rejoice and leap for joy on that day! Behold, your reward will be great in heaven. For their ancestors treated the prophets in the same way.
    But woe to you who are rich,
      for you have received your consolation.
    Woe to you who are filled now,
      for you will be hungry.
    Woe to you who laugh now,
      for you will grieve and weep.
    Woe to you when all speak well of you,
      for their ancestors treated the
        false prophets in this way."

Practice of Prayer

Psalm 1:1–2, 3, 4 and 6 (40:5a)

R. Blessed are they who hope in the Lord.

Blessed the man who follows not
    the counsel of the wicked,
nor walks in the way of sinners,
    nor sits in the company of the insolent,
but delights in the law of the LORD
    and meditates on his law day and night. R.

He is like a tree
    planted near running water,
that yields its fruit in due season,
    and whose leaves never fade.
Whatever he does, prospers. R.

Not so the wicked, not so;
    they are like chaff which the wind
        drives away.
For the LORD watches over the way of the just,
    but the way of the wicked vanishes. R.

Practice of Faith

The image of a tree planted beside running water is an apt one for any Sunday—the original Christian feast, the day of delight, the day of freedom. The world we inhabit sends out its messages incessantly. Twenty-four/seven we are assailed by images that can cause us to forget who (and Whose) we are. Billboards, commercials, displays of wealth, and affluence beguile us into thinking we are incomplete without whatever they are hawking. In the apostolic letter, *Dies Domini*, the late Pope John Paul II urged the faithful "to rediscover Sunday." He called the day "an opportunity given to us to turn the fleeting moments of this life into seeds of eternity." Sunday calls us back to the fundamental freedom of life as God's beloved. It is our invitation to refreshment—a day for rest, for special treats, for visits to extended family and other loved ones, for joyful acts of charity. How will you honor and celebrate the Lord's Day today?

Scripture Insights

It is amazing how many times throughout the Scriptures God's people are imaged as plants. Both today's first reading and psalm depict the just person, "rooted" in the Lord, as a flourishing tree, whose roots draw on life-giving waters—a tree ever-verdant, producing much fruit.

It is this interior depth that enables such a person to still produce fruit, even in a time of drought. A person rooted in the Lord knows a strength that can withstand turmoil. For the psalmist, that depth is reached through meditation on the Torah. Israel loved the law of the Lord, seeing it as a light for one's way and as the path to life.

In today's text from Jeremiah, the prophet is called to trust in the Lord and to find his strength in the Lord. Jeremiah was a man who suffered greatly in carrying out his ministry. He needed the encouragement of God's word. The psalmist likens the one who trusts in God's love to an olive tree, a beautiful tree known for its longevity and abundant productivity.

Interestingly, Luke employs the image of a fruit-bearing tree as part of Jesus' beatitude discourse. What can be more trying to sustain than situations of poverty, hunger, grief, and insults? In these—as well as in one's own inner disposition—the disciple is called to produce "good fruit."

Those who do so will be counted among the righteous, towering like the palm tree and the majestic cedar of Lebanon, "planted in the house of the Lord" and flourishing in his courts.

• How does the image of Christ as the "first fruit" relate to Jeremiah 17 and Psalm 1?

• What practices can help you to become more rooted in the Lord?

• Can you think of a time when trusting in the Lord calmed you during a rough time?

February 18, 2007

READING I   1 Samuel 26:2, 7—9, 12—13, 22—23

In those days, Saul went down to the desert of Ziph with three thousand picked men of Israel, to search for David in the desert of Ziph. So David and Abishai went among Saul's soldiers by night and found Saul lying asleep within the barricade, with his spear thrust into the ground at his head and Abner and his men sleeping around him.

Abishai whispered to David: "God has delivered your enemy into your grasp this day. Let me nail him to the ground with one thrust of the spear; I will not need a second thrust!" But David said to Abishai, "Do not harm him, for who can lay hands on the LORD's anointed and remain unpunished?" So David took the spear and the water jug from their place at Saul's head, and they got away without anyone's seeing or knowing or awakening. All remained asleep, because the LORD had put them into a deep slumber.

Going across to an opposite slope, David stood on a remote hilltop at a great distance from Abner, son of Ner, and the troops. He said: "Here is the king's spear. Let an attendant come over to get it. The LORD will reward each man for his justice and faithfulness. Today, though the LORD delivered you into my grasp, I would not harm the LORD's anointed."

READING II   1 Corinthians 15:45—49

Brothers and sisters: It is written, *The first man, Adam, became a living being,* the last Adam a life-giving spirit. But the spiritual was not first; rather the natural and then the spiritual. The first man was from the earth, earthly; the second man, from heaven. As was the earthly one, so also are the earthly, and as is the heavenly one, so also are the heavenly. Just as we have borne the image of the earthly one, we shall also bear the image of the heavenly one.

GOSPEL   Luke 6:27—38

Jesus said to his disciples: "To you who hear I say, love your enemies, do good to those who hate you, bless those who curse you, pray for those who mistreat you. To the person who strikes you on one cheek, offer the other one as well, and from the person who takes your cloak, do not withhold even your tunic. Give to everyone who asks of you, and from the one who takes what is yours do not demand it back. Do to others as you would have them do to you. For if you love those who love you, what credit is that to you? Even sinners love those who love them. And if you do good to those who do good to you, what credit is that to you? Even sinners do the same. If you lend money to those from whom you expect repayment, what credit is that to you? Even sinners lend to sinners, and get back the same amount. But rather, love your enemies and do good to them, and lend expecting nothing back; then your reward will be great and you will be children of the Most High, for he himself is kind to the ungrateful and the wicked. Be merciful, just as your Father is merciful.

"Stop judging and you will not be judged. Stop condemning and you will not be condemned. Forgive and you will be forgiven. Give and gifts will be given to you; a good measure, packed together, shaken down, and overflowing, will be poured into your lap. For the measure with which you measure will in return be measured out to you."

Practice of Prayer

Psalm 103:1 — 2, 3 — 4, 8, 10, 12 — 13 (8a)

R. The Lord is kind and merciful.

Bless the LORD, O my soul;
　　all my being, bless his holy name.
Bless the LORD, O my soul;
　　forget not all his benefits.　R.

He pardons all your iniquities,
　　heals all your ills.
He redeems your life from destruction,
　　crowns you with kindness and
　　　　compassion. R.

Merciful and gracious is the LORD,
　　slow to anger, and abounding in kindness.
Not according to our sins does he deal with us,
　　nor does he requite us according
　　　　to our crimes. R.

As far as the east is from the west,
　　so far has he put our transgressions from us.
As a father has compassion on his children,
　　so the LORD has compassion
　　　　on those who fear him.　R.

Practice of Hope

Jim McKinley grew up in Protestant West Belfast, Ireland. Leaving school at age 15, he joined a Loyalist paramilitary group. Arrested and imprisoned, gradually he came to believe that those who follow Jesus are called to be peacemakers. Released after 12 years, he met his future wife, a Catholic. "From the minute we met," he says, "we knew that God had brought us together to work in reconciliation and peacemaking. This has not occurred overnight—this journey has been slow and painful as both of us shed off the baggage that we carried with us from our upbringing in 'the troubles.'" The two have formed an organization called Pax Works, which facilitates conversation at the grassroots level. Their story, and many others, can be found in the book *Artisans of Peace*, edited by Mary Ann Cejka and Thomas Bamat Maryknoll, New York: Orbis Books, 2003).

Scripture Insights

"I would not harm the Lord's anointed" (1 Samuel 26:23). David's words seem incredulous. How could he pass up the chance to kill the man who was seeking to kill him? Actually, today's reading is not the first such incident. In chapter 24, David had likewise let a similar opportunity go by. "The Lord forbid that I should do such a thing to my master, the Lord's anointed, as to lay a hand on him, for he is the Lord's anointed"—consecrated for the Lord's service when the prophet poured oil on his head.

David's words call all of us to account. Who among us has this same attitude of reverence and respect for another because of what God has made that person to be?

Every human being is deserving of reverence and respect because of who God has made them to be—a person created in God's own image and likeness. Every human being—yes, even the "enemy," deserves our reverence and respect because God created them in his own image and likeness. And Jesus' words in today's Gospel tell us precisely how we are to treat them. If we do as we are commanded, not only will we be imitating David towards Saul, we will be like Jesus. We will act with mercy.

The Greek word used with reference to the Father's mercifulness, *oiktirmós,* is the same word used in the Septuagint (Greek) translation of Exodus 34:6. Mercy is a preeminent characteristic of God. Luke's Gospel, more than any of the others, gives this prominence. Let us take Jesus' words to heart that we might be and do mercy.

◆ How does Psalm 103 illustrate "mercy"?

◆ Identify one practice that will help you become more merciful.

◆ Does forgiving a murderer make sense to you?

Lent

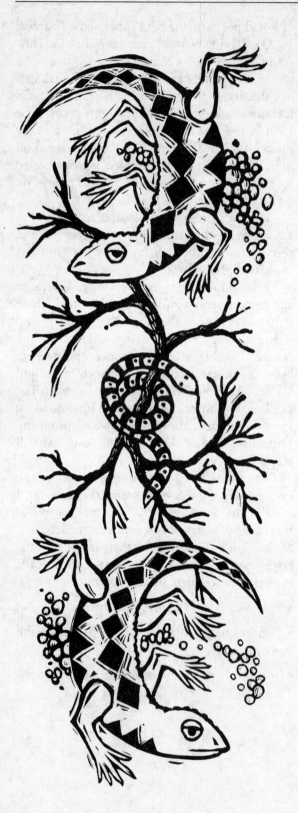

Prayer before Reading the Word

O Lord, great and faithful God,
it is good for us to be here!
Let us listen to your Son, your chosen One.

Shatter the hardness of our hearts
and open our minds to the wisdom of the gospel,
that we may grasp the lessons you teach us daily
and bring forth the fruit of true
and continual conversion.

We ask this through the One
into whom we have been baptized,
our Lord Jesus Christ, your Son,
and who lives and reigns with you
in the unity of the Holy Spirit,
God for ever and ever. Amen.

Prayer after Reading the Word

Infinite is your compassion, O God,
and gracious the pardon
that Jesus, the Teacher, offers
to every sinner who stands before him.

Gladden our hearts
at the word that sends us on our way in peace;
and grant that we who have been found
    by your grace
may gladly welcome to the table of your family
all who long to find their way home.

We ask this through Christ,
our peace and reconciliation,
the Lord who lives and reigns with you
in the unity of the Holy Spirit,
God for ever and ever. Amen.

Weekday Readings

February 21: Ash Wednesday
   Joel 2:12–18; 2 Corinthians 5:20–6:2; Matthew 6:1–6, 16–18

February 22: Feast of the Chair of Saint Peter
   1 Peter 5:1–4; Matthew 16:13–19

February 23: *Isaiah 58:1–9a; Matthew 9:14–15*
February 24: *Isaiah 58:9b–14; Luke 5:27–32*

February 26: *Leviticus 19:1–2, 11–18; Matthew 25:31–46*
February 27: *Isaiah 55:10–11; Matthew 6:7–15*
February 28: *Jonah 3:1–10; Luke 11:29–32*
March 1: *Esther C:12, 14–16, 23-25; Matthew 7:7–12*
March 2: *Ezekiel 18:21–28; Matthew 5:20–26*
March 3: *Deuteronomy 26:16–19; Matthew 5:43–48*

March 5: *Daniel 9:4b–10; Luke 6:36–38*
March 6: *Isaiah 1:10, 16–20; Matthew 23:1–12*
March 7: *Jeremiah 18:18–20; Matthew 20: 17–28*
March 8: *Jeremiah 17:5–10; Luke 16:19–31*
March 9: *Genesis 37:3–4, 12–13a, 17b–28a; Matthew 21:33–43, 45–46*
March 10: *Micah 7:14–15, 18–20; Luke 15:1–3, 11–32*

March 12: *2 Kings 5:1–15b; Luke 4:24–30*
March 13: *Daniel 3:25, 34–43; Matthew 18:21–35*
March 14: *Deuteronomy 4:1, 5–9; Matthew 5:17–19*
March 15: *Jeremiah 7:23–28; Luke 11:14–23*
March 16: *Hosea 14:2–10; Mark 12:28–34*
March 17: *Hosea 6:1–6; Luke 18:9–14*

March 19: Solemnity of Saint Joseph, husband of the Blessed Virgin Mary
   2 Samuel 7:4–5a, 12–14a, 16; Romans 4:13, 16–18, 22; Matthew 1:16, 18–21, 24a

March 20: *Ezekiel 47:1–9, 12; John 5:1–16*
March 21: *Isaiah 49:8–15; John 5:17–30*
March 22: *Exodus 32:7–14; John 5:31–47*
March 23: *Wisdom 2:1a, 12–22; John 7:1–2, 10, 25–30*
March 24: *Jeremiah 11:18–20; John 7:40–53*

March 26: Solemnity of the Annunciation of the Lord
   Isaiah 7:10–14; 8:10; Hebrews 10:4–10; Luke 1:26–38

March 27: *Numbers 21:4–9; John 8:21–30*
March 28: *Deuteronomy 3:14–20, 91–92, 95; John 8:31–42*
March 29: *Genesis 17:3–9; John 8:51–59*
March 30: *Jeremiah 20:10–13; John 10:31–42*
March 31: *Ezekiel 37:21–28; John 11:45–56*

April 2: *Isaiah 42:1–7; John 12:1–11*
April 3: *Isaiah 49:1–6; John 13:21–33, 36–38*
April 4: *Isaiah 50:4–9a; Matthew 26:14–25*

February 25, 2007

FIRST SUNDAY OF LENT

READING I   *Deuteronomy 26:4—10*

Moses spoke to the people, saying: "The priest shall receive the basket from you and shall set it in front of the altar of the LORD, your God. Then you shall declare before the LORD, your God, 'My father was a wandering Aramean who went down to Egypt with a small household and lived there as an alien. But there he became a nation great, strong, and numerous. When the Egyptians maltreated and oppressed us, imposing hard labor upon us, we cried to the LORD, the God of our fathers, and he heard our cry and saw our affliction, our toil, and our oppression. He brought us out of Egypt with his strong hand and outstretched arm, with terrifying power, with signs and wonders; and bringing us into this country, he gave us this land flowing with milk and honey. Therefore, I have now brought you the firstfruits of the products of the soil which you, O LORD, have given me.' And having set them before the LORD, your God, you shall bow down in his presence."

READING II   *Romans 10:8—13*

Brothers and sisters: What does Scripture say? *The word is near you, in your mouth and in your heart*—that is, the word of faith that we preach—, for, if you confess with your mouth that Jesus is Lord and believe in your heart that God raised him from the dead, you will be saved. For one believes with the heart and so is justified, and one confesses with the mouth and so is saved. For the Scripture says, *No one who believes in him will be put to shame.* For there is no distinction between Jew and Greek; the same Lord is Lord of all, enriching all who call upon him. For "everyone who calls on the name of the Lord will be saved."

GOSPEL   *Luke 4:1—13*

Filled with the Holy Spirit, Jesus returned from the Jordan and was led by the Spirit into the desert for forty days, to be tempted by the devil. He ate nothing during those days, and when they were over he was hungry. The devil said to him, "If you are the Son of God, command this stone to become bread." Jesus answered him, "It is written, *One does not live on bread alone.*" Then he took him up and showed him all the kingdoms of the world in a single instant. The devil said to him, "I shall give to you all this power and glory; for it has been handed over to me, and I may give it to whomever I wish. All this will be yours, if you worship me." Jesus said to him in reply, "It is written:

> You shall worship the Lord,
>> your God,
>> and him alone shall you serve."

Then he led him to Jerusalem, made him stand on the parapet of the temple, and said to him, "If you are the Son of God, throw yourself down from here, for it is written:

> He will command his angels
>> concerning you, to guard you,

and:

> With their hands they will support you,/lest you dash your foot against a stone."

Jesus said to him in reply, "It also says, *You shall not put the Lord, your God, to the test.*" When the devil had finished every temptation, he departed from him for a time.

Practice of Prayer

Psalm 91:1—2, 10—11, 12—13, 14—15 (see 15b)

R. Be with me, Lord, when I am in trouble.

You who dwell in the shelter of the Most High,
    who abide in the shadow of the Almighty,
say to the LORD, "My refuge and my fortress,
    my God, in whom I trust." R.

No evil shall befall you,
    nor affliction come near your tent.
For God commands the angels
    to guard you in all your ways. R.

Upon their hands they shall bear you up,
    lest you dash your foot against a stone.
You shall tread upon the asp and the viper;
    you shall trample down the lion and the
        dragon. R.

Because he clings to me, I will deliver him;
    I will set him on high because he
        acknowledges my name.
He shall call upon me, and I will answer him;
    I will be with him in distress;
I will deliver him and glorify him. R.

Practice of Hope

Prayer, fasting, and almsgiving are the year-round work of Christians. However, Lent is a season designed to call us back to the basics. St. Leo the Great said, "What Christians should be doing at all times should be done during Lent with greater care." That advice has never been more relevant. The gap between rich and poor grows greater. We on the affluent end of the scale can forget that so easily! Lent is a necessary spring tonic. Its triple disciplines of prayer, fasting, and almsgiving heal our hearts. Prayer calls us back to remembering that we are all one community. Fasting helps us recall that what we have was given to be shared. Almsgiving helps to address the injustices that forge stumbling blocks to peace and develops in us a generous spirit. Keep Lent well this year!

Scripture Insights

It is a modern American myth that there is such a thing as the "self-made" man or woman, an individual who succeeded on his or her own without seeking favors from family, friends, community, or society. The self-made individual is obliged to no one. Why is this an appealing portrait? After all, people who offer help to others with no thought of reward also are praised. Is the goal to be obliged to no one?

A credible depiction of hell is a place populated by souls trying to perpetually free themselves from bondage but refusing all offers to freedom that would imply obligation. The damnation is in the refusal. "Salvation," according to the *Catechism of the Catholic Church*, "comes from God alone" (paragraph 169). While there is much collective human effort required to cooperate with the salvation God offers people, there is simply no amount of will power, or work, that can achieve it absent God's help. Probably, at some time, everyone has tried to go it alone. But we all stand in need of God's help.

Some scholars believe today's verses from Deuteronomy are a creedal statement. There, Moses includes in his historical recitation, Israel's cry for salvation from slavery in Egypt. Under the boot of Egypt, Israel could only go to God. Neither for Jesus is there anyone to go to but his Father, despite the devil's promises of power and wealth. Taking these as examples to follow during this penitential season, we might give thanks when our obligations remind us that we need God's help.

• Why do you think Jesus answers the devil with scripture?

• Can you recall a time when you were struck with the realization that you needed God's power and not yours? Did life seem easier afterwards?

• How do you rely on the different communities of which you are a member?

READING I   *Genesis 15:5—12, 17—18*

The Lord God took Abram outside and said, "Look up at the sky and count the stars, if you can. Just so," he added, "shall your descendants be." Abram put his faith in the LORD, who credited it to him as an act of righteousness.

He then said to him, "I am the LORD who brought you from Ur of the Chaldeans to give you this land as a possession." "O Lord GOD," he asked, "how am I to know that I shall possess it?" He answered him, "Bring me a three-year-old heifer, a three-year-old she-goat, a three-year-old ram, a turtledove, and a young pigeon." Abram brought him all these, split them in two, and placed each half opposite the other; but the birds he did not cut up. Birds of prey swooped down on the carcasses, but Abram stayed with them. As the sun was about to set, a trance fell upon Abram, and a deep, terrifying darkness enveloped him.

When the sun had set and it was dark, there appeared a smoking fire pot and a flaming torch, which passed between those pieces. It was on that occasion that the LORD made a covenant with Abram, saying: "To your descendants I give this land, from the Wadi of Egypt to the Great River, the Euphrates."

READING II   *Philippians 3:17—4:1*

Shorter: Philippians 3:20—4:1

Join with others in being imitators of me, brothers and sisters, and observe those who thus conduct themselves according to the model you have in us. For many, as I have often told you and now tell you even in tears, conduct themselves as enemies of the cross of Christ. Their end is destruction. Their God is their stomach; their glory is in their "shame." Their minds are occupied with earthly things. But our citizenship is in heaven, and from it we also await a savior, the Lord Jesus Christ. He will change our lowly body to conform with his glorified body by the power that enables him also to bring all things into subjection to himself.

Therefore, my brothers and sisters, whom I love and long for, my joy and crown, in this way stand firm in the Lord.

GOSPEL   *Luke 9:28b—36*

Jesus took Peter, John and James and went up the mountain to pray. While he was praying, his face changed in appearance and his clothing became dazzling white. And behold, two men were conversing with him, Moses and Elijah, who appeared in glory and spoke of his exodus that he was going to accomplish in Jerusalem. Peter and his companions had been overcome by sleep, but becoming fully awake, they saw his glory and the two men standing with him. As they were about to part from him, Peter said to Jesus, "Master, it is good that we are here; let us make three tents, one for you, one for Moses, and one for Elijah." But he did not know what he was saying. While he was still speaking, a cloud came and cast a shadow over them, and they became frightened when they entered the cloud. Then from the cloud came a voice that said, "This is my chosen Son; listen to him." After the voice had spoken, Jesus was found alone. They fell silent and did not at that time tell anyone what they had seen.

Practice of Prayer

Psalm 27:1, 7 — 8, 8 — 9, 13 — 14

R. The Lord is my light and my salvation.

The LORD is my light and my salvation;
  whom should I fear?
The LORD is my life's refuge;
  of whom should I be afraid? R.

Hear, O LORD, the sound of my call;
  have pity on me, and answer me.
Of you my heart speaks; you my glance seeks. R.

Your presence, O LORD, I seek.
  Hide not your face from me;
do not in anger repel your servant.
  You are my helper; cast me not off. R.

I believe that I shall see the bounty of the LORD
  in the land of the living.
Wait for the LORD with courage;
  be stouthearted, and wait for the LORD. R.

Practice of Faith

In the gospels, Jesus' disciples are sometimes portrayed as oblivious to the seriousness of his mission and to the profound nature of what he is teaching. In this Transfiguration encounter, however, Peter, John, and James have a *kairos* moment, an experience of time out of time. In the profound silence, they are able to comprehend Jesus' true identity. Twenty-first century disciples of Jesus are still discovering the power of silence. The not-for-profit organization Contemplative Outreach teaches centering prayer, a method of prayer that prepares a person to receive the gift of God's presence. Centering prayer also quiets the spirit so that one is better able to cooperate with this gift. It emphasizes prayer as a personal relationship with God. People who practice centering prayer on a regular basis notice that it tends to build communities of faith. You can learn more about Contemplative Outreach at www.centering prayer.com.

Scripture Insights

You can find one of the great chases depicted in English literature in G. K. Chesterton's *The Man Who Was Thursday*. Six men, each named for a day of the week, pursue a figure known to them only as Sunday, whom they fear to be the most dangerous being imaginable. The men's pursuit is relentless, but their mysterious quarry eludes them by cab, fire engine, and even hot air balloon. At last, believing they have finally lost track of him, the six men discuss what they think of Sunday and discover their thoughts about him differ radically. Despite their intimate association with him, the six have scarcely comprehended Sunday.

In the gospels, Jesus frequently teaches his disciples privately. Today, we see Jesus select Peter, James, and John to go up the mountain with him. Peter's reaction to the transfiguration shows that he does not understand its significance. Neither does he understand the talk of the "exodus" among Jesus, Moses, and Elijah. Peter's offer to make tents seems peculiar, although easy to understand. Though grateful for what he's witnessing, Peter is in total awe and babbles.

The Christian life has been defined in many ways. One succinct definition is that it is the search for the triune God, and that it is the most important search there is. But the object of our search, even when shown as within reach, in reality always lies beyond our grasp. In these rare moments, grateful awe is perhaps the best a person can do.

• Deciding to believe in God was a leap in faith for Abram. Describe leaps of faith you have made and why you made them.

• How does Paul use political language in the second reading?

• Have you had anything like a "Transfiguration experience"?

READING I   *Exodus 3:1 — 8a, 13 — 15*

Moses was tending the flock of his father-in-law Jethro, the priest of Midian. Leading the flock across the desert, he came to Horeb, the mountain of God. There an angel of the LORD appeared to Moses in fire flaming out of a bush. As he looked on, he was surprised to see that the bush, though on fire, was not consumed. So Moses decided, "I must go over to look at this remarkable sight, and see why the bush is not burned."

When the LORD saw him coming over to look at it more closely, God called out to him from the bush, "Moses! Moses!" He answered, "Here I am." God said, "Come no nearer! Remove the sandals from your feet, for the place where you stand is holy ground. I am the God of your fathers," he continued, "the God of Abraham, the God of Isaac, the God of Jacob." Moses hid his face, for he was afraid to look at God. But the LORD said, "I have witnessed the affliction of my people in Egypt and have heard their cry of complaint against their slave drivers, so I know well what they are suffering. Therefore I have come down to rescue them from the hands of the Egyptians and lead them out of that land into a good and spacious land, a land flowing with milk and honey."

Moses said to God, "But when I go to the Israelites and say to them, 'The God of your fathers has sent me to you,' if they ask me, 'What is his name?' what am I to tell them?" God replied, "I am who am." Then he added, "This is what you shall tell the Israelites: I AM sent me to you."

God spoke further to Moses, "Thus shall you say to the Israelites: The LORD, the God of your fathers, the God of Abraham, the God of Isaac, the God of Jacob, has sent me to you.

"This is my name forever;
    thus am I to be remembered
       through all generations."

READING II   *1 Corinthians 10:1 — 6, 10 — 12*

I do not want you to be unaware, brothers and sisters, that our ancestors were all under the cloud and all passed through the sea, and all of them were baptized into Moses in the cloud and in the sea. All ate the same spiritual food, and all drank the same spiritual drink, for they drank from a spiritual rock that followed them, and the rock was the Christ. Yet God was not pleased with most of them, for they were struck down in the desert.

These things happened as examples for us, so that we might not desire evil things, as they did. Do not grumble as some of them did, and suffered death by the destroyer. These things happened to them as an example, and they have been written down as a warning to us, upon whom the end of the ages has come. Therefore, whoever thinks he is standing secure should take care not to fall.

GOSPEL   *Luke 13:1 — 9*

Some people told Jesus about the Galileans whose blood Pilate had mingled with the blood of their sacrifices. Jesus said to them in reply, "Do you think that because these Galileans suffered in this way they were greater sinners than all other Galileans? By no means! But I tell you, if you do not repent, you will all perish as they did! Or those eighteen people who were killed when the tower at Siloam fell on them— do you think they were more guilty than everyone else who lived in Jerusalem? By no means! But I tell you, if you do not repent, you will all perish as they did!"

And he told them this parable: "There once was a person who had a fig tree planted in his orchard, and when he came in search of fruit on it but found none, he said to the gardener, 'For three years now I have come in search of fruit on this fig tree but have found none. So cut it down. Why should it exhaust the soil?' He said to him in reply, 'Sir, leave it for this year also, and I shall cultivate the ground around it and fertilize it; it may bear fruit in the future. If not you can cut it down.'"

Practice of Prayer

Psalm 103:1—2, 3—4, 6—7, 8, 11

R. The LORD is kind and merciful.

Bless the LORD, O my soul;
    and all my being, bless his holy name.
Bless the LORD, O my soul,
    and forget not all his benefits. R.

He pardons all your iniquities,
    heals all your ills,
He redeems your life from destruction,
    he crowns you with kindness
        and compassion. R.

The LORD secures justice
    and the rights of all the oppressed.
He has made known his ways to Moses,
    and his deeds to the children of Israel. R.

Merciful and gracious is the LORD,
    slow to anger and abounding in kindness.
For as the heavens are high above the earth,
    so surpassing is his kindness toward those
        who fear him. R.

Practice of Hope

Powerful images of the Exodus in today's first and second readings have stirred the hearts of those who struggled for worker justice. One such person was John Corridan, SJ, known to his colleagues as "Pete." In 1946, shortly after arriving at the Xavier Institute of Industrial Relations in New York City, Corridan was assigned to work with dockworkers on nearby Chelsea Piers. He discovered that corruption, kickbacks, and organized crime were rampant. "Men are hired," he told a reporter, "as if they were beasts of burden, part of the slave market of a pagan era." His willingness to break the code of silence that had held sway until then—at considerable personal risk—led to a public outcry and eventual reform. The labor priest, portrayed by Karl Malden, in the film *On the Waterfront* was a character closely based on Father Corridan's life fand work.

Scripture Insights

It's hard not to envy Moses. God gave him specific instructions. When Moses became confused, he received clarification. Most of us are not so fortunate. So let scripture be our burning bush. We can devour and never consume it.

In today's passage from First Corinthians, Saint Paul shows how the early Church interpreted the sacred books of Israel. According to Saint Paul, God's help and punishments of Israel during the Exodus "happened to them as an example, and they have been written down as a warning to us." Speaking of the rock that quenched their thirst, he says that the rock "was the Christ." Saint Paul finds Christ in the Exodus, even where he is not explicitly mentioned and concludes that this account is aimed at Jesus' followers in Saint Paul's time.

Reading the story of the Exodus through the Christian awareness of Christ's presence in the sacraments, Saint Paul suggests that Christ accompanied the Israelites in sacramental experiences that they could not recognize. Their passage through the Red Sea was a kind of Baptism into Moses—an insight that helped Christians see themselves as heirs of Israel encountering a second Exodus in their baptisms into Christ. The spiritual food and drink the Israelites received was a prefiguration of Eucharist.

Saint Paul understands Israel's exodus, with its blessings and chastisements, as analogous to the Corinthians' situation. Divided Corinth is mirrored in quarrelsome Israel. Perhaps today's divided churches are similar to Saint Paul's view of both the Exodus and the situation he addresses at Corinth. In this season of penance, we might reflect on these scriptural examples.

• How does the parable of the fig tree underscore Jesus' earlier words about repentance?

• What significance (personal, religious, spiritual) do you see in the name "I AM"?

• Do you believe God punishes for sin? Why or why not?

READING I   *Exodus 17:3—7*

In those days, in their thirst for water, the people grumbled against Moses, saying, "Why did you ever make us leave Egypt? Was it just to have us die here of thirst with our children and our live-stock?" So Moses cried out to the LORD, "What shall I do with this people? A little more and they will stone me!" The LORD answered Moses, "Go over there in front of the people, along with some of the elders of Israel, holding in your hand, as you go, the staff with which you struck the river. I will be standing there in front of you on the rock in Horeb. Strike the rock, and the water will flow from it for the people to drink." This Moses did, in the presence of the elders of Israel. The place was called Massah and Meribah, because the Israelites quarreled there and tested the LORD, saying, "Is the LORD in our midst or not?"

READING II   *Romans 5:1—2, 5—8*

Brothers and sisters: Since we have been justified by faith, we have peace with God through our Lord Jesus Christ, through whom we have gained access by faith to this grace in which we stand, and we boast in hope of the glory of God.

And hope does not disappoint, because the love of God has been poured out into our hearts through the Holy Spirit who has been given to us. For Christ, while we were still helpless, died at the appointed time for the ungodly. Indeed, only with difficulty does one die for a just person, though perhaps for a good person one might even find courage to die. But God proves his love for us in that while we were still sinners Christ died for us.

GOSPEL   *John 4:5—15, 19b—26, 39a, 40—42*

Longer: John 4:5–42

Jesus came to a town of Samaria called Sychar, near the plot of land that Jacob had given to his son Joseph. Jacob's well was there. Jesus, tired from his journey, sat down there at the well. It was about noon.

A woman of Samaria came to draw water. Jesus said to her, "Give me a drink." His disciples had gone into the town to buy food. The Samaritan woman said to him, "How can you, a Jew, ask me, a Samaritan woman, for a drink?"—For Jews use nothing in common with Samaritans.—Jesus answered and said to her, "If you knew the gift of God and who is saying to you, 'Give me a drink,' you would have asked him and he would have given you living water." The woman said to him, "Sir, you do not even have a bucket and the cistern is deep; where then can you get this living water? Are you greater than our father Jacob, who gave us this cistern and drank from it himself with his children and his flocks?" Jesus answered and said to her, "Everyone who drinks this water will be thirsty again; but whoever drinks the water I shall give will never thirst; the water I shall give will become in him a spring of water welling up to eternal life." The woman said to him, "Sir, give me this water, so that I may not be thirsty or have to keep coming here to draw water.

"I can see that you are a prophet. Our ancestors worshiped on this mountain; but you people say that the place to worship is in Jerusalem." Jesus said to her, "Believe me, woman, the hour is coming when you will worship the Father neither on this mountain nor in Jerusalem. You people worship what you do not understand; we worship what we understand, because salvation is from the Jews. But the hour is coming, and is now here, when true worshipers will worship the Father in Spirit and truth; and indeed the Father seeks such people to worship him. God is Spirit, and those who worship him must worship in Spirit and truth." The woman said to him, "I know that the Messiah is coming, the one called the Christ; when he comes, he will tell us everything." Jesus said to her, "I am he, the one speaking with you."

Many of the Samaritans of that town began to believe in him. When the Samaritans came to him, they invited him to stay with them; and he stayed there two days. Many more began to believe in him because of his word, and they said to the woman, "We no longer believe because of your word; for we have heard for ourselves, and we know that this is truly the savior of the world."

Practice of Charity

In the fourth century in Milan, catechumens were baptized at Easter Vigil much as they are today. However, in those days the services were very long. So, after the baptisms, the newly baptized were offered a drink of milk and honey to sustain them. This let them know that they had found a homeland, just as the Israelites centuries earlier had found "a land flowing with milk and honey." Today in your parish, people are preparing for Baptism and for full reception into the Catholic Church through the Rite of Christian Initiation of Adults (RCIA). They, too, are in need of sustenance. How can you support them? You might carry the name of a catechumen in your pocket and pray for that person. Perhaps you could offer to assist the RCIA team, help to make a baptismal garment, or donate money for a baptismal candle. Your welcome will make a difference!

Scripture Insights

Imagine a reporter's random interview on prayer. A pedestrian is queried about her belief in God's answering prayer. "Oh yes," she replies. "That's what I believe." The reporter continues, "Do you mean that God gives you what you ask for?" "Oh no," she says, chuckling. "And I'm happy God doesn't." "Why?" asks the confused reporter. The pedestrian replies, "Well, what I want, and what I need aren't the same. If God let me have whatever I wanted, instead of giving me what I needed, then it wouldn't be long before I had totally short-changed myself."

The Samaritan woman desires a more convenient access to drinking water. Jesus offers her "a spring of water welling up to eternal life," a reference to the waters of Baptism. The woman does not understand Jesus' offer, and you can't blame her. Most people can probably identify with the woman. She is so dominated by personal cares that she is deaf to the appeal of the one closest to her.

In the Exodus reading, the Israelites believe their only options are slavery or death. They suppose that Moses led them out from under Pharaoh's whip only to let them perish in the wilderness. Despite their experience, they leave out God when considering options.

Who has not been like the Samaritan woman? Who has not been like the Israelites, refusing even to ask for help in the first place? We do well this season if we make our petitions to God in the hopes that we will receive what we need instead of what we want.

• Why do you think Jesus does not make himself clear to the Samaritan woman?

• What does the phrase "hope does not disappoint" mean? What kind of hope is this?

• How have your prayers of petitions changed in recent years?

READING I   *Joshua 5:9a, 10—12*

The LORD said to Joshua, "Today I have removed the reproach of Egypt from you."

While the Israelites were encamped at Gilgal on the plains of Jericho, they celebrated the Passover on the evening of the fourteenth of the month. On the day after the Passover, they ate of the produce of the land in the form of unleavened cakes and parched grain. On that same day after the Passover, on which they ate of the produce of the land, the manna ceased. No longer was there manna for the Israelites, who that year ate of the yield of the land of Canaan.

READING II   *2 Corinthians 5:17—21*

Brothers and sisters: Whoever is in Christ is a new creation: the old things have passed away; behold, new things have come. And all this is from God, who has reconciled us to himself through Christ and given us the ministry of reconciliation, namely, God was reconciling the world to himself in Christ, not counting their trespasses against them and entrusting to us the message of reconciliation. So we are ambassadors for Christ, as if God were appealing through us. We implore you on behalf of Christ, be reconciled to God. For our sake he made him to be sin who did not know sin, so that we might become the righteousness of God in him.

GOSPEL   *Luke 15:1—3, 11—32*

Tax collectors and sinners were all drawing near to listen to Jesus, but the Pharisees and scribes began to complain, saying, "This man welcomes sinners and eats with them." So to them Jesus addressed this parable: "A man had two sons, and the younger son said to his father, 'Father give me the share of your estate that should come to me.' So the father divided the property between them. After a few days, the younger son collected all his belongings and set off to a distant country where he squandered his inheritance on a life of dissipation. When he had freely spent everything, a severe famine struck that country, and he found himself in dire need. So he hired himself out to one of the local citizens who sent him to his farm to tend the swine. And he longed to eat his fill of the pods on which the swine fed, but nobody gave him any. Coming to his senses he thought, 'How many of my father's hired workers have more than enough food to eat, but here am I, dying from hunger. I shall get up and go to my father and I shall say to him, "Father, I have sinned against heaven and against you. I no longer deserve to be called your son; treat me as you would treat one of your hired workers."' So he got up and went back to his father. While he was still a long way off, his father caught sight of him, and was filled with compassion. He ran to his son, embraced him and kissed him. His son said to him, 'Father, I have sinned against heaven and against you; I no longer deserve to be called your son.' But his father ordered his servants, 'Quickly bring the finest robe and put it on him; put a ring on his finger and sandals on his feet. Take the fattened calf and slaughter it. Then let us celebrate with a feast, because this son of mine was dead, and has come to life again; he was lost, and has been found.' Then the celebration began. Now the older son had been out in the field and, on his way back, as he neared the house, he heard the sound of music and dancing. He called one of the servants and asked what this might mean. The servant said to him, 'Your brother has returned and your father has slaughtered the fattened calf because he has him back safe and sound.' He became angry, and when he refused to enter the house, his father came out and pleaded with him. He said to his father in reply, 'Look, all these years I served you and not once did I disobey your orders; yet you never gave me even a young goat to feast on with my friends. But when your son returns who swallowed up your property with prostitutes, for him you slaughter the fattened calf.' He said to him, 'My son, you are here with me always; everything I have is yours. But now we must celebrate and rejoice, because your brother was dead and has come to life again; he was lost and has been found.'"

Practice of Prayer

Psalm 34:2—3, 4—5, 6—7 (9a)

R. Taste and see the goodness of the Lord.

I will bless the LORD at all times;
  his praise shall be ever in my mouth.
Let my soul glory in the LORD;
  the lowly will hear me and be glad. R.

Glorify the LORD with me,
  let us together extol his name.
I sought the LORD, and he answered me
  and delivered me from all my fears. R.

Look to him that you may be radiant with joy,
  and your faces may not blush with shame.
When the poor one called out, the LORD heard,
  and from all his distress he saved him. R.

Practice of Charity

Unfortunately, the kind of severe famine experienced by the prodigal son is still all too common in the twenty-first century. The primary causes of famine remain the same—war, drought, and invading insects such as locusts. Catholic Relief Services attempts to build peace in countries around the world while also trying to meet the needs of the impoverished. A $75 donation to CRS will provide a goat that will yield fresh milk and cheese for a family. A $20 donation will buy hens for a household, and $50 will purchase a calf. To discover how you can help provide for the needs of people in other countries, check out the CRS Project Catalog at www.crsgifts.org/feeding.cfm. Through the catalog, you will find descriptions of projects in many countries, the cost of a share of a project, and how to make a donation.

Scripture Insights

Luke doesn't give a name to the main character in today's Gospel reading, and so traditionally he has been called the Prodigal Son. The man's name is one of many things we do not know about him. Did he sincerely repent of his sins against heaven and father or was the speech he delivered just a slick attempt to cut the best deal he could?

Jesus tells this story in response to the complaint that Jesus "welcomes sinners and eats with them." Tax collectors are obviously included among the undesirables with whom Jesus dines. These low-level officials were understandably hated. Backed by the threat of Roman violence, tax collectors took money and property from the poor, helped themselves to a nice cut, and gave the rest to their bosses. The complaint of the scribes and Pharisees is appropriate, for it is with willing participants in the impoverishment of Israel that Jesus chooses to spend his time.

Is all sin identical? Is the squandering of an inheritance the same as the impoverishment of an entire people? Is a loving, repentant son the same as a cynical son plotting to further manipulate his father? Of course, they are not. But despite the opinion of the scribes and Pharisees, sin is not the issue. The son's sincerity has no bearing on his father's compassion. Jesus tells the story of the Prodigal Son to illustrate that God's mercy is not subject to human restriction. The comforting conclusion is that God joyfully extends mercy to the very worst of us.

• What does Saint Paul mean when he says that God made "him to be sin who did not know sin"?

• How do you identify with one or more of the characters in the Gospel reading?

• Why is it so hard to offer mercy without conditions? Is there someone who needs your mercy?

READING I 1 Samuel 16:1b, 6–7, 10–13a

The LORD said to Samuel: "Fill your horn with oil, and be on your way. I am sending you to Jesse of Bethlehem, for I have chosen my king from among his sons."

As Jesse and his sons came to the sacrifice, Samuel looked at Eliab and thought, "Surely the LORD's anointed is here before him." But the LORD said to Samuel: "Do not judge from his appearance or from his lofty stature, because I have rejected him. Not as man sees does God see, because man sees the appearance but the LORD looks into the heart." In the same way Jesse presented seven sons before Samuel, but Samuel said to Jesse, "The LORD has not chosen any one of these." Then Samuel asked Jesse, "Are these all the sons you have?" Jesse replied, "There is still the youngest, who is tending the sheep." Samuel said to Jesse, "Send for him; we will not begin the sacrificial banquet until he arrives here." Jesse sent and had the young man brought to them. He was ruddy, a youth handsome to behold and making a splendid appearance. The LORD said, "There—anoint him, for this is the one!" Then Samuel, with the horn of oil in hand, anointed David in the presence of his brothers; and from that day on, the spirit of the LORD rushed upon David.

READING II Ephesians 5:8–14

Brothers and sisters: You were once darkness, but now you are light in the Lord. Live as children of light, for light produces every kind of goodness and righteousness and truth. Try to learn what is pleasing to the Lord. Take no part in the fruitless works of darkness; rather expose them, for it is shameful even to mention the things done by them in secret; but everything exposed by the light becomes visible, for everything that becomes visible is light. Therefore, it says:

"Awake, O sleeper,
and arise from the dead,
and Christ will give you light."

GOSPEL John 9:1–41

Shorter: John 9:1, 6–9, 13–17, 34–38

As Jesus passed by he saw a man blind from birth. His disciples asked him, "Rabbi, who sinned, this man or his parents, that he was born blind?" Jesus answered, "Neither he nor his parents sinned; it is so that the works of God might be made visible through him. We have to do the works of the one who sent me while it is day. Night is coming when no one can work. While I am in the world, I am the light of the world." When he had said this, he spat on the ground and made clay with the saliva, and smeared the clay on his eyes, and said to him, "Go wash in the Pool of Siloam"—which means Sent—. So he went and washed, and came back able to see.

His neighbors and those who had seen him earlier as a beggar said, "Isn't this the one who used to sit and beg?" Some said, "It is," but others said, "No, he just looks like him." He said, "I am." So they said to him, "How were your eyes opened?" He replied, "The man called Jesus made clay and anointed my eyes and told me, 'Go to Siloam and wash.' So I went there and washed and was able to see." And they said to him, "Where is he?" He said, "I don't know."

They brought the one who was once blind to the Pharisees. Now Jesus had made clay and opened his eyes on a sabbath. So then the Pharisees also asked him how he was able to see. He said to them, "He put clay on my eyes, and I washed, and now I can see." So some of the Pharisees said, "This man is not from God, because he does not keep the sabbath." But others said, "How can a sinful man do such signs?" And there was a division among them. So they said to the blind man again, "What do you have to say about him, since he opened your eyes?" He said, "He is a prophet."

Now the Jews did not believe that he had been blind and gained his sight until they summoned the parents of the one who had gained his sight. They asked them, "Is this your son, who you say was born blind? How does he now see?" His parents answered and said, "We know that this is our son and that he was born blind. We do not know how he sees now, nor do we know who opened his eyes. Ask him, he is of age; he can speak for himself." His parents said this because they were afraid of the Jews, for the Jews had already agreed that if anyone acknowledged him as the Christ, he would be expelled from the synagogue. For this reason his parents said, "He is of age; question him."

So a second time they called the man who had been blind and said to him, "Give God the praise! We know that this man is a sinner." He replied, "If he is a sinner, I do not know. One thing I do know is that I was blind and now I see." So they said to him, "What did he do to you? How did he open your eyes?" He answered them, "I told you already and you did not listen. Why do you want to hear it again? Do you want to become his disciples, too?" They ridiculed him and said, "You are that man's disciple; we are disciples of Moses! We know that God spoke to Moses, but we do not know where this one is from." The man answered and said to them, "This is what is so amazing, that you do not know where he is from, yet he opened my eyes. We know that God does not listen to sinners, but if one is devout and does his will, he listens to him. It is unheard of that anyone ever opened the eyes of a person born blind. If this man were not from God, he would not be able to do anything." They answered and said to him, "You were born totally in sin, and are you trying to teach us?" Then they threw him out.

When Jesus heard that they had thrown him out, he found him and said, "Do you believe in the Son of Man?" He answered and said, "Who is he, sir, that I may believe in him?" Jesus said to him, "You have seen him, the one speaking with you is he." He said, "I do believe, Lord," and he worshiped him. Then Jesus said, "I came into this world for judgment, so that those who do not see might see, and those who do see might become blind."

Some of the Pharisees who were with him heard this and said to him, "Surely we are not also blind, are we?" Jesus said to them, "If you were blind, you would have no sin; but now you are saying, 'We see,' so your sin remains."

You can still visit the pool of Siloam in Jerusalem. Today the pool's water is unsafe to drink. The pool is fed by the Gihon spring, which flows from the base of the ridge where the most ancient part of Jerusalem once stood. The spring was flowing when David captured Jerusalem by stealth and made it his capital. And it was flowing when a man born blind was commanded to rinse his eyes in its waters and saw the world clearly for the first time.

As the man born blind learns, seeing the world clearly has consequences. Since he testifies to the fact that Jesus healed him, the man is sold out by neighbors and family, interrogated by religious officials, and finally cast out of the only community he has ever known. The true blindness in the story belongs not to the man, but to his neighbors, who push him before the Pharisees, and the Pharisees, whose blindness consists in their mistaken belief that they see well enough to pass judgment on others.

The man born blind is open to Jesus' aid because he knows he cannot see. Unlike the Pharisees, who live in the darkness, the man born blind knows of his infirmity. Unlike his neighbors, who see so poorly they cannot agree on the identity of a man they have seen daily for years, the man born blind is under no such illusion. Can we say as much? How many modern tourists, in Jerusalem or elsewhere, excitedly view the place but remain blind to the adjacent injustice?

◆ What does the phrase "the spirit of the Lord rushed upon David" mean?

◆ Why is it hard to accept that someone has changed?

◆ From what blindness, if any, has God healed you? Were you surprised when you discovered this blindness?

READING I   *Isaiah 43:16 — 21*

Thus says the LORD,
    who opens a way in the sea
    and a path in the mighty waters,
who leads out chariots and horsemen,
    a powerful army,
till they lie prostrate together, never to rise,
    snuffed out and quenched like a wick.
Remember not the events of the past,
    the things of long ago consider not;
see, I am doing something new!
    Now it springs forth, do you not
        perceive it?
In the desert I make a way;
    in the wasteland, rivers.
Wild beasts honor me,
    jackals and ostriches,
for I put water in the desert
    and rivers in the wasteland
    for my chosen people to drink,
the people whom I formed for myself,
    that they might announce my praise.

READING II   *Philippians 3:8 — 14*

Brothers and sisters: I consider everything as a loss because of the supreme good of knowing Christ Jesus my Lord. For his sake I have accepted the loss of all things and I consider them so much rubbish, that I may gain Christ and be found in him, not having any righteousness of my own based on the law but that which comes through faith in Christ, the righteousness from God, depending on faith to know him and the power of his resurrection and the sharing of his sufferings by being conformed to his death, if somehow I may attain the resurrection from the dead.

It is not that I have already taken hold of it or have already attained perfect maturity, but I continue my pursuit in hope that I may possess it, since I have indeed been taken possession of by Christ Jesus. Brothers and sisters, I for my part do not consider myself to have taken possession. Just one thing: forgetting what lies behind but straining forward to what lies ahead, I continue my pursuit toward the goal, the prize of God's upward calling, in Christ Jesus.

GOSPEL   *John 8:1 — 11*

Jesus went to the Mount of Olives. But early in the morning he arrived again in the temple area, and all the people started coming to him, and he sat down and taught them. Then the scribes and the Pharisees brought a woman who had been caught in adultery and made her stand in the middle. They said to him, "Teacher, this woman was caught in the very act of committing adultery. Now in the law, Moses commanded us to stone such women. So what do you say?" They said this to test him, so that they could have some charge to bring against him. Jesus bent down and began to write on the ground with his finger. But when they continued asking him, he straightened up and said to them, "Let the one among you who is without sin be the first to throw a stone at her." Again he bent down and wrote on the ground. And in response, they went away one by one, beginning with the elders. So he was left alone with the woman before him. Then Jesus straightened up and said to her, "Woman, where are they? Has no one condemned you?" She replied, "No one, sir." Then Jesus said, "Neither do I condemn you. Go, and from now on do not sin any more."

Practice of Prayer

R. The Lord has done great things for us; we are
    filled with joy.

When the LORD brought back
    the captives of Zion,
  we were like men dreaming.
Then our mouth was filled with laughter,
    and our tongue with rejoicing. R.

Then they said among the nations,
    "The LORD has done great things for them."
The LORD has done great things for us;
  we are glad indeed. R.

Restore our fortunes, O LORD,
    like the torrents in the southern desert.
Those who sow in tears
  shall reap rejoicing. R.

Although they go forth weeping,
    carrying the seed to be sown,
they shall come back rejoicing,
    carrying their sheaves. R.

Practice of Hope

As today's Gospel demonstrates, the people loved to hear Jesus teach. The disciples addressed Jesus as Rabboni (teacher). Learning communities can still be places where the teaching of Jesus is proclaimed. Archbishop Oscar Romero High School in Edmonton, Alberta, is named for the courageous Guatemalan bishop killed while celebrating Mass because of his cries for justice. Students and faculty alike have taken to heart the compassionate spirit of their namesake. When the school's social justice club ran a clothing drive hoping to outfit 15 people, they obtained enough to clothe 190 people. Students are generating money to provide hot lunches in inner-city schools, and to fund the digging of a well in a developing community. Often the price of admission to a school sporting event is a donation of canned food for a local soup kitchen. This outreach results in an atmosphere where everyone feels welcome and safe.

Scripture Insights

For the sake of Christ, Saint Paul writes, "I have accepted the loss of all things." A drastic statement! It would have been interesting if Saint Paul had provided a list of his losses. It's hard not to be skeptical of such a claim? What things exactly?

Saint Paul writes from jail. Since he was imprisoned many times, it is uncertain whether he wrote this letter from a jail in Ephesus (modern Turkey) or in Rome. If we want to know what Saint Paul means by the loss of all things, we should consider his situation when he wrote the letter. Ancient jails were not penal institutions from which convicts were released upon completing terms of imprisonment. They were holding tanks, pending torture and often death. Saint Paul knows that death is likely. So when Saint Paul tells the Philippians he has "accepted the loss of all things," he refers to a dire situation.

Saint Maximilian Kolbe acted as a servant to others in an Auschwitz prison during World War II. The prisoner branded 16670 heard confessions while in the hospital recovering from a beating. He celebrated Mass with smuggled bread and wine. Finally, he offered to die for a father slated for death. Saint Maximilian never flinched from his life as a Christian. Can we say the same?

◆ In the Gospel, the elders are the first to leave. Why?

◆ Sometimes we throw stones at another's character. Describe a time when you have stood up for someone others verbally assassinated?

◆ What are you willing to lose for the sake of Jesus Christ?

READING I   Ezekiel 37:12—14

Thus says the Lord GOD: O my people, I will open your graves and have you rise from them, and bring you back to the land of Israel. Then you shall know that I am the LORD, when I open your graves and have you rise from them, O my people! I will put my spirit in you that you may live, and I will settle you upon your land; thus you shall know that I am the LORD. I have promised, and I will do it, says the LORD.

READING II   Romans 8:8—11

Brothers and sisters: Those who are in the flesh cannot please God. But you are not in the flesh; on the contrary, you are in the spirit, if only the Spirit of God dwells in you. Whoever does not have the Spirit of Christ does not belong to him. But if Christ is in you, although the body is dead because of sin, the spirit is alive because of righteousness. If the Spirit of the one who raised Jesus from the dead dwells in you, the one who raised Christ from the dead will give life to your mortal bodies also, through his Spirit dwelling in you.

GOSPEL   John 11:3—7, 17, 20—27, 33b—45

Longer: John 11:1–45

The sisters sent word to Jesus saying, "Master, the one you love is ill." When Jesus heard this he said, "This illness is not to end in death, but is for the glory of God, that the Son of God may be glorified through it." Now Jesus loved Martha and her sister and Lazarus. So when he heard that he was ill, he remained for two days in the place where he was. Then after this he said to his disciples, "Let us go back to Judea."

When Jesus arrived, he found that Lazarus had already been in the tomb for four days. When Martha heard that Jesus was coming, she went to meet him; but Mary sat at home. Martha said to Jesus, "Lord, if you had been here, my brother would not have died. But even now I know that whatever you ask of God, God will give you." Jesus said to her, "Your brother will rise." Martha said to him, "I know he will rise, in the resurrection on the last day." Jesus told her, "I am the resurrection and the life; whoever believes in me, even if he dies, will live, and everyone who lives and believes in me will never die. Do you believe this?" She said to him, "Yes, Lord. I have come to believe that you are the Christ, the Son of God, the one who is coming into the world."

He became perturbed and deeply troubled, and said, "Where have you laid him?" They said to him, "Sir, come and see." And Jesus wept. So the Jews said, "See how he loved him." But some of them said, "Could not the one who opened the eyes of the blind man have done something so that this man would not have died?"

So Jesus, perturbed again, came to the tomb. It was a cave, and a stone lay across it. Jesus said, "Take away the stone." Martha, the dead man's sister, said to him, "Lord, by now there will be a stench; he has been dead for four days." Jesus said to her, "Did I not tell you that if you believe you will see the glory of God?" So they took away the stone. And Jesus raised his eyes and said, "Father, I thank you for hearing me. I know that you always hear me; but because of the crowd here I have said this, that they may believe that you sent me." And when he had said this, he cried out in a loud voice, "Lazarus, come out!" The dead man came out, tied hand and foot with burial bands, and his face was wrapped in a cloth. So Jesus said to them, "Untie him and let him go."

Now many of the Jews who had come to Mary and seen what he had done began to believe in him.

Practice of Prayer

Psalm 130:1—2, 3—4, 4—6, 7—8 (7)

R. With the Lord there is mercy, and fullness
of redemption.

Out of the depths I cry to you, O LORD;
LORD, hear my voice!
Let your ears be attentive
to my voice in supplication. R.

If you, LORD, mark our iniquities,
LORD, who can stand?
But with you is forgiveness
and so you may be revered. R.

I trust in the LORD;
my soul trusts in his word.
More than sentinels wait for the dawn
let Israel wait for the LORD. R.

For with the LORD is kindness
and with him is plenteous redemption;
and he will redeem Israel
from all their iniquities. R.

Practice of Charity

In 1972 Sister Anne Brooks was wheelchair-bound. The diagnosis was rheumatoid arthritis; her condition had been worsening for twenty years. However, she so badly wanted to work with the poor and needy that she endured a year of excruciatingly painful medical treatment. Afterward, she was able to volunteer at a health clinic, and earned a degree in osteopathic medicine. She opened a clinic in Tutwiler, a Mississippi Delta town that had lost its agricultural jobs to technology years ago. About 80 percent of Sister Anne's patients have no health insurance. Nonetheless, she and several other Sisters of the Holy Names of Jesus and Mary have built a community health system and have transformed many other aspects of life in Tutwiler. When asked what she got out of all this, she responded, "More than a thousand percent job satisfaction!" Donations are welcome. Tutwiler Medical Clinic, 205 Alma Street, Tutwiler MS 38963.

Scripture Insights

"Lord, if you had been here, my brother would not have died." In what tone of voice do you imagine the sisters queried Jesus? The text says that while Mary remained at home, Martha "went out to meet him." Did Martha meet him in the certainty that he had a good reason for coming late? Did she run to ask why Jesus had dithered for two days while her brother wasted away? Does the author intend Martha's words to testify to her belief in her Lord's power and his identity as God's Son?

Martha's disposition toward Jesus becomes clearer while examining the Gospel of John in its original Greek. The word translated as "meet" in the text quoted above signifies the formal greeting of an important person. It is the verb used in the next chapter to describe how the Jerusalem crowds greet Jesus upon his triumphal entry into the city. The author wants readers to know that Martha greets her Lord with respect.

Also note that Martha qualifies whatever criticism her statement contains. "But even now," she continues, "I know that whatever you ask of God, God will give you." Is this a profession of faith in what Jesus is about to do for Lazarus? Not quite. Martha cannot imagine that, as Jesus says, her brother "will rise" except "in the resurrection on the last day." When Jesus raises Lazarus, it is a shock. There are few guarantees in a mature relationship with God. Surprise is usually a safe bet.

• In the reading from Ezekiel, how do you interpret the relationship between the opening of graves and the gift of God's spirit?

• How is a body "dead because of sin" but alive in spirit?

• Would you have gone out to meet Jesus like Martha? Or would you have stayed at home like Mary? Why?

READING I   *Isaiah 50:4—7*

The Lord GOD has given me
    a well-trained tongue,
that I might know how to speak to the weary
    a word that will rouse them.
Morning after morning
    he opens my ear that I may hear;
and I have not rebelled,
    have not turned back.
I gave my back to those who beat me,
    my cheeks to those who plucked
      my beard;
my face I did not shield
    from buffets and spitting.

The Lord GOD is my help,
    therefore I am not disgraced;
I have set my face like flint,
    knowing that I shall not be put to shame.

READING II   *Philippians 2:6—11*

Christ Jesus, though he was in the form of God,
    did not regard equality with God
    something to be grasped.
Rather, he emptied himself,
    taking the form of a slave,
    coming in human likeness;
and found human in appearance,
    he humbled himself,
    becoming obedient to the point of death,
    even death on a cross.
Because of this, God greatly exalted him
    and bestowed on him the name
    which is above every name,
    that at the name of Jesus
    every knee should bend,
    of those in heaven and on earth and under
      the earth,
    and every tongue confess that
Jesus Christ is Lord,
    to the glory of God the Father.

GOSPEL   *Luke 22:14—23:56*

Shorter: Luke 23:1–49

When the hour came, Jesus took his place at table with the apostles. He said to them, "I have eagerly desired to eat this Passover with you before I suffer, for, I tell you, I shall not eat it again until there is fulfillment in the kingdom of God." Then he took a cup, gave thanks, and said, "Take this and share it among yourselves; for I tell you that from this time on I shall not drink of the fruit of the vine until the kingdom of God comes." Then he took the bread, said the blessing, broke it, and gave it to them, saying, "This is my body, which will be given for you; do this in memory of me." And likewise the cup after they had eaten, saying, "This cup is the new covenant in my blood, which will be shed for you.

"And yet behold, the hand of the one who is to betray me is with me on the table; for the Son of Man indeed goes as it has been determined; but woe to that man by whom he is betrayed." And they began to debate among themselves who among them would do such a deed.

Then an argument broke out among them about which of them should be regarded as the greatest. He said to them, "The kings of the Gentiles lord it over them and those in authority over them are addressed as 'Benefactors'; but among you it shall not be so. Rather, let the greatest among you be as the youngest, and the leader as the servant. For who is greater: the one seated at table or the one who serves? Is it not the one seated at table? I am among you as the one who serves. It is you who have stood by me in my trials; and I confer a kingdom on you, just as my Father has conferred one on me, that you may eat and drink at my table in my kingdom; and you will sit on thrones judging the twelve tribes of Israel.

"Simon, Simon, behold Satan has demanded to sift all of you like wheat, but I have prayed that your own faith may not fail; and once you have turned back, you must strengthen your brothers." He said to him, "Lord, I am prepared to go to prison and to die with you." But he replied,

"I tell you, Peter, before the cock crows this day, you will deny three times that you know me."

He said to them, "When I sent you forth without a money bag or a sack or sandals, were you in need of anything?" "No, nothing," they replied. He said to them, "But now one who has a money bag should take it, and likewise a sack, and one who does not have a sword should sell his cloak and buy one. For I tell you that this Scripture must be fulfilled in me, namely, *He was counted among the wicked;* and indeed what is written about me is coming to fulfillment." Then they said, "Lord, look, there are two swords here." But he replied, "It is enough!"

Then going out, he went, as was his custom, to the Mount of Olives, and the disciples followed him. When he arrived at the place he said to them, "Pray that you may not undergo the test." After withdrawing about a stone's throw from them and kneeling, he prayed, saying, "Father, if you are willing, take this cup away from me; still, not my will but yours be done." And to strengthen him an angel from heaven appeared to him. He was in such agony and he prayed so fervently that his sweat became like drops of blood falling on the ground. When he rose from prayer and returned to his disciples, he found them sleeping from grief. He said to them, "Why are you sleeping? Get up and pray that you may not undergo the test."

While he was still speaking, a crowd approached and in front was one of the Twelve, a man named Judas. He went up to Jesus to kiss him. Jesus said to him, "Judas, are you betraying the Son of Man with a kiss?" His disciples realized what was about to happen, and they asked, "Lord, shall we strike with a sword?" And one of them struck the high priest's servant and cut off his right ear. But Jesus said in reply, "Stop, no more of this!" Then he touched the servant's ear and healed him. And Jesus said to the chief priests and temple guards and elders who had come for him, "Have you come out as against a robber, with swords and clubs? Day after day I was with you in the temple area, and you did not seize me; but this is your hour, the time for the power of darkness."

After arresting him they led him away and took him into the house of the high priest; Peter was following at a distance. They lit a fire in the middle of the courtyard and sat around it, and Peter sat down with them. When a maid saw him seated in the light, she looked intently at him and said, "This man too was with him." But he denied it saying, "Woman, I do not know him." A short while later someone else saw him and said, "You too are one of them"; but Peter answered, "My friend, I am not." About an hour later, still another insisted, "Assuredly, this man too was with him, for he also is a Galilean." But Peter said, "My friend, I do not know what you are talking about." Just as he was saying this, the cock crowed, and the Lord turned and looked at Peter; and Peter remembered the word of the Lord, how he had said to him, "Before the cock crows today, you will deny me three times." He went out and began to weep bitterly.

The men who held Jesus in custody were ridiculing and beating him. They blindfolded him and questioned him, saying, "Prophesy! Who is it that struck you?" And they reviled him in saying many other things against him.

When day came the council of elders of the people met, both chief priests and scribes, and they brought him before their Sanhedrin. They said, "If you are the Christ, tell us," but he replied to them, "If I tell you, you will not believe, and if I question, you will not respond. But from this time on the Son of Man will be seated at the right hand of the power of God." They all asked, "Are you then the Son of God?" He replied to them, "You say that I am." Then they said, "What further need have we for testimony? We have heard it from his own mouth."

Then the whole assembly of them arose and brought him before Pilate. They brought charges against him, saying, "We found this man misleading our people; he opposes the payment of taxes to Caesar and maintains that he is the Christ, a king." Pilate asked him, "Are you the king of the Jews?" He said to him in reply, "You say so." Pilate then addressed the chief priests and the crowds,

"I find this man not guilty." But they were adamant and said, "He is inciting the people with his teaching throughout all Judea, from Galilee where he began even to here."

On hearing this Pilate asked if the man was a Galilean; and upon learning that he was under Herod's jurisdiction, he sent him to Herod, who was in Jerusalem at that time. Herod was very glad to see Jesus; he had been wanting to see him for a long time, for he had heard about him and had been hoping to see him perform some sign. He questioned him at length, but he gave him no answer. The chief priests and scribes, meanwhile, stood by accusing him harshly. Herod and his soldiers treated him contemptuously and mocked him, and after clothing him in resplendent garb, he sent him back to Pilate. Herod and Pilate became friends that very day, even though they had been enemies formerly. Pilate then summoned the chief priests, the rulers and the people and said to them, "You brought this man to me and accused him of inciting the people to revolt. I have conducted my investigation in your presence and have not found this man guilty of the charges you have brought against him, nor did Herod, for he sent him back to us. So no capital crime has been committed by him. Therefore I shall have him flogged and then release him."

But all together they shouted out, "Away with this man! Release Barabbas to us."—Now Barabbas had been imprisoned for a rebellion that had taken place in the city and for murder.— Again Pilate addressed them, still wishing to release Jesus, but they continued their shouting, "Crucify him! Crucify him!" Pilate addressed them a third time, "What evil has this man done? I found him guilty of no capital crime. Therefore I shall have him flogged and then release him." With loud shouts, however, they persisted in calling for his crucifixion, and their voices prevailed. The verdict of Pilate was that their demand should be granted. So he released the man who had been imprisoned for rebellion and murder, for whom they asked, and he handed Jesus over to them to deal with as they wished.

As they led him away they took hold of a certain Simon, a Cyrenian, who was coming in from the country; and after laying the cross on him, they made him carry it behind Jesus. A large crowd of people followed Jesus, including many women who mourned and lamented him. Jesus turned to them and said, "Daughters of Jerusalem, do not weep for me; weep instead for yourselves and for your children for indeed, the days are coming when people will say, 'Blessed are the barren, the wombs that never bore and the breasts that never nursed.' At that time people will say to the mountains, 'Fall upon us!' and to the hills, 'Cover us!' for if these things are done when the wood is green, what will happen when it is dry?" Now two others, both criminals, were led away with him to be executed.

When they came to the place called the Skull, they crucified him and the criminals there, one on his right, the other on his left. Then Jesus said, "Father, forgive them, they know not what they do." They divided his garments by casting lots. The people stood by and watched; the rulers, meanwhile, sneered at him and said, "He saved others, let him save himself if he is the chosen one, the Christ of God." Even the soldiers jeered at him. As they approached to offer him wine they called out, "If you are King of the Jews, save yourself." Above him there was an inscription that read, "This is the King of the Jews."

Now one of the criminals hanging there reviled Jesus, saying, "Are you not the Christ? Save yourself and us." The other, however, rebuking him, said in reply, "Have you no fear of God, for you are subject to the same condemnation? And indeed, we have been condemned justly, for the sentence we received corresponds to our crimes, but this man has done nothing criminal." Then he said, "Jesus, remember me when you come into your kingdom." He replied to him, "Amen, I say to you, today you will be with me in Paradise."

It was now about noon and darkness came over the whole land until three in the afternoon because of an eclipse of the sun. Then the veil of the temple was torn down the middle. Jesus cried out in a loud voice, "Father, into your hands I commend my spirit"; and when he had said this he breathed his last.

The centurion who witnessed what had happened glorified God and said, "This man was innocent beyond doubt." When all the people who had gathered for this spectacle saw what had happened, they returned home beating their breasts; but all his acquaintances stood at a distance, including the women who had followed him from Galilee and saw these events.

Now there was a virtuous and righteous man named Joseph, who, though he was a member of the council, had not consented to their plan of action. He came from the Jewish town of Arimathea and was awaiting the kingdom of God. He went to Pilate and asked for the body of Jesus. After he had taken the body down, he wrapped it in a linen cloth and laid him in a rock-hewn tomb in which no one had yet been buried. It was the day of preparation, and the sabbath was about to begin. The women who had come from Galilee with him followed behind, and when they had seen the tomb and the way in which his body was laid in it, they returned and prepared spices and perfumed oils. Then they rested on the sabbath according to the commandment.

Scripture Insights

"Lord, I am prepared to go to prison and to die with you." Doubtlessly, Saint Peter meant this. But in a few hours, he had fled the scene of Jesus' arrest and denied three times that he knew the one he once called "the Christ of God" (Luke 9:20). Jesus foresaw the apostle's betrayal and told him so. We do not know how this made Saint Peter feel. One bitter lesson he surely learned when the cock crowed was that willingness without commensurate action is nothing more than fantasy.

The significance of Jesus' final week on earth—his triumphal entry into Jerusalem, disruption of the temple's commerce, disputes, teachings, last supper, arrest, trial, crucifixion, and death—is much greater than Saint Peter's betrayal of Jesus. But Saint Peter's courage in safety, and cowardice in danger comprise the sort of faithlessness with which most of us can identify.

The unexpected twists of an average human life have a way of raising situations in which cherished beliefs and images of character are exposed as frauds. These terrible moments are gifts. They are gateways to conversion.

Consider the example of Saint Paul, who persecuted the church until struck blind. In his letter to the Philippians, Saint Paul offers the self-sacrifice of Jesus as an example to a church enduring a feud. Saint Paul sits in jail facing the strong possibility of death. It is impossible to know for what one is willing to sacrifice everything until faced with a demanding situation. But Saints Peter and Paul show us that faith is more than declaring one's willingness to follow Christ. It is about taking up one's cross when the time comes.

◆ How does Isaiah exemplify the virtue of humility?

◆ Is Christ's example something people should follow? Or is Christ's example impossible for people to follow?

◆ Have you been called to deeper conversion by something that seemed disconcerting at the time?

Holy Thursday brings the end to the Forty Days of Lent, which make up the season of anticipation of the great Three Days. Composed of prayer, alms-giving, fasting, and the preparation of the cate-chumens for Baptism, the season of Lent is now brought to a close and the Three Days begin as we approach the liturgy of Holy Thursday evening. As those to be initiated into the Church have prepared themselves for their entrance into the fullness of life, so have we been awakening in our hearts, minds, and bodies our own entrances into the life of Christ, experienced in the life of the Church.

The Three Days, this Easter Triduum (Latin for "three days"), is the center, the core, of the entire year for Christians. These days mark the mystery around which our entire lives are played out. Adults in the community are invited to plan ahead so that the whole time from Thursday night until Easter Sunday is free of social engagements, free of entertainment, and free of meals except for the simplest nourishment. We measure these days—indeed, our very salvation in the life of God—in step with the catechumens themselves; our own rebirths are revitalized as we participate in their initiation rites and as we have supported them along the way.

We are asked to fast on Good Friday and to continue fasting, if possible, all through Holy Saturday as strictly as we can so that we come to the Easter Vigil hungry and full of excitement, parched and longing to feel the sacred water of the font on our skin. Good Friday and Holy Saturday are days of paring down distractions so that we may be free for prayer and anticipation, for reflection, preparation, and silence. The Church is getting ready for the Great Night of the Easter Vigil.

As one who has been initiated into the Church, as one whose life has been wedded to this community gathered at the table, you should antici-pate the Triduum with concentration and vigor. With you, the whole Church knows that our pres-ence for the liturgies of the Triduum is not just an invitation. Everyone is needed. We "pull out all the stops" for these days. As human persons, wedded to humanity by the joys and travails of life and grafted onto the body of the Church by the sanctifying waters of Baptism, we lead the new members into new life in this community of faith.

To this end, the Three Days are seen not as three liturgies distinct from one another but as one movement. These days have been connected intimately and liturgically from the early days of the Christian Church. As a member of this com-munity, you should be personally committed to preparing for and anticipating the Triduum and its culmination in the Vigil of the Great Night, Holy Saturday.

The Church proclaims the direction of the Triduum by the opening antiphon of Holy Thursday, which comes from Paul's Letter to the Galatians (6:14). With this verse the Church sets a spiritual environment into which we as com-mitted Christians enter the Triduum:

> We should glory in the cross of our Lord Jesus Christ, for he is our salvation, our life and resurrection; through him we are saved and made free.

HOLY THURSDAY

On Thursday evening we enter into this Triduum together. Whether presider, baker, lector, preacher, wine maker, greeter, altar server, minister of the Eucharist, decorator, or person in the remote cor-ner in the last pew of the church, we begin, as always, by hearkening to the word of God. These are the scriptures for the liturgy of Holy Thursday:

Exodus 12:1–8, 11–14
Ancient instructions for the meal of the Passover.

1 Corinthians 11:23–26
Eat the bread and drink the cup until the return of the Lord.

John 13:1–15
Jesus washes the feet of the disciples.

Then we, like Jesus, do something strange: We wash feet. Jesus gave us this image of what the church is supposed to look like, feel like, act like. Our position—whether as washer or washed, servant or served—is a difficult one for us to take. Yet we learn from the discomfort, from the awkwardness.

Then we celebrate the Eucharist. Because it is connected to the other liturgies of the Triduum on Good Friday and Holy Saturday night, the evening liturgy of Holy Thursday has no ending. Whether we stay to pray awhile or leave, we are now in the quiet, peace, and glory of the Triduum.

GOOD FRIDAY

We gather quietly in community on Friday and again listen to the Word of God:

Isaiah 52:13—53:12
The servant of the Lord was crushed for our sins.

Hebrews 4:14–16; 5:7–9
The Son of God learned obedience through his suffering.

John 18:1—19:42
The passion of Jesus Christ.

After the sermon, we pray at length for all the world's needs: for the Church; for the pope, the clergy and all the baptized; for those preparing for initiation; for the unity of Christians; for Jews; for non-Christians; for atheists; for all in public office; and for those in special need.

Then there is another once-a-year event: The holy cross is held up in our midst and we come forward one by one to do reverence with a kiss, bow, or genuflection. This communal reverence of an instrument of torture recalls the painful price, in the past and today, of salvation, the way in which our redemption is wrought, the stripes and humiliation of Jesus Christ that bring direction and life back to a humanity that is lost and dead. During the veneration of the cross, we sing not only of the sorrow but of the glory of the cross by which we have been saved.

Again, we bring to mind the words of Paul: "The cross of Jesus Christ . . . our salvation, our life and resurrection; through him we are saved and made free."

We continue in fasting and prayer and vigil, in rest and quiet, through Saturday. This Saturday for us is God's rest at the end of creation. It is Christ's repose in the tomb. It is Christ's visit with the dead.

EASTER VIGIL

Hungry now, pared down to basics, lightheaded from vigilance and full of excitement, we committed members of the Church, the already baptized, gather in darkness and light a new fire. From this blaze we light a great candle that will make this night bright for us and will burn throughout the Easter season.

We hearken again to the Word of God with some of the most powerful narratives and proclamations of our tradition:

Genesis 1:1—2:2
Creation of the world.

Genesis 22:1–18
The sacrifice of Isaac.

Exodus 14:15—15:1
The crossing of the Red Sea.

Isaiah 54:5–14
You will not be afraid.

Isaiah 55:1–11
Come, come to the water.

Baruch 3:9–15, 32—4:4
The shining light.

Ezekiel 36:16–28
The Lord says: I will sprinkle water.

Romans 6:3–11
United with him in death.

Mark 16:1–7
Jesus has been raised up.

After the readings, we pray to all our saints to stand with us as we go to the font and bless the waters. The chosen of all times and all places attend to what is about to take place. The catechumens renounce evil, profess the faith of the church, and are baptized and anointed.

All of us renew our baptism. For us these are the moments when death and life meet, when we reject evil and give our promises to God. All of this is in the communion of the Church. So together we go to the table and celebrate the Easter Eucharist.

Easter

Prayer before Reading the Word

God of our ancestors,
you have raised up Jesus
and exalted him at your right hand
as Leader and Savior.

Open our minds to understand the scriptures,
and, as with great joy we bless you in your temple,
make us witnesses who can proclaim
the repentance and forgiveness
you extend to all the nations
in the name of Jesus,
the Messiah, our great high priest,
who intercedes before you on our behalf,
living and reigning with you
in the unity of the Holy Spirit,
God for ever and ever. Amen.

Prayer after Reading the Word

O God, the fountain of joy and of peace,
into the hands of your risen Son
you have entrusted the destinies
of peoples and of nations.

Keep us safe in those arms
from which no one can snatch us,
that we may proclaim your word
in peace and in persecution,
until at last we stand before the Lamb,
with songs of praise on our lips.

We ask this through the Lord Jesus,
our Passover and our Peace,
who lives and reigns with you
in the unity of the Holy Spirit,
God for ever and ever. Amen.

Weekday Readings

April 9: Solemnity of Monday in the Octave of Easter
Acts 2:14, 22–23; Matthew 28:8–15
April 10: Solemnity of Tuesday in the Octave of Easter
Acts 2:36–41; John 20:11–18
April 11: Solemnity of Wednesday in the Octave of Easter
Acts 3:1–10; Luke 24:13–35
April 12: Solemnity of Thursday in the Octave of Easter
Acts 3:11–26; Luke 24:35–48
April 13: Solemnity of Friday in the Octave of Easter
Acts 4:1–12; John 21:1–14
April 14: Solemnity of Saturday in the Octave of Easter
Acts 4:13–21; Mark 16:9–15

April 16: *Acts 4:23–31; John 3:1–8*
April 17: *Acts 4:32–37; John 3:7b–15*
April 18: *Acts 5:17–26; John 3:16–21*
April 19: *Acts 5:27–33; John 3:31–36*
April 20: *Acts 5:34–42; John 6:1–15*
April 21: *Acts 6:1–7; John 6:16–21*

April 23: *Acts 6:8–15; John 6:22–29*
April 24: *Acts 7:51–8:1a; John 6:30-35*
April 25: Feast of Saint Mark
1 Peter 5:5b–14; Mark 16:15–20
April 26: *Acts 8:26–40; John 6:44–51*
April 27: *Acts 9:1–20; John 6:52–59*
April 28: *Acts 9:31–42; John 6:60–69*

April 30: *Acts 11:1–8; John 10:1–10*
May 1: *Acts 11:19–26; John 10:22–30*
May 2: *Acts 12:24–13:5a; John 12:44–50*
May 3: Feast of Saints Philip and James
1 Corinthians 15:1–8; John 14:6–14
May 4: *Acts 13:26–33; John 14:1–6*
May 5: *Acts 13:44–52; John 14:7–14*

May 7: *Acts 14:5–18; John 14:21–26*
May 8: *Acts 14:19–28; John 14:27–31a*
May 9: *Acts 15:1–6; John 15:1–8*
May 10: *Acts 15:7–21; John 15:9–11*
May 11: *Acts 15:22–31; John 15:12–17*
May 12: *Acts 16:1–10; John 15:18–21*

May 14: Feast of Saint Matthias
Acts 1:15–17; John 15:18–21
May 15: *Acts 16:22–34; John 16:5–11*
May 16: *Acts 17:15, 22–18:1; John 16:12–15*
May 17: Solemnity of the Ascension of the Lord [In some regions, transferred to Seventh Sunday of Easter]
Acts 1:1–11; Ephesians 1:17–23; Luke 24:46–53
May 18: *Acts 18:9–18; John 16:20–23*
May 19: *Acts 18:23–28; John 16:23b–28*

May 21: *Acts 19:1–8; John 16:29–33*
May 22: *Acts 20:17–27; John 17:1–11a*
May 23: *Acts 20:28–38; John 17:11b–19*
May 24: *Acts 22:30; 23:6–11; John 17:20–26*
May 25: *Acts 25:13b–21; John 21:15–19*
May 26: morning: *Acts 28:16–20, 30-31; John*

April 8, 2007

READING I   Acts 10:34a, 37—43

Peter proceeded to speak and said: "You know what has happened all over Judea, beginning in Galilee after the baptism that John preached, how God anointed Jesus of Nazareth with the Holy Spirit and power. He went about doing good and healing all those oppressed by the devil, for God was with him. We are witnesses of all that he did both in the country of the Jews and in Jerusalem. They put him to death by hanging him on a tree. This man God raised on the third day and granted that he be visible, not to all the people, but to us, the witnesses chosen by God in advance, who ate and drank with him after he rose from the dead. He commissioned us to preach to the people and testify that he is the one appointed by God as judge of the living and the dead. To him all the prophets bear witness, that everyone who believes in him will receive forgiveness of sins through his name."

READING II   Colossians 3:1—4

Alternate: 1 Corinthians 5:6b–8

Brothers and sisters: If then you were raised with Christ, seek what is above, where Christ is seated at the right hand of God. Think of what is above, not of what is on earth. For you have died, and your life is hidden with Christ in God. When Christ your life appears, then you too will appear with him in glory.

GOSPEL   John 20:1—9

On the first day of the week, Mary of Magdala came to the tomb early in the morning, while it was still dark, and saw the stone removed from the tomb. So she ran and went to Simon Peter and to the other disciple whom Jesus loved, and told them, "They have taken the Lord from the tomb, and we don't know where they put him." So Peter and the other disciple went out and came to the tomb. They both ran, but the other disciple ran faster than Peter and arrived at the tomb first; he bent down and saw the burial cloths there, but did not go in. When Simon Peter arrived after him, he went into the tomb and saw the burial cloths there, and the cloth that had covered his head, not with the burial cloths but rolled up in a separate place. Then the other disciple also went in, the one who had arrived at the tomb first, and he saw and believed. For they did not yet understand the Scripture that he had to rise from the dead.

Practice of Prayer

Psalm 118:1—2, 16—17, 22—23 (24)

R. This is the day the Lord has made; let us
    rejoice and be glad.
or: Alleluia.

Give thanks to the LORD, for he is good,
    for his mercy endures forever.
Let the house of Israel say,
    "His mercy endures forever." R.

"The right hand of the LORD is exalted;
    the right hand of the LORD
        has struck with power."
I shall not die, but live,
    and declare the works of the LORD. R.

The stone which the builders rejected
    has become the cornerstone.
By the LORD has this been done;
    it is wonderful in our eyes. R.

Practice of Faith

For some reason, the observance of the forty days of Lent is better known than the longer Easter season. Many people think Easter is over when the sun sets on Easter evening. Actually, the celebration of this greatest of feasts lasts fifty jubilant days! Liturgist Peter Mazar commented, "Fifty days are a seventh of the year, and so we keep our fifty-day Eastertime as a long Lord's Day, the 'Great Sunday.' Fifty days are a week of weeks, plus a day, a symbol of eternity. And so we keep Eastertime 'playing heaven,' living as if God's reign had already come. Christians—both the newly baptized and the long baptized—are ready to live in the wedding feast of heaven and earth, like a honeymoon, no fasting, no mourning, endlessly singing our alleluias." How will you live in the wedding feast today?

Scripture Insights

The events of Jesus' Passion are sacred history. Jesus enters Jerusalem acclaimed by crowds waving palms. He has a final Passover meal with his disciples and washes their feet. Then come his arrest, trial, torture, and death. In a dramatic reversal, the news of Jesus' resurrection spreads among his disciples, and he begins to appear to them. Since we know the sacred history, Good Friday cannot be the day of confusion and despair that it was for Jesus' first disciples. Neither can Easter be the surprise for us that it was for them. We know, from the first day of Lent, that Jesus' death in Jerusalem is the end of nothing, but falls at the beginning of everything.

What, then, is the death the author of Colossians describes? It is probably a reference to the metaphoric death that Christians experience in Baptism. Early Christian baptistries adopted the circular designs of Roman tombs to symbolize the believers' death to old ways of thinking and living, and as a ritual way to share in Christ's death that opened the way to new life. But it is wrong, as ancient commentators sometimes contended, that Christians are obsessed by death. The author of Colossians is reminding his readers that death to sin is a necessary step on the journey to becoming a resurrected people.

The news of Easter, it has been said, is that God turned death into life to dance on death's grave. This news is the beating heart of the Christian religion.

• Why does the Colossians' author talk about the resurrection of believers as though it has already been accomplished?

• Does knowing that the faithful will have their sins forgiven help you forgive?

• "Think of what is above, not what is on earth." How exactly have you done this in your daily life?

READING I   Acts 5:12—16

Many signs and wonders were done among the people at the hands of the apostles. They were all together in Solomon's portico. None of the others dared to join them, but the people esteemed them. Yet more than ever, believers in the Lord, great numbers of men and women, were added to them. Thus they even carried the sick out into the streets and laid them on cots and mats so that when Peter came by, at least his shadow might fall on one or another of them. A large number of people from the towns in the vicinity of Jerusalem also gathered, bringing the sick and those disturbed by unclean spirits, and they were all cured.

READING II   Revelation 1:9—11a, 12—13, 17—19

I, John, your brother, who share with you the distress, the kingdom, and the endurance we have in Jesus, found myself on the island called Patmos because I proclaimed God's word and gave testimony to Jesus. I was caught up in spirit on the Lord's day and heard behind me a voice as loud as a trumpet, which said, "Write on a scroll what you see." Then I turned to see whose voice it was that spoke to me, and when I turned, I saw seven gold lampstands and in the midst of the lampstands one like a son of man, wearing an ankle-length robe, with a gold sash around his chest.

When I caught sight of him, I fell down at his feet as though dead. He touched me with his right hand and said, "Do not be afraid. I am the first and the last, the one who lives. Once I was dead, but now I am alive forever and ever. I hold the keys to death and the netherworld. Write down, therefore, what you have seen, and what is happening, and what will happen afterwards."

GOSPEL   John 20:19—31

On the evening of that first day of the week, when the doors were locked, where the disciples were, for fear of the Jews, Jesus came and stood in their midst and said to them, "Peace be with you." When he had said this, he showed them his hands and his side. The disciples rejoiced when they saw the Lord. Jesus said to them again, "Peace be with you. As the Father has sent me, so I send you." And when he had said this, he breathed on them and said to them, "Receive the Holy Spirit. Whose sins you forgive are forgiven them, and whose sins you retain are retained."

Thomas, called Didymus, one of the Twelve, was not with them when Jesus came. So the other disciples said to him, "We have seen the Lord." But he said to them, "Unless I see the mark of the nails in his hands and put my finger into the nailmarks and put my hand into his side, I will not believe."

Now a week later his disciples were again inside and Thomas was with them. Jesus came, although the doors were locked, and stood in their midst and said, "Peace be with you." Then he said to Thomas, "Put your finger here and see my hands, and bring your hand and put it into my side, and do not be unbelieving, but believe." Thomas answered and said to him, "My Lord and my God!" Jesus said to him, "Have you come to believe because you have seen me? Blessed are those who have not seen and have believed."

Now Jesus did many other signs in the presence of his disciples that are not written in this book. But these are written that you may come to believe that Jesus is the Christ, the Son of God, and that through this belief you may have life in his name.

Practice of Prayer

R. Give thanks to the LORD, for he is good, his
     love is everlasting.
or: Alleluia.

Let the house of Israel say,
    "His mercy endures forever."
Let the house of Aaron say,
    "His mercy endures forever."
Let those who fear the LORD say,
    "His mercy endures forever." R.

I was hard pressed and was falling,
    but the LORD helped me.
My strength and my courage is the LORD,
    and he has been my savior.
The joyful shout of victory
    in the tents of the just. R.

The stone which the builders rejected
    has become the cornerstone.
By the LORD has this been done;
    it is wonderful in our eyes.
This is the day the LORD has made;
    let us be glad and rejoice in it. R.

Practice of Hope

Before the wars of the 1990s, people of varied eth-
nic groups and religious convictions in the Balkans
often lived side by side, sharing friendships and
sometimes intermarrying. The tragic violence rent
massive numbers of these relationships as people
fled for their lives. In the aftermath, Dutch filmmakers Eric van den Broek and Katarina Rejger
conceived a project called "Videoletters," recounted
in The New York Times (6/8/05). They invited
anyone in the former Yugoslavia who had lost
touch with a friend or neighbor of a different eth-
nic group to record a message. The filmmakers
would try to deliver the message anywhere in the
region. The project has led to many joyful
reunions. It was designed to demonstrate that reconciliation is possible. The directors of the project
hope that their idea can be expanded to other areas
of conflict, such as Israel and Palestine, Russia, and
Africa. Learn more at www.videoletters.net.

Scripture Insights

Dramatic spiritual experiences are rare. Few people can say that they met with God face-to-face,
in a dream, or a vision. It is not surprising that
doubts greet such claims. If we want to be reasonable and faithful disciples, a healthy skepticism
about extraordinary spiritual claims is in order.

We are not amazed to find extraordinary spiritual claims in Scripture. After all, we regard
sacred writings as the word of God. Today we read
in Acts of miraculous cures in Jerusalem and
the peoples' hope in the healing power of Saint
Peter—even of his shadow. In Revelation we read
of John of Patmos, "caught up in the spirit" and
commanded to write down his vision. And we
read in John's Gospel of the disciples' reception of
the Holy Spirit after Jesus overcomes Thomas'
doubts. Christianity is founded on the extraordinary claims surrounding Jesus of Nazareth. We
believe that he was killed, buried, and brought to
new life, and that his resurrection releases his followers from death. In that light, today's readings
are appropriately extraordinary. Perhaps our
recognition of Christ's presence has arrived in
seemingly mundane ways: in the births of children, in reconciliations, through falling in love,
through the promise of the first buds of spring.
Once we know how to sense Christ's presence,
is a child's birth ordinary? Is spring after winter
mundane? The Easter stories of scripture are
extraordinary. When we let them help us see in
new ways, we experience the extraordinary. We
experience a world brimming with God's grace.

• How is John's response to Christ in the reading
from Revelation similar to the disciples' response
in the Gospel?

• Do you greet people in a way that would calm
their fears?

• Have you ever had an extraordinary religious
experience or insight and how did it affect you?

READING I   Acts 5:27b — 32, 40b — 41

When the captain and the court officers had brought the apostles in and made them stand before the Sanhedrin, the high priest questioned them, "We gave you strict orders, did we not, to stop teaching in that name? Yet you have filled Jerusalem with your teaching and want to bring this man's blood upon us." But Peter and the apostles said in reply, "We must obey God rather than men. The God of our ancestors raised Jesus, though you had him killed by hanging him on a tree. God exalted him at his right hand as leader and savior to grant Israel repentance and forgiveness of sins. We are witnesses of these things, as is the Holy Spirit whom God has given to those who obey him."

The Sanhedrin ordered the apostles to stop speaking in the name of Jesus, and dismissed them. So they left the presence of the Sanhedrin, rejoicing that they had been found worthy to suffer dishonor for the sake of the name.

READING II   Revelation 5:11 — 14

I, John, looked and heard the voices of many angels who surrounded the throne and the living creatures and the elders. They were countless in number, and they cried out in a loud voice:

"Worthy is the Lamb that was slain
to receive power and riches,
wisdom and strength,
honor and glory and blessing."

Then I heard every creature in heaven and on earth and under the earth and in the sea, everything in the universe, cry out:

"To the one who sits on the
throne and to the Lamb
be blessing and honor, glory and might,
forever and ever."

The four living creatures answered, "Amen," and the elders fell down and worshiped.

GOSPEL   John 21:1 — 19

Shorter: John 21:1–14

At that time, Jesus revealed himself again to his disciples at the Sea of Tiberias. He revealed himself in this way. Together were Simon Peter, Thomas called Didymus, Nathanael from Cana in Galilee, Zebedee's sons, and two others of his disciples. Simon Peter said to them, "I am going fishing." They said to him, "We also will come with you." So they went out and got into the boat, but that night they caught nothing. When it was already dawn, Jesus was standing on the shore; but the disciples did not realize that it was Jesus. Jesus said to them, "Children, have you caught anything to eat?" They answered him, "No." So he said to them, "Cast the net over the right side of the boat and you will find something." So they cast it, and were not able to pull it in because of the number of fish. So the disciple whom Jesus loved said to Peter, "It is the Lord." When Simon Peter heard that it was the Lord, he tucked in his garment, for he was lightly clad, and jumped into the sea. The other disciples came in the boat, for they were not far from shore, only about a hundred yards, dragging the net with the fish. When they climbed out on shore, they saw a charcoal fire with fish on it and bread. Jesus said to them, "Bring some of the fish you just caught." So Simon Peter went over and dragged the net ashore full of one hundred fifty-three large fish. Even though there were so many, the net was not torn. Jesus said to them, "Come, have breakfast." And none of the disciples dared to ask him, "Who are you?" because they realized it was the Lord. Jesus came over and took the bread and gave it to them, and in like manner the fish. This was now the third time Jesus was revealed to his disciples after being raised from the dead.

When they had finished breakfast, Jesus said to Simon Peter, "Simon, son of John, do you love me more than these?" Simon Peter answered him, "Yes, Lord, you know that I love you." Jesus said to him, "Feed my lambs." He then said to Simon Peter a second time, "Simon, son of John, do you love me?" Simon Peter answered him, "Yes, Lord, you know that I love you." Jesus said to him, "Tend my sheep." Jesus said to him the third time, "Simon, son of John, do you love me?" Peter was distressed that Jesus had said to him a third time, "Do you love me?" and he said to him, "Lord, you know everything; you know that I love you." Jesus said to him, "Feed my sheep. Amen, amen, I say to you, when you were younger, you used to dress yourself and go where you wanted; but when you grow old, you will stretch out your hands, and someone else will dress you and lead you where you do not want to go." He said this signifying by what kind of death he would glorify God. And when he had said this, he said to him, "Follow me."

Practice of Prayer

Psalm 30:2, 4, 5 — 6, 11 — 12, 13 (2a)

R. I will praise you, LORD, for you have
      rescued me.
or: Alleluia.

I will extol you, O LORD, for you drew me clear
    and did not let my enemies rejoice over me.
O LORD, you brought me up
      from the netherworld;
      you preserved me from among those going
        down into the pit.   R.

Sing praise to the LORD, you his faithful ones,
    and give thanks to his holy name.
For his anger lasts but a moment;
    a lifetime, his good will.
At nightfall, weeping enters in,
    but with the dawn, rejoicing.   R.

Hear, O LORD, and have pity on me;
    O LORD, be my helper.
You changed my mourning into dancing;
    O LORD, my God, forever will I give
      you thanks.   R.

Practice of Charity

Laura Metzger chose an unlikely spot to demonstrate her math and business skills. Laura was a volunteer with Amate House, a young adult service program. Her deduction came in the midst of her work at a food pantry. Every bag of food distributed there gets one staple. Peanut butter is nutritious, needs no special handling, and is liked by just about everybody. However, purchasing peanut butter ate up the pantry's cash. Laura asked the sharing parishes to do peanut butter drives instead of canned food drives. The pantry's food bill was reduced by half. Find out more about Amate House at www.amatehouse.org.

Scripture Insights

The Acts of the Apostles is a gripping page turner. Today's account of the confrontation between the apostles and the members of the Sanhedrin is an example of a story from the early Church that is entertaining and instructive. While reading of the beginnings of the Church, Christians learn of the humorous, tragic, and inspiring events of their past. The apostles teach in the name of Jesus. But what does it mean to teach in the savior's name? Is starting a sentence with "In the name of Jesus . . . ." enough? The answer is in Peter's response to the Sanhedrin. Teaching in Jesus' name means bearing witness to his teachings and story, whatever the consequences. It means facing down opponents to tell of the astounding reversal that God vindicated a man who had been tried and executed.

It also may mean continuing a mission when those in power do not believe in your words and actions. Considering the Twelve to be false prophets, the Sanhedrin had forbidden them to spread the news of Jesus. Their disobedience brought imprisonment. Today's reading from Acts does not tell that a death sentence was nearly imposed on the apostles. In this story of our Christian family, the apostles stand against a combined might while teaching in the name of Jesus.

• How is Simon Peter portrayed in today's Gospel reading? How does he compare with the others?

• Why do the disciples find joy in dishonor? What experience of yours might be similar?

• When have you stood up to someone or something, convinced that any other course of action would be disobedience to God? Or imagine how you might do this.

READING I   Acts 13:14, 43–52

Paul and Barnabas continued on from Perga and reached Antioch in Pisidia. On the sabbath they entered the synagogue and took their seats. Many Jews and worshipers who were converts to Judaism followed Paul and Barnabas, who spoke to them and urged them to remain faithful to the grace of God.

On the following sabbath almost the whole city gathered to hear the word of the Lord. When the Jews saw the crowds, they were filled with jealousy and with violent abuse contradicted what Paul said. Both Paul and Barnabas spoke out boldly and said, "It was necessary that the word of God be spoken to you first, but since you reject it and condemn yourselves as unworthy of eternal life, we now turn to the Gentiles. For so the Lord has commanded us, *I have made you a light to the Gentiles, that you may be an instrument of salvation to the ends of the earth.*"

The Gentiles were delighted when they heard this and glorified the word of the Lord. All who were destined for eternal life came to believe, and the word of the Lord continued to spread through the whole region. The Jews, however, incited the women of prominence who were worshipers and the leading men of the city, stirred up a persecution against Paul and Barnabas, and expelled them from their territory. So they shook the dust from their feet in protest against them, and went to Iconium. The disciples were filled with joy and the Holy Spirit.

READING II   Revelation 7:9, 14b–17

I, John, had a vision of a great multitude, which no one could count, from every nation, race, people and tongue. They stood before the throne and before the Lamb, wearing white robes and holding palm branches in their hands.

Then one of the elders said to me, "These are the ones who have survived the time of great distress; they have washed their robes and made them white in the blood of the Lamb.

"For this reason they stand
> before God's throne
and worship him day and
> night in his temple.
The one who sits on the throne
> will shelter them.
They will not hunger or thirst anymore,
> nor will the sun or any heat strike them.
For the Lamb who is in the
> center of the throne
will shepherd them
and lead them to springs
> of life-giving water,
and God will wipe away every
> tear from their eyes."

GOSPEL   John 10:27–30

Jesus said: "My sheep hear my voice; I know them, and they follow me. I give them eternal life, and they shall never perish. No one can take them out of my hand. My Father, who has given them to me, is greater than all, and no one can take them out of the Father's hand. The Father and I are one."

Practice of Prayer

Psalm 100:1—2, 3, 5 (3c)

R. We are his people, the sheep of his flock.
or: Alleluia.

Sing joyfully to the LORD, all you lands;
    serve the LORD with gladness;
    come before him with joyful song. R.

Know that the LORD is God;
    he made us, his we are,
    his people, the flock he tends. R.

The LORD is good:
    his kindness endures forever,
    and his faithfulness, to all generations. R.

Practice of Hope

In 1933, Communists marching in their annual New York City May Day parade did a double take as they proceeded through Union Square. There, they discovered for sale the first issue of a newspaper called *The Catholic Worker*. Most of the marchers had believed until that moment that the Catholic Church was uninterested in the plight of unemployed and hungry workers. The new newspaper educated people about Catholic social teaching and promoted the peaceful transformation of society. Founders Dorothy Day and Peter Maurin called for a world where "it would be easier to be good." *The Catholic Worker* cost one cent (and does to this day). Within six months, 100,000 copies were being printed each month. The paper's stance for Christian hospitality soon brought homeless people to its doors. Now there are Catholic Worker houses of hospitality in many parts of the world. Learn more at www. catholicworker.org.

Scripture Insights

The best modern scholarship on the early days of Jesus' movement describes its membership as composed largely of Jews. But by the end of the first century, the Christian community was mostly Gentile. Interpreting this change must have been puzzling for early Christians. One attempt to explain the situation can be seen in Saint Paul's statement that the Jews needed to hear and reject the word of God before he and Barnabas could turn to the Gentiles.

Such confrontations as we see in today's reading drive the narrative of Acts and allow the apostles to teach about Jesus. Confrontations between Jesus and "the Jews" drive the first half of the Gospel of John. They usually arise from Jesus' signs, giving Jesus a chance to speak at length. These speeches often increase hostility. Our Gospel text breaks off before verse 31. There, Jews pick up stones to throw at Jesus.

Portions of Paul's letters indicate some Jews persecuted segments of the early Church. Such persecution may explain, but not justify, the harsh portrait of "the Jews" in John's Gospel and in other early Christian literature. Thinking of persecution in the context of Jewish-Christian relations today, the worst examples are of Christian persecution of Jews (Crusades, Holocaust, etc.). In the light of this history, the Second Vatican Council affirmed that the Church "deplores all hatreds, persecutions, displays of anti-Semitism leveled at any time or from any source against the Jews" (*Nostra Aetate*, 4).

◆ What images are in both the reading from Revelation and the Gospel?

◆ How do you understand Jesus' statement "The Father and I are one"? Does this influence your relationship to the persons of the Trinity?

◆ What do you think of Jesus' description of his followers as sheep? How do you feel like a sheep of his flock?

READING I Acts 14:21—27

After Paul and Barnabas had proclaimed the good news to that city and made a considerable number of disciples, they returned to Lystra and to Iconium and to Antioch. They strengthened the spirits of the disciples and exhorted them to persevere in the faith, saying, "It is necessary for us to undergo many hardships to enter the kingdom of God." They appointed elders for them in each church and, with prayer and fasting, commended them to the Lord in whom they had put their faith. Then they traveled through Pisidia and reached Pamphylia. After proclaiming the word at Perga they went down to Attalia. From there they sailed to Antioch, where they had been commended to the grace of God for the work they had now accomplished. And when they arrived, they called the church together and reported what God had done with them and how he had opened the door of faith to the Gentiles.

READING II Revelation 21:1—5a

Then I, John, saw a new heaven and a new earth. The former heaven and the former earth had passed away, and the sea was no more. I also saw the holy city, a new Jerusalem, coming down out of heaven from God, prepared as a bride adorned for her husband. I heard a loud voice from the throne saying, "Behold, God's dwelling is with the human race. He will dwell with them and they will be his people and God himself will always be with them as their God. He will wipe every tear from their eyes, and there shall be no more death or mourning, wailing or pain, for the old order has passed away."

The One who sat on the throne said, "Behold, I make all things new."

GOSPEL John 13:31—33a, 34—35

When Judas had left them, Jesus said, "Now is the Son of Man glorified, and God is glorified in him. If God is glorified in him, God will also glorify him in himself, and God will glorify him at once. My children, I will be with you only a little while longer. I give you a new commandment: love one another. As I have loved you, so you also should love one another. This is how all will know that you are my disciples, if you have love for one another."

Practice of Prayer

Psalm 145:8—9, 10—11, 12—13 (see 1)

R. I will praise your name for ever, my king
     and my God.
or: Alleluia.

The LORD is gracious and merciful,
     slow to anger and of great kindness.
The LORD is good to all
     and compassionate toward all his works. R.

Let all your works give you thanks, O LORD,
     and let your faithful ones bless you.
Let them discourse of the glory of your kingdom
     and speak of your might. R.

Let them make known your might to the
          children of Adam,
     and the glorious splendor of your kingdom.
Your kingdom is a kingdom for all ages,
     and your dominion endures through all
          generations. R.

Practice of Faith

On Sundays during slave times, African American women sometimes adorned their bandannas with wildflowers. Thus, they silently voiced their irrepressible conviction that they were beloved by God. When slavery ended, Sunday churchgoing offered liberated slave women one of their few opportunities to dress up, even though their hats might be made from feedbags stiffened with starch. In ensuing years, black women have taken delight in wearing elegant hats to church as an expression of their creativity. This long-standing spiritual practice is detailed in *Crowns: Portraits of Black Women in Church Hats,* by Michael Cunningham and Craig Marberry (New York: Doubleday, 2000). The book shows how black women's "hattitude" encouraged them to stand up tall and confident in their churches—churches that formed the heart of the abolition, Underground Railroad, and civil rights movements. *Crowns* was so successful as a book that it has been adapted into a popular musical theater piece.

Scripture Insights

The language of divine glory is central to the theology of the Gospel of John. In the Old Testament, God's glory is typically a "brilliant" supernatural quality. There, illumination depicts God's presence and power. John, however, relates Jesus' death on the cross with the divine glory he shares with his Father. This is a stunning and ironic revision of the Gospel writer's inheritance from Judaism. For John, Jesus is exalted on the cross. What would have been a humiliating death became a means of revelation greater than prophecy or God's gift of the law at Mount Sinai.

Perhaps the most peculiar aspect of the *Left Behind* media series is the seeming delight of its authors in the violence and sweeping damnation of souls they suppose will accompany the return of Jesus. The book of Revelation is little more than fuel for the authors' imaginations. Our readings conclude today with the love command. But there is more to Jesus' words than the command to love. He also claims "all will know that you are my disciples, if you have love for one another." The defining mark of discipleship, according to Jesus, is that "all," insiders and outsiders, see love shared among the disciples. "Dare we hope all men shall be saved?" asked the Jesuit theologian Urs von Balthasar in his book of the same title. His answer, in light of the traditions of the ancient church he loved, was "yes." One way to show our love for one another and for the world God loves is to work and pray that no one is left behind.

◆ What do you find glorious about the Easter season?

◆ What are your thoughts about Judas and the role he played in Jesus' death?

◆ How can a strict literal reading of the Bible be misleading?

READING I   Acts 15:1—2, 22—29

Some who had come down from Judea were instructing the brothers, "Unless you are circumcised according to the Mosaic practice, you cannot be saved." Because there arose no little dissension and debate by Paul and Barnabas with them, it was decided that Paul, Barnabas, and some of the others should go up to Jerusalem to the apostles and elders about this question.

The apostles and elders, in agreement with the whole church, decided to choose representatives and to send them to Antioch with Paul and Barnabas. The ones chosen were Judas, who was called Barsabbas, and Silas, leaders among the brothers. This is the letter delivered by them:

"The apostles and the elders, your brothers, to the brothers in Antioch, Syria, and Cilicia of Gentile origin: greetings. Since we have heard that some of our number who went out without any mandate from us have upset you with their teachings and disturbed your peace of mind, we have with one accord decided to choose representatives and to send them to you along with our beloved Barnabas and Paul, who have dedicated their lives to the name of our Lord Jesus Christ. So we are sending Judas and Silas who will also convey this same message by word of mouth: 'It is the decision of the Holy Spirit and of us not to place on you any burden beyond these necessities, namely, to abstain from meat sacrificed to idols, from blood, from meats of strangled animals, and from unlawful marriage. If you keep free of these, you will be doing what is right. Farewell.'"

READING II   Revelation 21:10—14, 22—23

The angel took me in spirit to a great, high mountain and showed me the holy city Jerusalem coming down out of heaven from God. It gleamed with the splendor of God. Its radiance was like that of a precious stone, like jasper, clear as crystal. It had a massive, high wall, with twelve gates where twelve angels were stationed and on which names were inscribed, the names of the twelve tribes of the Israelites. There were three gates facing east, three north, three south, and three west. The wall of the city had twelve courses of stones as its foundation, on which were inscribed the twelve names of the twelve apostles of the Lamb.

I saw no temple in the city for its temple is the Lord God almighty and the Lamb. The city had no need of sun or moon to shine on it, for the glory of God gave it light, and its lamp was the Lamb.

GOSPEL   John 14:23—29

Jesus said to his disciples: "Whoever loves me will keep my word, and my Father will love him, and we will come to him and make our dwelling with him. Whoever does not love me does not keep my words; yet the word you hear is not mine but that of the Father who sent me.

"I have told you this while I am with you. The Advocate, the Holy Spirit, whom the Father will send in my name, will teach you everything and remind you of all that I told you. Peace I leave with you; my peace I give to you. Not as the world gives do I give it to you. Do not let your hearts be troubled or afraid. You heard me tell you, 'I am going away and I will come back to you.' If you loved me, you would rejoice that I am going to the Father; for the Father is greater than I. And now I have told you this before it happens, so that when it happens you may believe."

Practice of Prayer

Psalm 67:2—3, 5, 6, 8 (2a)

R. O God, let all the nations praise you!
or: Alleluia.

May God have pity on us and bless us;
    may he let his face shine upon us.
So may your way be known upon earth;
    among all nations, your salvation. R.

May the nations be glad and exult
    because you rule the peoples in equity;
    the nations on the earth you guide. R.

May the peoples praise you, O God;
    may all the peoples praise you!
May God bless us,
    and may all the ends of the earth
        fear him! R.

Practice of Hope

American gardens are resplendent for Mother's Day today, among them Conrad's Garden in Wicker Park, Chicago—also known as Resurrection Garden. The garden was created in 1998 for Conrad Cwiertnia, who was suffering from cancer. His house was filled with medical equipment, so Conrad's neighbors, Doug Wood and Denise Browning, planted a garden where his many friends could continue to visit. Artists began painting there, people wandered through, and one night a dance was held. Conrad died in 2003. The two loyal neighbors hoped to purchase the property eventually, but it was sold. So they obtained permission from the new owner and from the city to move the garden plant-by-plant to the park. They dug up 1,800 plants, wrapped each in burlap and moved every one to its new home via shopping cart. Since its beauty draws so many visitors, the garden has made the park safer.

Scripture Insights

Twenty-seven books comprise the New Testament. The majority are letters. These letters, also known as epistles, were vital to the Church's early development. Sometimes, as the apostle Paul says, they were more persuasive than the writer's presence (see 2 Corinthians 10:7–11). In today's reading from Acts, we have what some biblical scholars call an "embedded letter." This is a letter placed in, or perhaps composed for, a larger text.

The account of the Council in Antioch describes the struggles of the early Christian communities. Specifically addressed is the issue of circumcision. Parish council members may marvel at how simply the issue is worked out. However, it is worth checking another New Testament letter, Saint Paul's epistle to the Galatians (see especially 2:11–14), before deciding on the ease of the resolution.

Any group of people undergoing change will face conflicts. When all agree on what binds the group, issues are settled easier. Today's Gospel reading provides one of the traditional bases for understanding what holds the Church together. We are disciples of Jesus joined by the Holy Spirit. Our understanding and experience of the Spirit is a source of our unity, our "catholicity." Our Catholic family conflicts may not be so quickly resolved as in today's reading from Acts, but the resource for their resolution has been offered. It is our choice to accept or reject what it has to teach us.

• How does the second reading explain the absence of the temple in the New Jerusalem?

♦ On the Fourth Sunday of Easter, we read Jesus' declaration that "The Father and I are one." Today Jesus says, "the Father is greater than I." How do you reconcile these passages?

♦ When have you been aware of the Holy Spirit resolving a conflict in your life? How do you open yourself to the work of the Spirit?

READING I   Acts 1:1—11

In the first book, Theophilus, I dealt with all that Jesus did and taught until the day he was taken up, after giving instructions through the Holy Spirit to the apostles whom he had chosen. He presented himself alive to them by many proofs after he had suffered, appearing to them during forty days and speaking about the kingdom of God. While meeting with them, he enjoined them not to depart from Jerusalem, but to wait for "the promise of the Father about which you have heard me speak; for John baptized with water, but in a few days you will be baptized with the Holy Spirit."

When they had gathered together they asked him, "Lord, are you at this time going to restore the kingdom to Israel?" He answered them, "It is not for you to know the times or seasons that the Father has established by his own authority. But you will receive power when the Holy Spirit comes upon you, and you will be my witnesses in Jerusalem, throughout Judea and Samaria, and to the ends of the earth." When he had said this, as they were looking on, he was lifted up, and a cloud took him from their sight. While they were looking intently at the sky as he was going, suddenly two men dressed in white garments stood beside them. They said, "Men of Galilee, why are you standing there looking at the sky? This Jesus who has been taken up from you into heaven will return in the same way as you have seen him going into heaven."

READING II   Hebrews 9:24—28;
10:19—23 or Ephesians 1:17—23

Christ did not enter into a sanctuary made by hands, a copy of the true one, but heaven itself, that he might now appear before God on our behalf. Not that he might offer himself repeatedly, as the high priest enters each year into the sanctuary with blood that is not his own; if that were so, he would have had to suffer repeatedly from the foundation of the world. But now once for all he has appeared at the end of the ages to take away sin by his sacrifice. Just as it is appointed that men and women die once, and after this the judgment, so also Christ, offered once to take away the sins of many, will appear a second time, not to take away sin but to bring salvation to those who eagerly await him.

Therefore, brothers and sisters, since through the blood of Jesus we have confidence of entrance into the sanctuary by the new and living way he opened for us through the veil, that is, his flesh, and since we have "a great priest over the house of God," let us approach with a sincere heart and in absolute trust, with our hearts sprinkled clean from an evil conscience and our bodies washed in pure water. Let us hold unwaveringly to our confession that gives us hope, for he who made the promise is trustworthy.

GOSPEL   Luke 24:46—53

Jesus said to his disciples: "Thus it is written that the Christ would suffer and rise from the dead on the third day and that repentance, for the forgiveness of sins, would be preached in his name to all the nations, beginning from Jerusalem. You are witnesses of these things. And behold I am sending the promise of my Father upon you; but stay in the city until you are clothed with power from on high."

Then he led them out as far as Bethany, raised his hands, and blessed them. As he blessed them he parted from them and was taken up to heaven. They did him homage and then returned to Jerusalem with great joy, and they were continually in the temple praising God.

Practice of Prayer

Psalm 47:2—3, 6—7, 8—9 (6)

R. God mounts his throne to shouts of joy:
    a blare of trumpets for the Lord.
or: Alleluia.

All you peoples, clap your hands,
    shout to God with cries of gladness,
For the LORD, the Most High, the awesome,
    is the great king over all the earth. R.

God mounts his throne amid shouts of joy;
    the LORD, amid trumpet blasts.
Sing praise to God, sing praise;
    sing praise to our king, sing praise. R.

For king of all the earth is God;
    sing hymns of praise.
God reigns over the nations,
    God sits upon his holy throne. R.

Practice of Charity

More people have died in the HIV/AIDS pandemic so far than in all the wars of the twentieth century. In Africa, where the disease has struck with special severity, an estimated 15 million children have lost one or both parents to the illness. Many of these young persons are growing up totally bereft—no home, no education, no care of any kind. Catholic Relief Services' Africa campaign, "Africa Rising! Hope and Healing," provides ways for U.S. citizens to work for legislation that combats HIV/AIDS and poverty issues on the continent. Educational resources are available for classroom and parish use. The free Africa campaign packet includes a poster, map, brochures, and handouts. For more information, go to www.crs.org/africacampaign.cfm.

Scripture Insights

Most biblical scholars think the same author composed the Gospel of Luke and the Acts of the Apostles. Today we encounter one of the major pieces of evidence that supports this theory. Compare the first reading, the introduction to the Acts of the Apostles, with the introduction to Luke (1:1–4). You will find each addresses someone called Theophilus. In Greek the name means "God-lover." Whoever Theophilus was, it is likely that today's first reading was the introduction to part two of a longer work, conventionally called Luke-Acts.

The reading from Acts tells us that, before Jesus ascended, the apostles asked him about the restoration of the Kingdom of Israel. We know from prophetic and apocalyptic Jewish writings that many Jews in Jesus' day believed that a royal messiah of King David's line would rise to restore their kingdom. The apostles' question about Israel's political fortune makes sense in this context. Almost like parents querying a recently graduated son or daughter, the disciples want to know (now that forty days have passed) when Jesus plans to get to work meeting their expectations. And how does Jesus respond? By telling the apostles that *they* will receive power when the Holy Spirit comes upon them; and then ascending before their eyes.

The Ascension is a vivid story demonstrating a truth we learn over and over again: God is not subject to human expectations. If we imagine God will act as we expect, perhaps we will find that we, like the apostles, are the actors God has in mind.

◆ Why do you think Jesus commands the disciples to remain "in the city"?

◆ Do you ever expect someone else in the church to do something only to realize later that the Holy Spirit has given you power to act?

◆ When has God frustrated you? Angered you? Surprised you?

READING I   *Acts 7:55 — 60*

Stephen, filled with the Holy Spirit, looked up intently to heaven and saw the glory of God and Jesus standing at the right hand of God, and Stephen said, "Behold, I see the heavens opened and the Son of Man standing at the right hand of God." But they cried out in a loud voice, covered their ears, and rushed upon him together. They threw him out of the city, and began to stone him. The witnesses laid down their cloaks at the feet of a young man named Saul. As they were stoning Stephen, he called out, "Lord Jesus, receive my spirit." Then he fell to his knees and cried out in a loud voice, "Lord, do not hold this sin against them"; and when he said this, he fell asleep.

READING II   *Revelation 22:12 — 14, 16 — 17, 20*

I, John, heard a voice saying to me: "Behold, I am coming soon. I bring with me the recompense I will give to each according to his deeds. I am the Alpha and the Omega, the first and the last, the beginning and the end."

Blessed are they who wash their robes so as to have the right to the tree of life and enter the city through its gates.

"I, Jesus, sent my angel to give you this testimony for the churches. I am the root and offspring of David, the bright morning star."

The Spirit and the bride say, "Come." Let the hearer say, "Come." Let the one who thirsts come forward, and the one who wants it receive the gift of life-giving water.

The one who gives this testimony says, "Yes, I am coming soon." Amen! Come, Lord Jesus!

GOSPEL   *John 17:20 — 26*

Lifting up his eyes to heaven, Jesus prayed saying: "Holy Father, I pray not only for them, but also for those who will believe in me through their word, so that they may all be one, as you, Father, are in me and I in you, that they also may be in us, that the world may believe that you sent me. And I have given them the glory you gave me, so that they may be one, as we are one, I in them and you in me, that they may be brought to perfection as one, that the world may know that you sent me, and that you loved them even as you loved me. Father, they are your gift to me. I wish that where I am they also may be with me, that they may see my glory that you gave me, because you loved me before the foundation of the world. Righteous Father, the world also does not know you, but I know you, and they know that you sent me. I made known to them your name and I will make it known, that the love with which you loved me may be in them and I in them."

Practice of Prayer

Psalm 97:1 − 2, 6 − 7, 9 (1a, 9a)

R. The Lord is king, the most high over all
    the earth.

or: Alleluia.

The LORD is king; let the earth rejoice;
    let the many islands be glad.
Justice and judgment are the foundation
    of his throne. R.

The heavens proclaim his justice,
    and all peoples see his glory.
All gods are prostrate before him. R.

You, O LORD, are the Most High over all
    the earth,
    exalted far above all gods. R.

Practice of Faith

In a specially appointed room, a group of young children work quietly. One removes a group of objects from a handmade wooden box, telling herself the scripture story they portray. Another traces designs of various crosses, while a third marks cities named in the New Testament on a map of ancient Israel. All are deeply engaged. They are catechumens, and their room is called an atrium. In early Christianity, the atrium was the place where catechumens studied and prayed. Everything in the atrium is chosen for its beauty and usefulness to the children. The catechists study and pray with the Scriptures before presenting them to the children. This is the Catechesis of the Good Shepherd, which biblical scholar Sofia Cavaletti developed using a Montessori model. Cavaletti understood that the child has a deep inborn spirituality that needs only to be evoked and nurtured. To learn more, visit www.cgsusa.org.

Scripture Insights

The theological discipline devoted to the study of Jesus Christ is called Christology. It was hard for the early church to arrive at an understanding of Jesus. The disciples grappled with accepting that the messiah was subject to a brutal execution and glorious resurrection. In the fourth century, the Council of Nicea (325) explained Jesus' relation to the Father, and the Council of Chalcedon (341) clarified the two natures of Christ.

Three of the most important facets of John's Christology are that Jesus has been sent by the Father, that he reveals the Father, and that he and the Father are one. But all this was difficult for the disciples to comprehend. In the Gospels of Matthew, Mark, and Luke, the disciples do not understand the importance of Jesus' claims that the Son of Man must suffer, die, and rise. In John, they do not grasp Jesus' talk of sending, revelation, and unity.

Jesus' prayer in today's Gospel reading is largely a prayer for us, "for those who will believe" through the disciples' proclamation. It is a prayer that the Church will reveal that the Father has sent Jesus. Clear in today's reading is that we must find unity in the world. In showing God to others, we will be acting as Jesus did when he revealed the Father to our ancestors in faith.

• How does Saint Stephen reveal the glory of God?

• As Saint Stephen is stoned, he forgives his killers. Have you ever forgiven someone while they were doing you wrong? Has anyone ever forgiven you while you were doing wrong to them?

• What do you think you can do (or what do you do already) to foster greater unity among Christians?

READING I   Acts 2:1—11

When the time for Pentecost was fulfilled, they were all in one place together. And suddenly there came from the sky a noise like a strong driving wind, and it filled the entire house in which they were. Then there appeared to them tongues as of fire, which parted and came to rest on each one of them. And they were all filled with the Holy Spirit and began to speak in different tongues, as the Spirit enabled them to proclaim.

Now there were devout Jews from every nation under heaven staying in Jerusalem. At this sound, they gathered in a large crowd, but they were confused because each one heard them speaking in his own language. They were astounded, and in amazement they asked, "Are not all these people who are speaking Galileans? Then how does each of us hear them in his native language? We are Parthians, Medes, and Elamites, inhabitants of Mesopotamia, Judea and Cappadocia, Pontus and Asia, Phrygia and Pamphylia, Egypt and the districts of Libya near Cyrene, as well as travelers from Rome, both Jews and converts to Judaism, Cretans and Arabs, yet we hear them speaking in our own tongues of the mighty acts of God."

READING II   Romans 8:8—17 or 1 Corinthians 12:3b—7, 12—13

Brothers and sisters: Those who are in the flesh cannot please God. But you are not in the flesh; on the contrary, you are in the spirit, if only the Spirit of God dwells in you. Whoever does not have the Spirit of Christ does not belong to him. But if Christ is in you, although the body is dead because of sin, the spirit is alive because of righteousness. If the Spirit of the one who raised Jesus from the dead dwells in you, the one who raised Christ from the dead will give life to your mortal bodies also, through his Spirit that dwells in you. Consequently, brothers and sisters, we are not debtors to the flesh, to live according to the flesh. For if you live according to the flesh, you will die, but if by the Spirit you put to death the deeds of the body, you will live.

For those who are led by the Spirit of God are sons of God. For you did not receive a spirit of slavery to fall back into fear, but you received a spirit of adoption, through whom we cry, "Abba, Father!" The Spirit himself bears witness with our spirit that we are children of God, and if children, then heirs, heirs of God and joint heirs with Christ, if only we suffer with him so that we may also be glorified with him.

GOSPEL   John 14:15—16, 23b—26 or John 20:19—23

Jesus said to his disciples: "If you love me, you will keep my commandments. And I will ask the Father, and he will give you another Advocate to be with you always.

"Whoever loves me will keep my word, and my Father will love him, and we will come to him and make our dwelling with him. Those who do not love me do not keep my words; yet the word you hear is not mine but that of the Father who sent me.

"I have told you this while I am with you. The Advocate, the Holy Spirit whom the Father will send in my name, will teach you everything and remind you of all that I told you."

Practice of Prayer

Practice of Hope

Since the early 1990s, the people of Christ the Redeemer parish in Mount Orion, Michigan, had been following a simple guideline. At every choir rehearsal, administrative meeting, or other gathering, they asked: "What impact will what we do here have on the poor?" Considering this question faithfully led them to designate a percentage of all parish income for the poor and to develop a vibrant Christian service ministry. Then in 1996, as the congregation prepared to build a new church, the pastor, Father Joe Dailey, commented, "Here we are getting ready to build a house for ourselves, and there are a lot of homeless people in our world today." A sacrificial giving program collected funds, not only for the new church, but also for a new Habitat for Humanity dwelling in nearby Pontiac. Parish volunteers built that house and several more since. More than 300 parishioners have contributed their labor.

Scripture Insights

According to traditional teaching, Pentecost is the birthday of the church. In today's reading from Acts, the Holy Spirit appears dramatically. This is not, of course, the first time we have encountered the Spirit in Luke-Acts. We meet the Holy Spirit at the beginning of this two-part work, when the angel Gabriel informs Mary that the "overshadowing" of the spirit will permit her to conceive Jesus. It is the advent of the Holy Spirit that John the Baptist and Jesus promise. The gift of the Holy Spirit ushers in the era of the church.

In the writings of Saint Paul, "flesh" is often opposed to "spirit." This is the case in the reading for today. Note some of the other oppositions present in this passage. Death is opposed to life, slavery to adoption, and inheritance and fear to the cry of "Abba, Father!" Who would argue that adoption is better than slavery? Life than death? It must follow, therefore, that spirit is better than flesh.

Saint Paul conceives of spirit in its opposition to flesh in the reading from Romans differently than the author of Luke-Acts thinks of the Holy Spirit in the selection from Acts. For Saint Paul, flesh and spirit describe contradictory ways of life and relationships with God. For the author of Luke-Acts, the Holy Spirit is a powerful divine actor on the church's behalf. However we argue the case for Catholic Christianity, we do well to remember that we are a people joined by the Holy Spirit. Our power is not our own.

◆ What does Saint Paul mean by the body being dead to sin?

◆ In the Gospel reading, the Greek word translated as "Advocate" can also be rendered as "Comforter." Why do you prefer one translation more than the other?

◆ What does being filled with the Spirit mean to you?

Summer Ordinary Time

Prayer before Reading the Word

Wise and merciful God,
Grant us a heart
Thirsting for your truth,
Longing for your presence,
And ready to hear you in the word of your Son.
Grant us the wisdom of your Spirit,
the understanding bestowed on the true disciples,
that we may carry the cross each day
and follow after your Son, our Lord Jesus Christ,
who lives and reigns with you
in the unity of the Holy Spirit,
God for ever and ever. Amen.

Prayer after Reading the Word

Your word resounds in your church, O God,
As a fountain of wisdom and a rule of life;
Make us, O God, faithful disciples of that wisdom
Whose Teacher and Master is Christ
And whose chair of learning is the cross.
Schooled in this unique wisdom,
May we be prepared to conquer our fears
        and temptations,
To take up our cross daily
And to follow Jesus toward true life.
We ask this through our Lord Jesus Christ,
        your Son,
Who lives and reigns with you
In the unity of the Holy Spirit,
God for ever and ever. Amen.

Weekday Readings

May 28: *Sirach 17:20–24; Mark 10:17–27*
May 29: *Sirach 35:1–12; Mark 10:28–31*
May 30: *Sirach 36:1, 4–5a, 10–17; Mark 10:32–45*
May 31: Feast of the Visitation of the Blessed Virgin Mary
    Zephaniah 3:14–18a; Luke 1:39–56
June 1: *Sirach 44:1, 9–13; Mark 11:11–26*
June 2: *Sirach 51:12cd–20; Mark 11:27–33*

June 4: *Tobit 1:3, 2:1a–8; Mark 12:1–12*
June 5: *Tobit 2:9–14; Mark 12:13–17*
June 6: *Tobit 3:1–11 a, 16–17a; Mark 12:18–27*
June 7: *Tobit 6:10–11; 7:1bcde, 9–17; 8:4–9a; Mark 12:28–34*
June 8: *Tobit 11:5–17; Mark 12:35–37*
June 9: *Tobit 12:1, 5–15, 20; Mark 12:38–44*

June 11: *Acts 11:21b–26; 13: 1–3; Matthew 5:1–12*
June 12: *2 Corinthians 1:18–22; Matthew 5:13–16*
June 13: *2 Corinthians 3:4–11; Matthew 5:17–19*
June 14: *2 Corinthians 3:15–4:1, 3–6; Matthew 5:20–26*
June 15: Solemnity of the Most Sacred Heart of Jesus
    Ezekiel 34:11–16; Romans 5:5b–11; Luke 15:3–7
June 16: *2 Corinthians 5:14–21; Luke 2:41–51;*

June 18: *2 Corinthians 6:1–10; Matthew 5:38–42*
June 19: *2 Corinthians 8:1–9; Matthew 5:43–48*
June 20: *2 Corinthians 9:6–11; Matthew 6:1–6, 16–18*
June 21: *2 Corinthians 11:1–11; Matthew 6:7–15*
June 22: *2 Corinthians 11:18, 21–30; Matthew 6:19–23*
June 23: *2 Corinthians 12:1–10; Matthew 6:24–34*

June 25: *Genesis 12:1–9; Matthew 7:1–5*
June 26: *Genesis 13:2, 5–18; Matthew 7:6, 12–14*
June 27: *Genesis 15:1–12, 17–18; Matthew 7:15–20*
June 28: *Genesis 16:1–12, 15–16; Matthew 7:21–29*
June 29: Solemnity of Saints Peter and Paul
    Acts 12:1–11; 2 Timothy 4:6–8; 17–18; Matthew 16:13–19
June 30: *Genesis 18:1–15; Matthew 8:5–17*

July 2: *Genesis 18:16–33; Matthew 8:18–22*
July 3: Feast of Saint Thomas the Apostle
    Ephesians 2:19–22; John 20:24–29
July 4: *Genesis 21:5, 8–20a; Matthew 8:28–34*
July 5: *Genesis 22:1b–19; Matthew 9:1–8*
July 6: *Genesis 23:1–4, 19; 24:1–8, 62–67; Matthew 9:9–13*
July 7: *Genesis 27:1–5, 15–29; Matthew 9:14–17*

July 9: *Genesis 28:10–22a; Matthew 9:18–26*
July 10: *Genesis 32:23–33; Matthew 9:32–38*
July 11: *Genesis 41:55–57; 42:5–7a, 17–24a; Matthew 10:1–7*
July 12: *Genesis 44:18–21, 23b–29; 45:1–5; Matthew 10:7–15*
July 13: *Genesis 46:1–7, 28–30; Matthew 10:16–23*
July 14: *Genesis 49:29–32; 50:15–26a; Matthew 10:24–33*

July 16: *Exodus 1:8–14, 22; Matthew 10:34–11:1*
July 17: *Exodus 2:1–15a; Matthew 11:20–24*
July 18: *Exodus 3:1–6, 9–12; Matthew 11:25–27*
July 19: *Exodus 3:13–20; Matthew 11:28–30*
July 20: *Exodus 11:10–12:14; Matthew 12:1–8*
July 21: *Exodus 12:37–42; Matthew 12:14–21*

July 23: *Exodus 14:5–18; Matthew 12:38–42*
July 24: *Exodus 14:21–15:1; Matthew 12:46–50*
July 25: Feast of Saint James
    2 Corinthians 4:7–15; Matthew 20:20–28

July 26: *Exodus 19:1–2, 9–11, 16–20b; Matthew 13:10–17*
July 27: *Exodus 20:1–17; Matthew 13:18–23*
July 28: *Exodus 24:3–8; Matthew 13:24–30*

July 30: *Exodus 32:15–24, 30–34; Matthew 13:31–35*
July 31 *Exodus 33: 7–11; 34:5b–9, 28; Matthew 13:36–43*
August 1: *Exodus 34:29–35; Matthew 13:44–46*
August 2: *Exodus 40:16–21, 34–38; Matthew 13:47–53*
August 3: *Leviticus 23:1, 4–11, 15–16, 27, 34b–37;*
    Matthew 13:54–58
August 4: *Leviticus 25:1, 8–17; Matthew 14:1–12*

August 6: Feast of the Transfiguration of the Lord
    Daniel 7:9–10, 13–14; 2 Peter 1:16–19; Luke 9:28b–36
August 7: *Numbers 12:1–13; Matthew 14:22–36*
August 8: *Numbers 13:1–2, 25–14:1, 26–29a, 34–35;*
    Matthew 15:21–28
August 9: *Numbers 20:1–13; Matthew 16:13–23*
August 10: Feast of Saint Lawrence
    2 Corinthians 9:6–10; John 12:24–26
August 11: *Deuteronomy 6:4–13; Matthew 17:14–20*

August 13: *Deuteronomy 10:12–22; Matthew 17:22–27*
August 14: *Deuteronomy 31:1–8; Matthew 18:1–5, 10, 12–14*
August 15: Solemnity of the Assumption of the Blessed
    Virgin Mary
    Revelation 11:19a; 12:1–6a, 10ab/1 Corinthians
    15:20–27; Luke 1:39–56
August 16: *Joshua 3:7–10a, 11, 13–17; Matthew 18:21–19:1*
August 17: *Joshua 24:1–13; Matthew19:3–12*
August 18: *Joshua 24:14–29; Matthew 19:13–15*

August 20: *Judges 2:11–19; Matthew 19:16–22*
August 21: Judges 6:11–24a; Matthew 19:23–30
August 22: *Judges 9:6–15; Matthew 20:1–16*
August 23: *Judges 11:29–39a; Matthew 22:1–14*
August 24: Feast of Saint Bartholomew
    Revelation 21:9b–14; John 1:45–51
August 25: *Ruth 2:1–3, 8–11; 4:13–17; Matthew 23:1–12*

August 27: *1 Thessalonians 1:1–5, 8b–10; Matthew 23:13–22*
August 28: *1 Thessalonians 2: 1–8; Matthew 23:23–26*
August 29: *1 Thessalonians 2:9–13; Mark 6:17–29*
August 30: *1 Thessalonians 3:7–13; Matthew 24:42–51*
August 31: *1 Thessalonians 4:1–8; Matthew 25:1–13*
September 1: *1 Thessalonians 4:9–11; Matthew 25:14–30*

September 3: *1 Thessalonians 4:13–18; Luke 4:16–30*
September 4: *1 Thessalonians 5:1–6, 9–11; Luke 4:31–37*
September 5: *Colossians 1:1–8; Luke 4:38–44*
September 6: *Colossians 1:9–14; Luke 5:1–11*
September 7: *Colossians 1:15–20; Luke 5:33–39*
September 8: Feast of the Birth of the Blessed Virgin Mary
    Micah 5:1–4a; Matthew 1:1–16, 18–23

September 10: *Colossians 1:24–2:3; Luke 6:6–11*
September 11: *Colossians 2:6–15; Luke 6:12–19*
September 12: *Colossians 3:1–11; Luke 6:20–26*
September 13: *Colossians 3:12–17; Luke 6:27–38*
September 14: Feast of the Exaltation of the Holy Cross
    Numbers 21:4b–9; Philippians 2:6–11; John 3:13–17
September 15: *1 Timothy 1:15–17; John 19:25–27*

READING I   *Proverbs 8:22—31*

Thus says the wisdom of God:

"The LORD possessed me, the beginning of
    his ways,
      the forerunner of his prodigies of
      long ago;
from of old I was poured forth,
    at the first, before the earth.
When there were no depths I was
    brought forth,
when there were no fountains or springs
    of water;
before the mountains were settled into place,
    before the hills, I was brought forth;
while as yet the earth and fields were
    not made,
    nor the first clods of the world.

"When the Lord established the heavens
    I was there,
    when he marked out the vault over the
    face of the deep;
when he made firm the skies above,
    when he fixed fast the foundations
    of the earth;
when he set for the sea its limit,
    so that the waters should not transgress
    his command;
then was I beside him as his craftsman,
    and I was his delight day by day,
playing before him all the while,
    playing on the surface of his earth;
    and I found delight in the human race."

READING II   *Romans 5:1—5*

Brothers and sisters: Therefore, since we have been justified by faith, we have peace with God through our Lord Jesus Christ, through whom we have gained access by faith to this grace in which we stand, and we boast in hope of the glory of God. Not only that, but we even boast of our afflictions, knowing that affliction produces endurance, and endurance, proven character, and proven character, hope, and hope does not disappoint, because the love of God has been poured out into our hearts through the Holy Spirit that has been given to us.

GOSPEL   *John 16:12—15*

Jesus said to his disciples: "I have much more to tell you, but you cannot bear it now. But when he comes, the Spirit of truth, he will guide you to all truth. He will not speak on his own, but he will speak what he hears, and will declare to you the things that are coming. He will glorify me, because he will take from what is mine and declare it to you. Everything that the Father has is mine; for this reason I told you that he will take from what is mine and declare it to you."

Practice of Prayer

Psalm 8:4 — 5, 6 — 7, 8 — 9 (2a)

R. O Lord, our God, how wonderful your name
      in all the earth!

When I behold your heavens, the work of
      your fingers,
    the moon and the stars which you
        set in place—
what is man that you should be mindful of him,
    or the son of man that you should care
      or him? R.

You have made him little less than the angels,
    and crowned him with glory
      and honor.
You have given him rule over the works of
      your hands,
    putting all things under his feet. R.

All sheep and oxen,
    yes, and the beasts of the field,
the birds of the air, the fishes of the sea,
    and whatever swims the paths
      of the seas. R.

Practice of Hope

The Trinity is a God of relationship. One person who discovered this in a delightful way was Saint Catherine of Siena (14th century). A dynamic, creative woman, she tended plague victims, fought corruption in church and state, and worked tirelessly for peace. People so desired Catherine's guidance and practical wisdom that, once when she visited Rome, people from all over Tuscany followed her there. At any given time, up to thirty of them might be staying in her lodgings. So her life was busy and active, often full of uproar. However, Catherine was also a mystic who reveled in the prayer of quiet. Sometimes she grieved because she could not find enough time to dwell on the mystery of the Trinity, the delight of her heart. "Oh, where were you, Lord?" she burst out once. The answer came: "There was I, daughter, in the midst of them."

Scripture Insights

The Catholic doctrine of the Most Holy Trinity received a definitive description at the Council of Nicea in 325. In less than a generation, Christians had exchanged periodic persecution for the protection and patronage of Emperor Constantine. At Nicea, bishops and theologians now met in full safety to debate the relationship among the Father, Jesus Christ, and the Holy Spirit. The great legacy of that council is the Nicene Creed.

One reason for the council was that Scripture did not clearly answer some pressing questions some Christians had about the Trinity. When did the Father beget Jesus? Were Jesus and the Father of the same nature? Reread the selections for today. Does Proverbs, Romans, or John offer clear answers to these questions? Is the Wisdom of God in Proverbs the same as the Advocate in John? If so, are they to be identified with the Holy Spirit?

The work of Nicea and of subsequent ecumenical councils was in part to explain scriptural truths not immediately apparent. The doctrine of the Trinity painstakingly crafted in the early centuries of the church affirms, above all, the unity of the three persons, Father, Son, and Holy Spirit. As is clearly apparent in the second and third readings, the Trinity is the pulse of the common life of the Church. May the unity of the persons of the Trinity replace our strife and division with reconciliation in anticipation of "the entry of God's creatures into the perfect unity of the Blessed Trinity" (Catechism of the Catholic Church, paragraph 259).

◆ In the reading from Proverbs, wisdom describes itself as a force existing before the time of creation. What do you think this has to do with the doctrine of the Trinity?

◆ What are some of the ways the Trinity figures in your prayer life?

◆ What are some mysteries of the Roman Catholic faith that you puzzle over?

June 10, 2007

READING I *Genesis 14:8—20*

In those days, Melchizedek, king of Salem, brought out bread and wine, and being a priest of God Most High, he blessed Abram with these words:/ "Blessed be Abram by God Most High,/the creator of heaven and earth;/and blessed be God Most High,/who delivered your foes into your hand." Then Abram gave him a tenth of everything.

READING II *1 Corinthians 11:23—26*

Brothers and sisters: I received from the Lord what I also handed on to you, that the Lord Jesus, on the night he was handed over, took bread, and, after he had given thanks, broke it and said, "This is my body that is for you. Do this in remembrance of me." In the same way also the cup, after supper, saying, "This cup is the new covenant in my blood. Do this, as often as you drink it, in remembrance of me." For as often as you eat this bread and drink the cup, you proclaim the death of the Lord until he comes.

GOSPEL *Luke 9:11b—17*

Jesus spoke to the crowds about the kingdom of God, and he healed those who needed to be cured. As the day was drawing to a close, the Twelve approached him and said, "Dismiss the crowd so that they can go to the surrounding villages and farms and find lodging and provisions; for we are in a deserted place here." He said to them, "Give them some food yourselves." They replied, "Five loaves and two fish are all we have, unless we ourselves go and buy food for all these people." Now the men there numbered about five thousand. Then he said to his disciples, "Have them sit down in groups of about fifty." They did so and made them all sit down. Then taking the five loaves and the two fish, and looking up to heaven, he said the blessing over them, broke them, and gave them to the disciples to set before the crowd. They all ate and were satisfied. And when the leftover fragments were picked up, they filled twelve wicker baskets.

Practice of Prayer

Psalm 110:1, 2, 3, 4 (4b)

R. You are a priest for ever, in the line
    of Melchizedek.

The LORD said to my Lord: "Sit at my right hand
    till I make your enemies your footstool."   R.

The scepter of your power the LORD will stretch
    forth from Zion:
    "Rule in the midst of your enemies."   R.

"Yours is princely power in the day of your birth,
    in holy splendor;
before the daystar, like the dew,
    I have begotten you."   R.

The LORD has sworn, and he will not repent:
    "You are a priest forever, according to the
    order of Melchizedek."   R.

Practice of Charity

More than 34,000 registered lobbyists work in Washington, D.C. Their job is to influence legislation for the corporations and trade organizations that pay their salaries. One lobby is different. Established in 1970 by forty-seven Catholic sisters who wanted to speak out for peace and justice, it is called Network. Network speaks to members of Congress for those who otherwise would have no voice in our society: the poor, the homeless, and children. It strives to close the gap between rich and poor, and to dismantle policies rooted in racism, greed, and violence. Member organizations and individuals, including religious congregations, parishes and dioceses around the country, sponsor Network's ongoing mission. When quick action is needed, Network contacts these members to phone, write, or e-mail their senators and representatives. Great good is being done! You can contact Network at www.networklobby.org.

Scripture Insights

The word "eucharist" comes from a Greek word meaning "thanksgiving." It is the central sacrament of Roman Catholic life. Participating in the rite links us with those who shared the Last Supper. It links us with the earliest church, which remembered Christ at a common meal in believers' homes, and with the Church universal throughout the world under the leadership and guidance of our Holy Father, the pope, the bishop of Rome. In today's second reading, we hear how Paul received the tradition (see also 1 Corinthians 15:3–8) and passed it on to the Corinthians.

Roman Catholic tradition typically has given a Eucharistic interpretation to the miracle of the loaves and fishes. The connection is fairly clear in John, but not as evident in Matthew, Mark, and Luke. Many biblical scholars also see a relationship between Jesus' multiplication of the loaves and fishes and the prophet Elisha's feeding people in Gilgal in 2 Kings 4:44. Both the multiplication miracles and the Eucharist nourish the hungry.

It is worth considering the second reading in its larger context of 1 Corinthians 1:17–34. In these verses, Saint Paul chides the Corinthians for permitting some members of the church to feast while others go hungry. "The Eucharist is not a Eucharist," Saint Paul is saying, "when the food is not shared equally." In most parishes, the Body and Blood of Christ are distributed equally, so the issue Saint Paul encountered does not arise. However, members of a congregation may feel left out in other ways. Are people with disabilities welcomed into ministries, or do they encounter obstacles? Is it possible, for example, for a wheelchair-bound person to serve as a lector? As we share the Eucharist, let us be sure to welcome all.

◆ Why do you think that Christ asked that the people sit in groups of fifty?

◆ How does the Eucharist nourish you?

◆ Describe how the second reading enhances your understanding of the Eucharist.

READING I   2 Samuel 12: 7—10, 13

Nathan said to David: "Thus says the LORD God of Israel: 'I anointed you king of Israel. I rescued you from the hand of Saul. I gave you your lord's house and your lord's wives for your own. I gave you the house of Israel and of Judah. And if this were not enough, I could count up for you still more. Why have you spurned the Lord and done evil in his sight? You have cut down Uriah the Hittite with the sword; you took his wife as your own, and him you killed with the sword of the Ammonites. Now, therefore, the sword shall never depart from your house, because you have despised me and have taken the wife of Uriah to be your wife.'" Then David said to Nathan, "I have sinned against the LORD." Nathan answered David: "The LORD on his part has forgiven your sin: you shall not die."

READING II   Galatians 2:16, 19—21

Brothers and sisters: We who know that a person is not justified by works of the law but through faith in Jesus Christ, even we have believed in Christ Jesus that we may be justified by faith in Christ and not by works of the law, because by works of the law no one will be justified. For through the law I died to the law, that I might live for God. I have been crucified with Christ; yet I live, no longer I, but Christ lives in me; insofar as I now live in the flesh, I live by faith in the Son of God who has loved me and given himself up for me. I do not nullify the grace of God; for if justification comes through the law, then Christ died for nothing.

GOSPEL   Luke 7:36 — 8:3

Shorter Luke 7:36—50

A Pharisee invited Jesus to dine with him, and he entered the Pharisee's house and reclined at table. Now there was a sinful woman in the city who learned that he was at table in the house of the Pharisee. Bringing an alabaster flask of ointment, she stood behind him at his feet weeping and began to bathe his feet with her tears. Then she wiped them with her hair, kissed them, and anointed them with the ointment. When the Pharisee who had invited him saw this he said to himself, "If this man were a prophet, he would know who and what sort of woman this is who is touching him, that she is a sinner." Jesus said to him in reply, "Simon, I have something to say to you." "Tell me, teacher," he said. "Two people were in debt to a certain creditor; one owed five hundred days' wages and the other owed fifty. Since they were unable to repay the debt, he forgave it for both. Which of them will love him more?" Simon said in reply, "The one, I suppose, whose larger debt was forgiven." He said to him, "You have judged rightly."

Then he turned to the woman and said to Simon, "Do you see this woman? When I entered your house, you did not give me water for my feet, but she has bathed them with her tears and wiped them with her hair. You did not give me a kiss, but she has not ceased kissing my feet since the time I entered. You did not anoint my head with oil, but she anointed my feet with ointment. So I tell you, her many sins have been forgiven because she has shown great love. But the one to whom little is forgiven, loves little." He said to her, "Your sins are forgiven." The others at table said to themselves, "Who is this who even forgives sins?" But he said to the woman, "Your faith has saved you; go in peace."

Afterward he journeyed from one town and village to another, preaching and proclaiming the good news of the kingdom of God. Accompanying him were the Twelve and some women who had been cured of evil spirits and infirmities, Mary, called Magdalene, from whom seven demons had gone out, Joanna, the wife of Herod's steward Chuza, Susanna, and many others who provided for them out of their resources.

Practice of Prayer

Psalm 32:1— 2, 5, 7, 11

R. Lord, forgive the wrong I have done.

Blessed is the one whose fault is taken away,
    whose sin is covered.
Blessed the man to whom the LORD imputes
    not guilt,
    in whose spirit there is no guile. R.

I acknowledged my sin to you,
    my guilt I covered not.
I said, "I confess my faults to the LORD,"
    and you took away the guilt of my sin. R.

You are my shelter; from distress you will
    preserve me;
    with glad cries of freedom you will ring me
    round. R.

Be glad in the LORD and rejoice, you just;
    exult, all you upright of heart. R.

Practice of Faith

This week we bask in sunlight. Not only is June 21 the official start of summer, but it is also the longest day of the year. This doesn't bring everyone joy. For my brother, this is the saddest day of the year, because it means that from now on the darkness will gain on the light, making every day shorter. While we have no power over how long the sun will shine daily, it is our choice whether our lives of faith will be "summer" or "winter." Will we embrace the light of Christ that was entrusted to us at our baptism and bask in the warmth of God's grace or fall into shadow through sin? Before next dipping your hand into the holy water, consider what "season" you are in with God. If it's "summer," give thanks. If it's "winter," perhaps it's time for the Son.

Scripture Insights

What a study in character today's scriptures afford us: King David, Paul the Pharisee, Simon the Pharisee, the unnamed woman who greets Jesus in his house—all viewed through the lens of their perceptions of their righteousness.

In biblical terms, to be righteous meant to be in the right relationship with God, a concept measured by fidelity to the Law. Both David and the woman in the Gospel recognized their unrighteousness and acknowledged it. There was no defense, no pretense of being what they were not. They epitomized the words of the psalmist: "I acknowledge my sin to you, my guilt I covered not. I said, 'I confess my faults to the Lord' and you took away the guilt of my sin."

Such an acknowledgement was far from Simon's mind. The Pharisees were a sect within Judaism who promoted adherence to the Law. In their strict adherence to the letter of the Law, they sometimes lost sight of other, equally important aspects of the Covenant, for example, God's mercy.

In verse 39, Simon shows his self-righteousness. He makes it evident that he, not the woman, is worthy of association with God's prophet. What is more, Simon scorns Jesus for not recognizing this. From Simon's perspective, Jesus was "defiled" by her sinfulness. Simon thinks less of Jesus because of this.

Simon has missed the point. Jesus welcomes sinners that he might bring them the reality of God's love and forgiveness. The woman, recognizing her great need, was able to receive what Jesus offered. Simon was not.

◆ In what ways do the women in this gospel passage show hospitality to Jesus?

◆ Why do you think acknowledgment of sin and the knowledge of God's forgiveness may lead to great love?

◆ How has another's humility helped you to know God better?

READING I *Isaiah 49:1—6*

Hear me, O coastlands
    listen, O distant peoples.
The LORD called me from birth,
    from my mother's womb he gave me
        my name.
He made of me a sharp-edged sword
    and concealed me in the shadow of his arm.
He made me a polished arrow,
    in his quiver he hid me.
You are my servant, he said to me,
    Israel, through whom I show my glory.

Though I thought I had toiled in vain,
    and for nothing, uselessly, spent my strength,
yet my reward is with the LORD,
    my recompense is with my God.
For now the LORD has spoken
    who formed me as his servant from
        the womb,
that Jacob may be brought back to him
    and Israel gathered to him;
and I am made glorious in the sight of the LORD,
    and my God is now my strength!
It is too little, he says, for you to be my servant,
    to raise up the tribes of Jacob,
    and restore the survivors of Israel;
I will make you a light to the nations,
    that my salvation may reach to the ends of
        the earth.

READING II *Acts 13:22—26*

In those days, Paul said:
"God raised up David as their king;
    of him he testified,
    I have found David, son of Jesse,
        a man after my own heart;
    he will carry out my every wish.
From this man's descendants God, according to
        his promise,
    has brought to Israel a savior, Jesus.
John heralded his coming by proclaiming a
        baptism of repentance
    to all the people of Israel;
and as John was completing his course, he
        would say,

'What do you suppose that I am? I am not he.
Behold, one is coming after me;
    I am not worthy to unfasten the sandals of
        his feet.'

"My brothers, children of the family
        of Abraham,
    and those others among you who are
        God-fearing,
    to us this word of salvation has been sent."

GOSPEL *Luke 1:57—66, 80*

When the time arrived for Elizabeth to have her child she gave birth to a son. Her neighbors and relatives heard that the Lord had shown his great mercy toward her, and they rejoiced with her. When they came on the eighth day to circumcise the child, they were going to call him Zechariah after his father, but his mother said in reply, "No. He will be called John." But they answered her, "There is no one among your relatives who has this name." So they made signs, asking his father what he wished him to be called. He asked for a tablet and wrote, "John is his name," and all were amazed. Immediately his mouth was opened, his tongue freed, and he spoke blessing God. Then fear came upon all their neighbors, and all these matters were discussed throughout the hill country of Judea. All who heard these things took them to heart, saying, "What, then, will this child be?" For surely the hand of the Lord was with him.

The child grew and became strong in spirit, and he was in the desert until the day of his manifestation to Israel.

Practice of Prayer

Psalm 139:1—3, 13—14ab, 14c—15 (14a)

R. I praise you for I am wonderfully made.

O LORD you have probed me and you know me;
> you know when I sit and when I stand;
> you understand my thoughts from afar.
My journeys and my rest you scrutinize,
> with all my ways you are familiar. R.

Truly you have formed my inmost being;
> you knit me in my mother's womb.
I give you thanks that I am fearfully,
> > wonderfully made;
> wonderful are your works. R.

My soul also you knew full well;
> nor was my frame unknown to you
when I was made in secret,
> when I was fashioned in the depths of
> > he earth. R.

Practice of Hope

Does your parish or youth group send teens on a mission trip in the summer? Many do, and these opportunities for service are often life-changing experiences. One organization that offers week-long, Christ-centered mission opportunities for 12-to 19-year-olds is YouthWorks! Based in Minneapolis, Minn., YouthWorks! has sites in urban and rural settings in the United States, Puerto Rico, and Mexico. Organizers say that when the youth cross borders of race and culture and leave their comfort zones behind, they offer more than hope and help. The 'works' in the name is about what God does in lives when allowed. Would you like to support someone who is acting as "a light to the nations"? Go to www. youth-works. com—and don't forget to pray for these young people as they learn what "servant leadership" is about.

Scripture Insights

"What, then, will this child be?" The biblical narratives of the birth of John the Baptist, filled with echoes and allusions to numerous birth narratives from the Old Testament, leave no doubt. This child "will be great in the sight of the Lord." As with many of the great patriarchs and prophets of Israel, a heavenly messenger foretold John's birth. As with many of these figures, he was born to a barren woman. In the Old Testament, "children are a gift from the Lord"; and barrenness, a disgrace. Elizabeth, like Sarah before her, was not only barren, she was beyond child-bearing years. Thus, this child signified God's special favor, as his name "John" implies ("Yahweh has shown favor").

Not only was the birth of John a sign of God's favor for Elizabeth, but for all Israel. As with the Servant in Isaiah 49:1–6, and Jeremiah, whose call is recounted in the first reading for the Vigil for today's Solemnity, God named and missioned this child before he was born. He would be one who would go forth "in the spirit and power of Elijah . . . to prepare a people fit for the Lord."

The last line of today's Gospel moves us beyond the birth to those hidden years of growth and becoming "strong in spirit," years in the desert— that traditional place of encounter with God. John stayed in the desert, until the day of his "manifestation" to Israel, when at the bidding of "the word of God," he came forth, proclaiming a baptism of repentance, preparing the way of the Lord. Look, then, at what this child became.

♦ Why do you think Psalm 139 is a particularly appropriate response for today's feast?

♦ In what sense are you "named"? Do you have a sense of the mission to which God may be calling you?

♦ Do you see yourself as a light to the nations?

July 1, 2007

READING I   *1 Kings 19:16b, 19 — 21*

The LORD said to Elijah: "You shall anoint Elisha, son of Shaphat of Abel-meholah, as prophet to succeed you."

Elijah set out and came upon Elisha, son of Shaphat, as he was plowing with twelve yoke of oxen; he was following the twelfth. Elijah went over to him and threw his cloak over him. Elisha left the oxen, ran after Elijah, and said, "Please, let me kiss my father and mother goodbye, and I will follow you." Elijah answered, "Go back! Have I done anything to you?" Elisha left him, and taking the yoke of oxen, slaughtered them; he used the plowing equipment for fuel to boil their flesh, and gave it to his people to eat. Then Elisha left and followed Elijah as his attendant.

READING II   *Galatians 5:1, 13 — 18*

Brothers and sisters: For freedom Christ set us free; so stand firm and do not submit again to the yoke of slavery.

For you were called for freedom, brothers and sisters. But do not use this freedom as an opportunity for the flesh; rather, serve one another through love. For the whole law is fulfilled in one statement, namely, *You shall love your neighbor as yourself.* But if you go on biting and devouring one another, beware that you are not consumed by one another.

I say, then: live by the Spirit and you will certainly not gratify the desire of the flesh. For the flesh has desires against the Spirit, and the Spirit against the flesh; these are opposed to each other, so that you may not do what you want. But if you are guided by the Spirit, you are not under the law.

GOSPEL   *Luke 9:51 — 62*

When the days for Jesus' being taken up were fulfilled, he resolutely determined to journey to Jerusalem, and he sent messengers ahead of him. On the way they entered a Samaritan village to prepare for his reception there, but they would not welcome him because the destination of his journey was Jerusalem. When the disciples James and John saw this they asked, "Lord, do you want us to call down fire from heaven to consume them?" Jesus turned and rebuked them, and they journeyed to another village.

As they were proceeding on their journey someone said to him, "I will follow you wherever you go." Jesus answered him, "Foxes have dens and birds of the sky have nests, but the Son of Man has nowhere to rest his head."

And to another he said, "Follow me." But he replied, "Lord, let me go first and bury my father." But he answered him, "Let the dead bury their dead. But you, go and proclaim the kingdom of God." And another said, "I will follow you, Lord, but first let me say farewell to my family at home." To him Jesus said, "No one who sets a hand to the plow and looks to what was left behind is fit for the kingdom of God."

Practice of Prayer

Psalm 16:1—2, 5, 7—8, 9—10, 11 (11a)

R. Lord, you will show us the path of life.

Keep me, O God, for in you I take refuge;
    I say to the LORD, "My Lord are you."
O LORD, my allotted portion and my cup,
    you it is who hold fast my lot.   R.

I bless the LORD who counsels me;
    even in the night my heart exhorts me.
I set the LORD ever before me;
    with him at my right hand,
        I shall not be disturbed.   R.

Therefore my heart is glad and my soul rejoices;
    my body, too, abides in confidence,
because you will not abandon my soul to
        the netherworld,
    nor will you suffer your faithful one to
        undergo corruption.   R.

You will show me the path to life,
    abounding joy in your presence,
    the delights at your right hand forever.   R.

Practice of Charity

In this Sunday's readings we are reminded that freedom and service are linked. Saint Paul tells us that Christ set us free so that we might "serve one another through love." In doing so, the One who has nowhere to lay his head will find a home. Taking that to heart is West Suburban PADS (Public Action to Deliver Shelter) in Oak Park, Ill. This volunteer-driven organization offers services for the homeless and advocates on their behalf. The religious congregations that offer shelter on a rotating basis are vital to the agency. The group welcomes donations of money, goods, and services. For more information, call (708) 488-1745 or go to www. westsuburbs. As we mark our nation's independence, consider the ways that you can help someone who is seeking "life, liberty, and the pursuit of happiness."

Scripture Insights

"When the days for Jesus' being taken up were fulfilled, he resolutely determined to journey to Jerusalem . . . . " (Luke 9:51). At first glance, the opening line of today's Gospel seems but an introduction to two incidents about the reception of Jesus and the nature of discipleship. Indeed, the verse is an introduction to these incidents, and the rest of the Gospel. As a result, it deserves our attention.

This is a turning point in the Gospel. Prior to this, Jesus has been ministering in Galilee. Here, he begins his journey to Jerusalem, where he will suffer, die, and rise from the dead.

The Greek text reads literally, "he set his face to go to Jerusalem." While the English translation conveys the sense well, one is likely to miss the allusion to Isaiah 50:7, where the Suffering Servant of God "set his face like flint" in the face of the suffering and opposition he endured in fulfillment of his mission. Such was the way of Jesus, who proceeded on his way, knowing what awaited him.

Suffering and death would not be the end. Rather, his destiny was to be "taken up" to the Father. Significantly, the related verb *analambán* is used with reference to Jesus' ascension in Acts. It is also used in 2 Kings with reference to Elijah's translation into heaven via the fiery chariot. As with Elijah, Jesus' destiny is heaven. For Jesus, this was accomplished through his death, resurrection, and ascension. And so it will be for us. May we set out on his way with confidence, knowing that he shows the path to life.

♦ What characteristics of discipleship are set forth in today's readings?

♦ How can you be more aware that the Father is the ultimate goal of my life's journey?

♦ Have you thought of the waters of baptism as waters that free you?

READING I   Isaiah 66:10—14c

Thus says the LORD:
Rejoice with Jerusalem and be glad because
     of her,
   all you who love her;
exult, exult with her,
   all you who were mourning over her!
Oh, that you may suck fully
   of the milk of her comfort,
that you may nurse with delight
   at her abundant breasts!
   For thus says the LORD:
Lo, I will spread prosperity over Jerusalem
     like a river,
   and the wealth of the nations
     like an overflowing torrent.
As nurslings, you shall be carried in her arms,
   and fondled in her lap;
as a mother comforts her child,
   so will I comfort you;
   in Jerusalem you shall find your comfort.

When you see this, your heart shall rejoice
   and your bodies flourish like the grass;
the LORD's power shall be known to
   his servants.

READING II   Galatians 6:14—18

Brothers and sisters: May I never boast except in the cross of our Lord Jesus Christ, through which the world has been crucified to me, and I to the world. For neither does circumcision mean anything, nor does uncircumcision, but only a new creation. Peace and mercy be to all who follow this rule and to the Israel of God.

From now on, let no one make troubles for me; for I bear the marks of Jesus on my body.

The grace of our Lord Jesus Christ be with your spirit, brothers and sisters. Amen.

GOSPEL   Luke 10:1—12, 17—20

Shorter: Luke 10:1–9

At that time the Lord appointed seventy-two others whom he sent ahead of him in pairs to every town and place he intended to visit. He said to them, "The harvest is abundant but the laborers are few; so ask the master of the harvest to send out laborers for his harvest. Go on your way; behold, I am sending you like lambs among wolves. Carry no money bag, no sack, no sandals; and greet no one along the way. Into whatever house you enter, first say, 'Peace to this household.' If a peaceful person lives there, your peace will rest on him; but if not, it will return to you. Stay in the same house and eat and drink what is offered to you, for the laborer deserves his payment. Do not move about from one house to another. Whatever town you enter and they welcome you, eat what is set before you, cure the sick in it and say to them, 'The kingdom of God is at hand for you.' Whatever town you enter and they do not receive you, go out into the streets and say, 'The dust of your town that clings to our feet, even that we shake off against you.' Yet know this: the kingdom of God is at hand. I tell you, it will be more tolerable for Sodom on that day than for that town."

The seventy-two returned rejoicing, and said, "Lord, even the demons are subject to us because of your name." Jesus said, "I have observed Satan fall like lightning from the sky. Behold, I have given you the power to 'tread upon serpents' and scorpions and upon the full force of the enemy and nothing will harm you. Nevertheless, do not rejoice because the spirits are subject to you, but rejoice because your names are written in heaven."

Practice of Prayer

Psalm 66:1—3, 4—5, 6—7, 16, 20 (1)

R. Let all the earth cry out to God with joy, alleluia.

Shout joyfully to God, all the earth;
   sing praise to the glory of his name;
   proclaim his glorious praise.
Say to God, "How tremendous are
      your deeds!" R.

"Let all on earth worship and sing praise to you,
      sing praise to your name!"
Come and see the works of God,
   his tremendous deeds among the children
      of Adam. R.

He changed the sea into dry land;
   through the river they passed on foot;
   therefore let us rejoice in him.
He rules by his might forever. R.

Hear now, all you who fear God,
   while I declare what he has been done for me.
Blessed be God, who refused me not
   my prayer or his kindness! R.

Practice of Faith

One of the ways that doctors heal is by touch. A gentle hand can determine the source of what ails us, but it can also reassure us when we're frightened or in pain. This was brought home powerfully when we celebrated the Rite of Acceptance with a young doctor preparing to come into the Catholic Church at Easter. As his sponsor traced the Sign of the Cross on his hands, we were awestruck as we realized all the good these hands had done and would continue to do as they touched others in love. And there was no telling how much more he would be able to offer the suffering Body of Christ through the marks of Christ he now bore on his body. We are called to do the same. Through the cross we are all called to reach out as Christ to touch Christ in one another.

Scripture Insights

"May I never boast except in the cross of our Lord Jesus Christ . . . ." The cross: a barbaric instrument of pain and humiliation that the Romans would not inflict on their citizens. Saint Paul, in effect, says, "May I never boast or take pride in anything but the unjust, unwarranted, humiliating death of our Lord . . . ." Saint Paul believed that the power and wisdom of God was revealed in the crucified Christ. In the cross, utter powerlessness is manifest. In the cross, the power of God broke through humiliation and helplessness into glorious new life. No wonder Saint Paul takes pride in the cross.

It was Saint Paul's conviction, that through baptism, believers receive a share in this new life. As Saint Paul taught elsewhere, through baptism, believers are "crucified together with Christ" and "buried together with Christ" that "we too might live in newness of life."

In today's reading, Saint Paul even speaks of "bearing the marks of Jesus on his body," a reference, perhaps, to the scars Saint Paul received in carrying out his apostolic ministry. Saint Paul may also be speaking in a figurative sense to express his conviction that by virtue of his baptism, he bears the marks, the sign, of the Crucified One in his very body.

In antiquity, the bodies of slaves were branded with "marks," signifying their owners. For the Jews, circumcision was the "mark" of belonging to God. Saint Paul disagrees. The cross is the Christian mark.

Saint Paul's words call us to reflect on the mark of the cross with which we are signed and to recognize to whom we belong. In his cross, is our life.

• What themes of "new life/creation" are found in today's Scriptures?

• What is the significance of making the Sign of the Cross?

• Do you consider the Sign of the Cross a prayer?

READING I *Deuteronomy 30:10—14*

Moses said to the people: "If only you would heed the voice of the LORD, your God, and keep his commandments and statutes that are written in this book of the law, when you return to the LORD, your God, with all your heart and all your soul.

"For this command that I enjoin on you today is not too mysterious and remote for you. It is not up in the sky, that you should say, 'Who will go up in the sky to get it for us and tell us of it, that we may carry it out?' Nor is it across the sea, that you should say, 'Who will cross the sea to get it for us and tell us of it, that we may carry it out?' No, it is something very near to you, already in your mouths and in your hearts; you have only to carry it out."

READING II *Colossians 1:15—20*

Christ Jesus is the image of the invisible God,
> the firstborn of all creation.
For in him were created all things
>> in heaven and on earth,
> the visible and the invisible,
> whether thrones or dominions or
>> principalities or powers;
> all things were created through him and
>> for him.
He is before all things,
> and in him all things hold together.
He is the head of the body, the church.
He is the beginning, the firstborn from
>> the dead,
> that in all things he himself might
>> be preeminent.
For in him all the fullness was pleased
>> to dwell,
> and through him to reconcile
>> all things for him,
> making peace by the blood of his cross
> through him, whether those on earth or
>> those in heaven.

GOSPEL *Luke 10:25—37*

There was a scholar of the law who stood up to test him and said, "Teacher, what must I do to inherit eternal life?" Jesus said to him, "What is written in the law? How do you read it?" He said in reply,
> *"You shall love the Lord, your God,*
> *with all your heart,*
> *with all your being,*
> *with all your strength,*
> *and with all your mind,*
> *and your neighbor as yourself."*
He replied to him, "You have answered correctly; do this and you will live."

But because he wished to justify himself, he said to Jesus, "And who is my neighbor?" Jesus replied, "A man fell victim to robbers as he went down from Jerusalem to Jericho. They stripped and beat him and went off leaving him half-dead. A priest happened to be going down that road, but when he saw him, he passed by on the opposite side. Likewise a Levite came to the place, and when he saw him, he passed by on the opposite side. But a Samaritan traveler who came upon him was moved with compassion at the sight. He approached the victim, poured oil and wine over his wounds and bandaged them. Then he lifted him up on his own animal, took him to an inn, and cared for him. The next day he took out two silver coins and gave them to the innkeeper with the instruction, 'Take care of him. If you spend more than what I have given you, I shall repay you on my way back.' Which of these three, in your opinion, was neighbor to the robbers' victim?" He answered, "The one who treated him with mercy." Jesus said to him, "Go and do likewise."

Practice of Prayer

Psalm 69:14, 17, 30–31, 33–34, 36, 37 (see 33) or Psalm 19:8, 9, 10, 11 (9a)

R. Turn to the Lord in your need, and you
 will live.

I pray to you, O LORD,
 for the time of your favor, O God!
In your great kindness answer me
 with your constant help.
Answer me, O LORD, for bounteous is
 your kindness;
 in your great mercy turn toward me. R.

I am afflicted and in pain;
 let your saving help, O God, protect me.
I will praise the name of God in song,
 and I will glorify him with thanksgiving. R.

"See, you lowly ones, and be glad;
 you who seek God, may your hearts revive!
For the LORD hears the poor,
 and his own who are in bonds
 he spurns not." R.

For God will save Zion
 and rebuild the cities of Judah.
The descendants of his servants shall inherit it,
 and those who love his name shall inhabit it.

Practice of Faith

While today's Gospel tells of extraordinary acts of mercy offered to someone who had been robbed and brutally beaten, even the simplest actions can have a great impact. The Peoria (Illinois) Journal-Star demonstrates that each day in a series detailing "random acts of kindness." One mother told of the stranger who fixed a flat tire when she had a carload of kids. She thanked her Good Samaritan for giving her family back precious time. Another person told of how her lunch tab had been paid by someone who noticed the despair on her face after she received bad news. These simple stories remind us that hope comes in all shapes and sizes. You don't have to have superhuman strength to change the world. You just have to have the willingness to love with all the strength you have.

Scripture Insights

"And who is my neighbor?" There's a poignancy to the question posed by the "scholar of the Law" in today's Gospel. Who does not resonate with his desire to know *exactly* what must be done to fulfill the Law in order to obtain the hoped for reward? For the Jews, observing the law of God was the way to life. Jesus' questioner was a professional in the law, and as Luke demonstrates by having him answer his own questions, the commandments of the Lord were very near to him, already in his mouth and in his heart. The story of the Good Samaritan is well-known and much loved. As shocking as the actions of the priest and Levite *seem* to be, they *were* members of the temple staff and contact with what was presumably a corpse would have rendered them ritually unclean, unfit for their respective services. In effect, they were keeping the law by moving on. The Samaritan, a member of a group despised by the Jerusalem Jews, turned out to be the one most faithful to it in Jesus' eyes. He is the one who *was* neighbor. Although Luke's text focuses on the word "neighbor," because this is the issue for the scholar, his response to Jesus echoes other biblical texts that were likewise in his heart: "It is mercy I desire, and not sacrifice" (Hosea 6:6; see also Micah 6:8). The scholar of the Law recognized this mercy in action. What remained for him to fulfill was Jesus' command: "go and do likewise."

♦ Name the actions of the Samaritan that demonstrate his "neighborliness" or mercy.

♦ Identify one situation in which you could be "neighbor" (show mercy) for another.

♦ Have you ever judged someone for not acting on behalf of another?

READING I *Genesis 18:1—10a*

The LORD appeared to Abraham by the terebinth of Mamre, as he sat in the entrance of his tent, while the day was growing hot. Looking up, Abraham saw three men standing nearby. When he saw them, he ran from the entrance of the tent to greet them; and bowing to the ground, he said: "Sir, if I may ask you this favor, please do not go on past your servant. Let some water be brought, that you may bathe your feet, and then rest yourselves under the tree. Now that you have come this close to your servant, let me bring you a little food, that you may refresh yourselves; and afterward you may go on your way." The men replied, "Very well, do as you have said."

Abraham hastened into the tent and told Sarah, "Quick, three measures of fine flour! Knead it and make rolls." He ran to the herd, picked out a tender, choice steer, and gave it to a servant, who quickly prepared it. Then Abraham got some curds and milk, as well as the steer that had been prepared, and set these before the three men; and he waited on them under the tree while they ate.

They asked Abraham, "Where is your wife Sarah?" He replied, "There in the tent." One of them said, "I will surely return to you about this time next year, and Sarah will then have a son."

READING II *Colossians 1:24—28*

Brothers and sisters: Now I rejoice in my sufferings for your sake, and in my flesh I am filling up what is lacking in the afflictions of Christ on behalf of his body, which is the church, of which I am a minister in accordance with God's stewardship given to me to bring to completion for you the word of God, the mystery hidden from ages and from generations past. But now it has been manifested to his holy ones, to whom God chose to make known the riches of the glory of this mystery among the Gentiles; it is Christ in you, the hope for glory. It is he whom we proclaim, admonishing everyone and teaching everyone with all wisdom, that we may present everyone perfect in Christ.

GOSPEL *Luke 10:38—42*

Jesus entered a village where a woman whose name was Martha welcomed him. She had a sister named Mary who sat beside the Lord at his feet listening to him speak. Martha, burdened with much serving, came to him and said, "Lord, do you not care that my sister has left me by myself to do the serving? Tell her to help me." The Lord said to her in reply, "Martha, Martha, you are anxious and worried about many things. There is need of only one thing. Mary has chosen the better part and it will not be taken from her."

Practice of Prayer

Psalm 15:2 — 3, 3 — 4, 5 (1a)

R. He who does justice will live in the presence of
the Lord.

One who walks blamelessly and does justice;
   who thinks the truth in his heart
   and slanders not with his tongue. R.

Who harms not his fellow man,
   nor takes up a reproach against his neighbor;
by whom the reprobate is despised,
   while he honors those who fear the LORD. R.

Who lends not his money at usury
   and accepts no bribe against the innocent.
One who does these things
   shall never be disturbed. R.

Practice of Faith

We Americans tend to compartmentalize everything. But life and faith defy that kind of definition. Despite our tendency to think of ourselves as
either Martha or Mary, we need to be both whole
and holy disciples. We must welcome Christ into
our lives as Martha did, but we can't be so busy
that we fail to listen to what our soul's most welcome guest is saying. Doing that is what com-
pelled Susan, a recent graduate of Franciscan
University of Steubenville (Ohio), to walk 3,200
miles with the organization Crossroads. She
decided to undertake this walking witness on
behalf of life after much prayer and reflection. "It's
not what you do, but what God asks you to do,"
Susan said. In the end, the walk became her prayer.
In what ways are you being called to pray and
act today?

Scripture Insights

Hospitality: the Middle Eastern virtue, par excel-
lence, as anyone who has traveled there knows!
Literally, the Greek word *philoxenía* means "love of
the stranger"—an alien concept in western culture
today where "fear of the stranger" predominates.

   "Do not neglect hospitality," writes the author
of the letter to the Hebrews, "for through it some
have unknowingly entertained angels," a clear
allusion in today's first reading. Little did Abraham
know that the three men whom he saw from the
entrance to this tent were the Lord and two of his
angels. (In the Old Testament, God and his heavenly messengers are frequently manifested under
the guise of a human being.) In receiving Jesus
into her home, Martha welcomed the very Son of
the Most High. Was Jesus a stranger to her at this
point? Possibly. This is the first mention of Martha
and her sister, Mary, in Luke's Gospel. Their meeting takes place as Jesus "continues his journey"
to Jerusalem. Here, as in John's story of the
Samaritan woman, Jesus' hosts, like Abraham and
Sarah, are always recipients of what God has to
give. Luke's Jesus warns against the preoccupations
and distractions that can impede reception of
these gifts. "Martha, Martha, you are anxious and
worried about many things. There is need of only
one thing." Mary, portrayed as a disciple sitting at
the feet of the Master, listening to his every word,
"has chosen the better part." Throughout his
Gospel, Luke highlights the themes of listening to
the Word and acting on the word. Those who do
so have chosen the better part. They are blessed.

◆ What is the "word" Paul speaks of in today's second reading?

◆ What distractions or anxieties impede my
discipleship?

◆ Do you find it hard to make prayer a priority
when you have a lot of work to do?

July 29, 2007

READING I   *Genesis 18:20—32*

In those days, the LORD said: "The outcry against Sodom and Gomorrah is so great, and their sin so grave, that I must go down and see whether or not their actions fully correspond to the cry against them that comes to me. I mean to find out."

While Abraham's visitors walked on farther toward Sodom, the LORD remained standing before Abraham. Then Abraham drew nearer and said: "Will you sweep away the innocent with the guilty? Suppose there were fifty innocent people in the city; would you wipe out the place, rather than spare it for the sake of the fifty innocent people within it? Far be it from you to do such a thing, to make the innocent die with the guilty so that the innocent and the guilty would be treated alike! Should not the judge of all the world act with justice?" The LORD replied, "If I find fifty innocent people in the city of Sodom, I will spare the whole place for their sake." Abraham spoke up again: "See how I am presuming to speak to my Lord, though I am but dust and ashes! What if there are five less than fifty innocent people? Will you destroy the whole city because of those five?" He answered, "I will not destroy it, if I find forty-five there." But Abraham persisted, saying "What if only forty are found there?" He replied, "I will forbear doing it for the sake of the forty." Then Abraham said, "Let not my Lord grow impatient if I go on. What if only thirty are found there?" He replied, "I will forbear doing it if I can find but thirty there." Still Abraham went on, "Since I have thus dared to speak to my Lord, what if there are no more than twenty?" The LORD answered, "I will not destroy it, for the sake of the twenty." But he still persisted: "Please, let not my Lord grow angry if I speak up this last time. What if there are at least ten there?" He replied, "For the sake of those ten, I will not destroy it."

READING II   *Colossians 2:12—14*

Brothers and sisters: You were buried with him in baptism, in which you were also raised with him through faith in the power of God, who raised him from the dead. And even when you were dead in transgressions and the uncircumcision of your flesh, he brought you to life along with him, having forgiven us all our transgressions; obliterating the bond against us, with its legal claims, which was opposed to us, he also removed it from our midst, nailing it to the cross.

GOSPEL   *Luke 11:1—13*

Jesus was praying in a certain place, and when he had finished, one of his disciples said to him, "Lord, teach us to pray just as John taught his disciples." He said to them, "When you pray, say:
Father, hallowed be your name,
    your kingdom come.
    Give us each day our daily bread
    and forgive us our sins
    for we ourselves forgive
        everyone in debt to us,
    and do not subject us to the final test."

And he said to them, "Suppose one of you has a friend to whom he goes at midnight and says, 'Friend, lend me three loaves of bread, for a friend of mine has arrived at my house from a journey and I have nothing to offer him,' and he says in reply from within, 'Do not bother me; the door has already been locked and my children and I are already in bed. I cannot get up to give you anything.' I tell you, if he does not get up to give the visitor the loaves because of their friendship, he will get up to give him whatever he needs because of his persistence.

"And I tell you, ask and you will receive; seek and you will find; knock and the door will be opened to you. For everyone who asks, receives; and the one who seeks, finds; and to the one who knocks, the door will be opened. What father among you would hand his son a snake when he asks for a fish? Or hand him a scorpion when he asks for an egg? If you then, who are wicked, know how to give good gifts to your children, how much more will the Father in heaven give the Holy Spirit to those who ask him?"

Practice of Prayer

Psalm 138:1—2, 2—3, 6—7, 7—8 (3a)

R. Lord, on the day I called for help, you
    answered me.

I will give thanks to you, O LORD, with all my heart,
    for you have heard the words of my mouth;
    in the presence of the angels
        I will sing your praise;
I will worship at your holy temple
    and give thanks to your name. R.

Because of your kindness and your truth;
    for you have made great above all things
    your name and your promise.
When I called you answered me;
    you built up strength within me. R.

The LORD is exalted, yet the lowly he sees,
    and the proud he knows from afar.
Though I walk amid distress, you preserve me;
    against the anger of my enemies you raise
        your hand. R.

Your right hand saves me.
    The LORD will complete
        what he has done for me;
your kindness, O LORD, endures forever;
    forsake not the work of your hands. R.

Practice of Faith

If you look at your parish calendar, night after night is likely to be devoted to classes, social activities, and outreach to various people in need. Putting faith into action is a good thing. It shows that we take discipleship seriously. A popular columnist in the Catholic press recently pondered what would happen if all parish activities were suspended for a year so that people could learn how to pray—really pray. In doing so, he said, "I have to believe that all the other ways a parish serves its people not only would fall into place, but would become driven by a fresh and awesome spirit." As impractical as that might sound on first hearing, Jesus shows us again and again that prayer isn't a last resort. For him, it was the beginning of everything. Do we trust enough to persist? If we seek, what will we find?

Scripture Insights

"Persistence pays." Today's readings afford apt illustration of this proverbial truth: Abraham bartering with God in typical Middle Eastern fashion; a man begging from his friend at an unseemly hour. Persistence pays. So Jesus would have us persist in prayer.

Not only do today's readings tell us how to pray, but they speak volumes about God. Abraham recognized the Lord as the judge of all the world—a judge who will show justice toward the innocent who are undeserving of punishment as well as to the wicked.

But God is much more than judge, today's Scriptures tell us, much more than "friend." God is *Father,* one who brings us into life from the realm of the death wrought by our transgressions. "Father" is the relationship we are not only taught" by Jesus, but the reality in which we are established through baptism.

The relationship between parent and child at the human level pales in comparison with that of the heavenly Father and his children. "If you, who are wicked, know how to give good gifts to your children, how much more will the Father in heaven give the Holy Spirit to those who ask him."

Note that this saying comes at the end of Jesus' teaching on persistence. "Be persistent," Jesus tells us, in beseeching your heavenly Father for the gift of the Holy Spirit, that principle of life, that power from on high that enables us to do far more than we can ask or imagine. So may we be in asking for this gift and may we not neglect what we are given.

• How are themes of God's fatherhood evident in today's second reading?

• Do you pray for the gift of the Spirit? Why or why not?

• Do you forgive as you would like the Father to forgive?

August 5, 2007

READING I   *Ecclesiastes 1:2, 2:21 — 23*

Vanity of vanities, says Qoheleth, vanity of vanities! All things are vanity!

Here is one who has labored with wisdom and knowledge and skill, and yet to another who has not labored over it, he must leave property. This also is vanity and a great misfortune. For what profit comes to man from all the toil and anxiety of heart with which he has labored under the sun? All his days sorrow and grief are their occupation; even at night his mind is not at rest. This also is vanity.

READING II   *Colossians 3:1 — 5, 9 — 11*

Brothers and sisters: If you were raised with Christ, seek what is above, where Christ is seated at the right hand of God. Think of what is above, not of what is on earth. For you have died, and your life is hidden with Christ in God. When Christ your life appears, then you too will appear with him in glory.

Put to death, then, the parts of you that are earthly: immorality, impurity, passion, evil desire, and the greed that is idolatry. Stop lying to one another, since you have taken off the old self with its practices and have put on the new self, which is being renewed, for knowledge, in the image of its creator. Here there is not Greek and Jew, circumcision and uncircumcision, barbarian, Scythian, slave, free; but Christ is all and in all.

GOSPEL   *Luke 12:13 — 21*

Someone in the crowd said to Jesus, "Teacher, tell my brother to share the inheritance with me." He replied to him, "Friend, who appointed me as your judge and arbitrator?" Then he said to the crowd, "Take care to guard against all greed, for though one may be rich, one's life does not consist of possessions."

Then he told them a parable. "There was a rich man whose land produced a bountiful harvest. He asked himself, 'What shall I do, for I do not have space to store my harvest?' And he said, 'This is what I shall do: I shall tear down my barns and build larger ones. There I shall store all my grain and other goods and I shall say to myself, "Now as for you, you have so many good things stored up for many years, rest, eat, drink, be merry!"' But God said to him, 'You fool, this night your life will be demanded of you; and the things you have prepared, to whom will they belong?' Thus will it be for all who store up treasure for themselves but are not rich in what matters to God."

Practice of Prayer

Psalm 90:3—4, 5—6, 12—13, 14, 17 (1)

R. If today you hear his voice, harden not
    your hearts.

You turn man back to dust,
    saying, "Return, O children of men."
For a thousand years in your sight
    are as yesterday, now that it is past,
    or as a watch of the night. R.

You make an end of them in their sleep;
    the next morning they are like
      the changing grass,
which at dawn springs up anew,
    but by evening wilts and fades. R.

Teach us to number our days aright,
    that we may gain wisdom of heart.
Return, O LORD! How long?
    Have pity on your servants! R.

Fill us at daybreak with your kindness,
    that we may shout for joy
      and gladness all our days.
And may the gracious care of the LORD our God
    be ours;
    prosper the work of our hands for us!
    Prosper the work of our hands! R.

Practice of Charity

If you listen carefully, you might hear the sounds of hammers and power saws in communities across the United States this weekend. That's the sound of Habitat for Humanity providing affordable housing for people who wouldn't have it otherwise. Making this possible are volunteers, many of whom have no previous construction experience, working under the supervision of skilled managers. Homes are generally built by coalitions of businesses or churches. At a Midwest parish, members constructed a home for Habitat at the same time they were building their new church. For them, the foundation for their new spiritual home had to be their love for Christ and their willingness to make him present to others. Habitat for Humanity can use whatever "treasure" you have to share. Don't store it up. Go to www.habitat.org to see how you can help.

Scripture Insights

"If you were raised with Christ . . . ." (Colossians 3:1)—not *when* you *are* raised—but *since* you *have been* raised." An accomplished fact. Unfortunately, the Greek particle *oûn* (then) is not translated in the Lectionary text, for it clearly indicates that the teaching given here is the logical consequence of all that Saint Paul has written so far. A prayerful reading of the first two chapters of Colossians will be most helpful in understanding the richness of Saint Paul's teaching, or rather, the richness of the reality that is ours through baptism into Christ.

For Saint Paul, Baptism initiates us into the very life of Christ. Baptism brings us to life with Christ, the same resurrected life that the risen Christ lives. Saint Paul truly believes that through baptism he has died *with* Christ and been raised *with* Christ in newness of life.

There is, to be sure, a "hidden" dimension of this reality, as it is not yet fully realized and won't be until that end-time day when Christ is fully revealed in glory. On that day, Christ's life in us will be fully realized as we are revealed in glory *with* him. In the meantime, seeking the things that are above, believers are being transformed into Christ's very image by his Spirit.

Saint Paul's words in today's second reading call believers to live out this reality faithfully. Our post-baptismal identity is a markedly different reality from our pre-baptismal one. Our behavior, then, should reflect our calling to act as Christ in the world.

◆ What behaviors and attitudes are called forth in today's Scriptures?

◆ Have you regretted some of the time you have worked hard to make your future secure? Could there have been another way?

◆ Do I know and celebrate the date of my Baptism?

READING I   *Wisdom 18:6—9*

The night of the passover was known beforehand
        to our fathers,
    that, with sure knowledge of the oaths
        in which they put their faith,
    they might have courage.
Your people awaited the salvation of the just
    and the destruction of their foes.
For when you punished our adversaries,
    in this you glorified us whom you
        had summoned.
For in secret the holy children of the good were
        offering sacrifice
    and putting into effect with one accord the
        divine institution.

READING II   *Hebrews 11:1—2, 8—12*

Longer: Hebrews 11:1–2, 8–19

Brothers and sisters: Faith is the realization of what is hoped for and evidence of things not seen. Because of it the ancients were well attested.

   By faith Abraham obeyed when he was called to go out to a place that he was to receive as an inheritance; he went out, not knowing where he was to go. By faith he sojourned in the promised land as in a foreign country, dwelling in tents with Isaac and Jacob, heirs of the same promise; for he was looking forward to the city with foundations, whose architect and maker is God. By faith he received power to generate, even though he was past the normal age—and Sarah herself was sterile—for he thought that the one who had made the promise was trustworthy. So it was that there came forth from one man, himself as good as dead, descendants as numerous as the stars in the sky and as countless as the sands on the seashore.

GOSPEL   *Luke 12:32—48*

Shorter: Luke 12:35–40

Jesus said to his disciples: "Do not be afraid any longer, little flock, for your Father is pleased to give you the kingdom. Sell your belongings and give alms. Provide money bags for yourselves that do not wear out, an inexhaustible treasure in heaven that no thief can reach nor moth destroy. For where your treasure is, there also will your heart be.

   "Gird your loins and light your lamps and be like servants who await their master's return from a wedding, ready to open immediately when he comes and knocks. Blessed are those servants whom the master finds vigilant on his arrival. Amen, I say to you, he will gird himself, have them recline at table, and proceed to wait on them. And should he come in the second or third watch and find them prepared in this way, blessed are those servants. Be sure of this: if the master of the house had known the hour when the thief was coming, he would not have let his house be broken into. You also must be prepared, for at an hour you do not expect, the Son of Man will come."

   Then Peter said, "Lord, is this parable meant for us or for everyone?" And the Lord replied, "Who, then, is the faithful and prudent steward whom the master will put in charge of his servants to distribute the food allowance at the proper time? Blessed is that servant whom his master on arrival finds doing so. Truly, I say to you, the master will put the servant in charge of all his property. But if that servant says to himself, 'My master is delayed in coming,' and begins to beat the menservants and the maidservants, to eat and drink and get drunk, then that servant's master will come on an unexpected day and at an unknown hour and will punish the servant severely and assign him a place with the unfaithful. That servant who knew his master's will but did not make preparations nor act in accord with his will shall be beaten severely; and the servant who was ignorant of his master's will but acted in a way deserving of a severe beating shall be beaten only lightly. Much will be required of the person entrusted with much, and still more will be demanded of the person entrusted with more."

Practice of Prayer

Psalm 33:1, 12, 18—19, 20—22 (12b)

R. Blessed the people the Lord has chosen to be
   his own.

Exult, you just, in the LORD;
   praise from the upright is fitting.
Blessed the nation whose God is the LORD,
   the people he has chosen for his own
      inheritance. R.

See, the eyes of the LORD are upon those who
   fear him,
   upon those who hope for his kindness,
to deliver them from death
   and preserve them in spite of famine. R.

Our soul waits for the LORD,
   who is our help and our shield.
May your kindness, O LORD, be upon us
   who have put our hope in you. R.

Practice of Faith

For a second week, we are invited to consider the "treasure" in our lives. If we were left in any doubt of what that might be last week, we are given a hint today: "Where your treasure is, there also will your heart be. I heard the story of a man who awoke one Saturday to realize he had fewer Saturdays ahead of him than behind him. It made him take a long, hard look at how he spent his time and with whom. He plotted out how many Saturdays he probably had left and bought that number of marbles, which he put in a jar. It was a visible reminder of how precious time is and each time he removed a marble from the jar, he made a conscious effort to spend that "treasure" with his family and friends. How are you choosing to spend your "marbles"?

Scripture Insights

With faith in God's promises, "they acknowledged themselves to be strangers and aliens on earth . . . ." Today's Scriptures set before us our ancestors in faith. They were a people who moved and acted on the basis of God's promise.

Chapter 11 of Hebrews is a veritable "who's who" among God's faithful people of old. These were people who traveled in obedience to new directives from their God, making their way to the place that God had promised.

Today's reading focuses on Abraham, our father in faith. Especially emphasized is his initial response to God's call to leave his homeland for a new, promised land. Both Lectionary options include a "spiritualized" interpretation of this "land," with reference to the heavenly homeland.

In a related vein, our reading from Wisdom emphasizes the faith of the Israelites at the time of the Exodus. The history of God's people is the story of faith called forth. It is a dynamic, living faith that empowers people to act on God's word.

In today's Gospel, Jesus calls his disciples to consciously and deliberately make their way to the kingdom. The command to "gird your loins" echoes that of Exodus 12:11. Then, the Hebrews were to be ready to flee from the land of Egypt to the land that God had promised. God's people must be alert, "prepared" to "pass over" into the kingdom of the Father at the coming of the Son of Man.

May we, too, acknowledge ourselves "to be strangers and aliens on earth," called to the same faith, the same courageous "moving on," constantly looking forward to our heavenly homeland.

◆ How do our "ancestors" in Hebrews 11 exemplify lives of faith?

◆ Who among your personal "ancestors" exemplifies a "living faith"? Why?

◆ When have you been tempted to delay working on your spiritual life until later?

READING I   *Jeremiah 38:4 — 6, 8 — 10*

In those days, the princes said to the king: "Jeremiah ought to be put to death; he is demoralizing the soldiers who are left in this city, and all the people, by speaking such things to them; he is not interested in the welfare of our people, but in their ruin." King Zedekiah answered: "He is in your power"; for the king could do nothing with them. And so they took Jeremiah and threw him into the cistern of Prince Malchiah, which was in the quarters of the guard, letting him down with ropes. There was no water in the cistern, only mud, and Jeremiah sank into the mud.

Ebed-melech, a court official, went there from the palace and said to him: "My lord king, these men have been at fault in all they have done to the prophet Jeremiah, casting him into the cistern. He will die of famine on the spot, for there is no more food in the city." Then the king ordered Ebed-melech the Cushite to take three men along with him, and draw the prophet Jeremiah out of the cistern before he should die.

READING II   *Hebrews 12: 1 — 4*

Brothers and sisters: Since we are surrounded by so great a cloud of witnesses, let us rid ourselves of every burden and sin that clings to us and persevere in running the race that lies before us while keeping our eyes fixed on Jesus, the leader and perfecter of faith. For the sake of the joy that lay before him he endured the cross, despising its shame, and has taken his seat at the right of the throne of God. Consider how he endured such opposition from sinners, in order that you may not grow weary and lose heart. In your struggle against sin you have not yet resisted to the point of shedding blood.

GOSPEL   *Luke 12: 49 — 53*

Jesus said to his disciples: "I have come to set the earth on fire, and how I wish it were already blazing! There is a baptism with which I must be baptized, and how great is my anguish until it is accomplished! "Do you think that I have come to establish peace on the earth? No, I tell you, but rather division. From now on a household of five will be divided, three against two and two against three; a father will be divided against his son and a son against his father, a mother against her daughter and a daughter against her mother, a mother-in-law against her daughter-in-law and a daughter-in-law against her mother-in-law."

Practice of Prayer

Psalm 40:2, 3, 4, 18 (14b)

R. Lord, come to my aid!

I have waited, waited for the Lord,
  and he stooped toward me. R.

The LORD heard my cry.
He drew me out of the pit of destruction,
  out of the mud of the swamp;
he set my feet upon a crag;
  he made firm my steps. R.

And he put a new song into my mouth,
  a hymn to our God.
Many shall look on in awe
  and trust in the LORD. R.

Though I am afflicted and poor,
  yet the LORD thinks of me.
You are my help and my deliverer;
  O my God, hold not back! R.

Practice of Hope

In 2005, the Midwest suffered a drought so severe that the governor of Illinois declared all 102 counties a disaster. While some may have thought the situation to be without hope, those who worked the land continued to keep their eyes fixed on the sky—and on Jesus. They acknowledged their dependence on God, saying it was this trust in divine providence that gave them peace in such times. They proved that hope is contagious as our hearts leapt with joy each time we heard the sound of approaching thunder. The next time you pick up an ear of corn, or eat or drink something made from soy beans, stop to think about what makes it possible for you to enjoy these things. Then thank God for the people whose hope, prayer, and hard work are resting in your hands.

Scripture Insights

". . . in order that you may not grow weary and lose heart. . ." (Hebrews 12:3). Isn't it comforting to know that the Scriptures understand that from time to time, we all get tired? Sometimes the struggles can be overwhelming.

No one knew this better than the prophet Jeremiah. Today's first reading records one such episode from his life. Even more revealing of the inner conflicts he experienced are his so-called "Confessions," prayers scattered throughout the book. Even these, however, reveal the deep-seated conviction that God will deliver him. *This* is the faith that enables one to persevere. And that's exactly what today's second reading, a continuation from last Sunday, would have us do. Hebrews 11 recounts the "great cloud of (faithful) witnesses" that surround us. As great as these were, Hebrews would have us look not so much at them, but at Jesus, *fixing our eyes* on him.

Earlier in the letter, the author tells of the struggle Jesus went through in embracing what lay before him. In lived fidelity in the midst of struggle and suffering, he was "perfected," matured, and accomplished his work. Hebrews 12:2 calls Jesus both *Leader* and *perfecter* of faith. Jesus believed in the promised joy that lay before him in the glory of the Father and acted accordingly. Unlike our ancestors in faith, he *did* receive what was promised in all its fullness. So too will we, if we are faithful.

• How does today's responsorial Psalm 40 relate to each of the other readings?

• How can reflection on Jesus' struggles and sufferings help us in dealing with our own? Apply that wisdom to something in your life now.

• Was there a time when you no longer wanted to "persevere in running the race"? What made you decide to continue with your faith?

READING I   *Isaiah 66:18 — 21*

Thus says the LORD: I know their works and their thoughts, and I come to gather nations of every language; they shall come and see my glory. I will set a sign among them; from them I will send fugitives to the nations: to Tarshish, Put and Lud, Mosoch, Tubal and Javan, to the distant coastlands that have never heard of my fame, or seen my glory; and they shall proclaim my glory among the nations. They shall bring all your brothers and sisters from all the nations as an offering to the Lord, on horses and in chariots, in carts, upon mules and dromedaries, to Jerusalem, my holy mountain, says the LORD, just as the Israelites bring their offering to the house of the LORD in clean vessels. Some of these I will take as priests and Levites, says the LORD.

READING II   *Hebrews 12:5 — 7, 11 — 13*

Brothers and sisters, You have forgotten the exhortation addressed to you as children: "My son, do not disdain the discipline of the Lord or lose heart when reproved by him; for whom the Lord loves, he disciplines; he scourges every son he acknowledges." Endure your trials as "discipline"; God treats you as sons. For what "son" is there whom his father does not discipline? At the time, all discipline seems a cause not for joy but for pain, yet later it brings the peaceful fruit of righteousness to those who are trained by it.

So strengthen your drooping hands and your weak knees. Make straight paths for your feet, that what is lame may not be disjointed but healed.

GOSPEL   *Luke 13:22 — 30*

Jesus passed through towns and villages, teaching as he went and making his way to Jerusalem. Someone asked him, "Lord, will only a few people be saved?" He answered them, "Strive to enter through the narrow gate, for many, I tell you, will attempt to enter but will not be strong enough. After the master of the house has arisen and locked the door, then will you stand outside knocking and saying, 'Lord, open the door for us.' He will say to you in reply, 'I do not know where you are from.' And you will say, 'We ate and drank in your company and you taught in our streets.' Then he will say to you, 'I do not know where you are from. Depart from me, all you evildoers!' And there will be wailing and grinding of teeth when you see Abraham, Isaac and Jacob and all the prophets in the kingdom of God and you yourselves cast out. And people will come from the east and the west and from the north and the south and will recline at table in the kingdom of God. For behold, some are last who will be first, and some are first who will be last."

Practice of Prayer

Psalm 117:1, 2 (Mark 16:15)

R. Go out to all the world and tell the good news. or: Alleluia.

Praise the Lord, all you nations;
  glorify him, all you peoples!   R.

For steadfast is his kindness toward us,
  and the fidelity of the Lord endures
    forever.   R.

Practice of Faith

When the prophet Isaiah wrote about setting a sign among the people so they would know and proclaim God's glory, I doubt he was referring to watermelon. Then again, he didn't know Arvilla. The pastoral administrator of a small Catholic parish in northwest Kansas, Arvilla knew that Baptist missionaries were canvassing the area as they built their church. One hot summer day, she called on her new neighbors, but she didn't take a business card or a Bible. She took cold slices of fresh watermelon and a smile. In that moment, she became a sign of the One who makes straight our paths, the One who is "the way, the truth, and the life." She opened the door to dialogue and Good News. This week—this day—someone around you needs a sign of God's love and joy. Don't be afraid to reach out and help them find it.

Scripture Insights

"Depart from me . . . ." What jarring words on a Sunday that celebrates the coming of the patriarchs, prophets, and people from all nations to the table of God's kingdom. Even more unsettling is the fact that these words are spoken to the very people who protest: "We ate and drank in your company." How is it that some who listened to Jesus' teaching in their streets, who ate and drank with him in table fellowship, will be denied entrance to the heavenly banquet in the kingdom of God?

Jesus' answer is simple: "I do not know where you are from." The seriousness of his response is emphasized by the fact that it is repeated. Those sent away from the Lord's presence have quite obviously not come from the way through the narrow gate.

Note that Jesus' questioner is identified only as "someone," not specified, not categorized as disciple or hypocrite, simply someone from the crowd who hasn't yet made a commitment. Jesus' words would invite precisely this response.

Jesus commands his hearers to "strive to enter through the narrow gate." The "narrow gate" is said to be wrought with difficulties ("constricted" in the New American Bible). Paradoxically, it is the only way that leads to life.

Strength is needed if one is to enter the narrow gate. Jesus encourages his listeners to "strive" to enter it. The Greek verb is *agōnízomai*—agonize, struggle. It takes discipline and work.

Blessed will be those who build up their strength so as to be able to come through the narrow gate. They will surely be invited to recline at table in the kingdom of God.

◆ How does today's reading from Hebrews address the "narrow" way?

◆ What narrow gate(s) are in your life now?

◆ How does regarding suffering as a discipline change your attitude toward it?

September 2, 2007

TWENTY-SECOND SUNDAY
IN ORDINARY TIME

READING I   Sirach 3:17—18, 20, 28—29

My child, conduct your affairs with humility,
    and you will be loved more than a giver
        of gifts.
Humble yourself the more, the greater you are,
    and you will find favor with God.
What is too sublime for you, seek not,
    into things beyond your strength
        search not.
The mind of a sage appreciates proverbs,
    and an attentive ear is the joy of
        the wise.
Water quenches a flaming fire,
    and alms atone for sins.

READING II   Hebrews 12:18—19, 22—24a

Brothers and sisters: You have not approached that which could be touched and a blazing fire and gloomy darkness and storm and a trumpet blast and a voice speaking words such that those who heard begged that no message be further addressed to them. No, you have approached Mount Zion and the city of the living God, the heavenly Jerusalem, and countless angels in festal gathering, and the assembly of the firstborn enrolled in heaven, and God the judge of all, and the spirits of the just made perfect, and Jesus, the mediator of a new covenant, and the sprinkled blood that speaks more eloquently than that of Abel.

GOSPEL   Luke 14:1, 7—14

On a sabbath Jesus went to dine at the home of one of the leading Pharisees, and the people there were observing him carefully.

He told a parable to those who had been invited, noticing how they were choosing the places of honor at the table. "When you are invited by someone to a wedding banquet, do not recline at table in the place of honor. A more distinguished guest than you may have been invited by him, and the host who invited both of you may approach you and say, 'Give your place to this man,' and then you would proceed with embarrassment to take the lowest place. Rather, when you are invited, go and take the lowest place so that when the host comes to you he may say, 'My friend, move up to a higher position.' Then you will enjoy the esteem of your companions at the table. For every one who exalts himself will be humbled, but the one who humbles himself will be exalted." Then he said to the host who invited him, "When you hold a lunch or a dinner, do not invite your friends or your brothers or your relatives or your wealthy neighbors, in case they may invite you back and you have repayment. Rather, when you hold a banquet, invite the poor, the crippled, the lame, the blind; blessed indeed will you be because of their inability to repay you. For you will be repaid at the resurrection of the righteous."

Practice of Prayer

Psalm 68:4—5, 6—7, 10—11 (see 11b)

R. God, in your goodness, you have made a
   home for the poor.

The just rejoice and exult before God;
   they are glad and rejoice.
Sing to God, chant praise to his name;
   whose name is the LORD.   R.

The father of orphans and the defender
      of widows
   is God in his holy dwelling.
God gives a home to the forsaken;
   he leads forth prisoners to prosperity.   R.

A bountiful rain you showered down, O God,
      upon your inheritance;
   you restored the land when it languished;
your flock settled in it;
   in your goodness, O God, you provided it for
      the needy.   R.

Practice of Charity

For most of us, work gives structure to our lives
as it provides a sense of identity. On the first
Monday of September, as a nation we consider the
rights and benefits we enjoy as a result of our
labors and the blessings God has bestowed on us.
While you're celebrating what your blood, sweat,
and tears have made possible, don't forget that
blood is a gift that can be shared. The American
Red Cross estimates that someone in the United
States needs blood every two seconds, and on hol-
idays the need is likely to be greater. Giving blood
is fairly easy and it saves lives. If your parish does-
n't sponsor an annual blood drive, now would be
a good time to start. Call your local chapter of the
American Red Cross to find out how you can
donate or go to www.givelife.org.

Scripture Insights

"Learn from me, for I am meek and humble of
heart" (Matthew 11:29b, Gospel acclamation).
Today's scriptures present Jesus as the sage who
embodies wisdom, one who had taken the wisdom of his ancestors to heart.

From his youth, Jesus would have faithfully
studied texts such as our first reading from Sirach,
who had allowed his study of scripture to influence the way he lived. Today's text focuses on
humility and almsgiving—as does the Gospel.
Two words are used for humility in verses 17–18.
The first, *praütes,* can also be translated as gentleness, meekness, or courtesy. The second, *tapeinó,*
means to assume the lowest position, to be undis-
tinguished. Both words occur in today's gospel
acclamation.

More is at stake in the Gospel "parable" than
simply preventing embarrassment. The attentive
disciple will recognize in the wedding feast an
image of the heavenly banquet. Earlier in the
Gospel, drawing upon prophetic traditions, Luke
had acclaimed Jesus as Bridegroom. Only the
humble, who will subsequently be exalted by God,
shall partake of this feast.

The sharing of a meal signified that there was
a relationship between the host and the guests.
The poor, the crippled, the blind, and the lame
were the "outcasts" of society. In their poverty,
they would lack the means to reciprocate. But it is
precisely because of this that the host will be
blessed in the age to come.

To give without any thought of return is itself a
form of humility, the very opposite of *self*-exaltation
and *self*-promotion. So did Jesus live. Blessed
indeed is the one who truly learns from him.

• How did Jesus fulfill the command of Sirach
3:18?

• What opportunities for almsgiving do you have?

• Name a time that you were changed by receiving
from someone who expected nothing in return.

September 9, 2007

READING I   Wisdom 9:13 — 18b

Who can know God's counsel,
> or who can conceive what the
>> LORD intends?
For the deliberations of mortals are timid,
> and unsure are our plans.
For the corruptible body burdens the soul
> and the earthen shelter weighs down the
>> mind that has many concerns.
And scarce do we guess the things on earth,
> and what is within our grasp
>> we find with difficulty;
>> but when things are in heaven, who can
>> search them out?
Or who ever knew your counsel, except you
> had given wisdom
> and sent your holy spirit from on high?
And thus were the paths of those
> on earth made straight.

READING II   Philemon 9 — 10, 12 — 17

I, Paul, an old man, and now also a prisoner for Christ Jesus, urge you on behalf of my child Onesimus, whose father I have become in my imprisonment; I am sending him, that is, my own heart, back to you. I should have liked to retain him for myself, so that he might serve me on your behalf in my imprisonment for the gospel, but I did not want to do anything without your consent, so that the good you do might not be forced but voluntary. Perhaps this is why he was away from you for a while, that you might have him back forever, no longer as a slave but more than a slave, a brother, beloved especially to me, but even more so to you, as a man and in the Lord. So if you regard me as a partner, welcome him as you would me.

GOSPEL   Luke 14:25 — 33

Great crowds were traveling with Jesus, and he turned and addressed them, "If anyone comes to me without hating his father and mother, wife and children, brothers and sisters, and even his own life, he cannot be my disciple. Whoever does not carry his own cross and come after me cannot be my disciple. Which of you wishing to construct a tower does not first sit down and calculate the cost to see if there is enough for its completion? Otherwise, after laying the foundation and finding himself unable to finish the work the onlookers should laugh at him and say, 'This one began to build but did not have the resources to finish.' Or what king marching into battle would not first sit down and decide whether with ten thousand troops he can successfully oppose another king advancing upon him with twenty thousand troops? But if not, while he is still far away, he will send a delegation to ask for peace terms. In the same way, anyone of you who does not renounce all his possessions cannot be my disciple."

Practice of Prayer

Psalm 90:3—4, 5—6, 12—13, 14—17 (1)

R. In every age, O Lord,
  you have been our refuge.

You turn man back to dust,
  saying, "Return, O children of men."
For a thousand years in your sight
  are as yesterday, now that it is past,
  or as a watch of the night. R.

You make an end of them in their sleep;
  the next morning they are
    like the changing grass,
which at dawn springs up anew,
  but by evening wilts and fades. R.

Teach us to number our days aright,
  that we may gain wisdom of heart.
Return, O LORD! How long?
  Have pity on your servants! R.

Fill us at daybreak with your kindness,
  that we may shout for joy and gladness all
    our days.
And may the gracious care of the LORD our God
  be ours;
  prosper the work of our hands for us!
  Prosper the work of our hands! R.

Practice of Faith

This Sunday's readings start with the question, "who can conceive what the Lord intends?" And it ends with the answer, "anyone of you who does not renounce all his possessions cannot be my disciple." The enormity of that response may leave us with another question. We may wonder, "What could God be thinking?" Many people are taking these questions of faith for a walk by journeying through a labyrinth. These walking meditations started in the Middle Ages as a way for people to make spiritual pilgrimages to the Holy Land, even if they couldn't bear the physical or financial burden. Of all shapes and sizes, many modern-day labyrinths are patterned after those that originated in the spiritual centers of Europe hundreds of years ago. To learn more about this spiritual exercise or to find a labyrinth in your area, go to www.labyrinthsociety.org.

Scripture Insights

Today's Gospel minces no words: discipleship costs. The thrice-repeated phrase "cannot be my disciple" leaves no doubt: there *are* "prerequisites." Notice how Luke distinguishes between the "crowds" and the "disciples." Merely "traveling with Jesus" is not enough. More is required.

The "prerequisites" involve ties with all that human beings hold dear: family relationships; possessions; even life itself. One's relationship to Jesus has priority over all others. For some in the early Church, "discipleship" resulted in estrangement from family members who could accept neither Jesus nor the disciple's commitment. Is the would-be disciple strong enough to sustain this rejection?

Does the would-be disciple love his or her own life/self and all that entails more than Jesus? Is he or she able to sacrifice that life—whether literally, as the Church's martyrs were called to do, or in a figurative sense—dying to self for the sake of another?

Possessions can likewise become what is most important for a person. Consequently, they must be "given-up" or "parted with" In the Lucan saying, Jesus tells the crowd: ". . . one's life does not consist of possessions." Rather, the disciple's true treasure is in heaven (12:33–34).

Discipleship will involve a cross, a great suffering that will lead to death, something uniquely personal. The disciple must be *able* to carry it, *willing* to carry it for the sake of Jesus.

Jesus' words cut to the core of our existence, exacting great price—but they point the way to everlasting life.

◆ How does today's Gospel fulfill Wisdom 9:18?

◆ What does your discipleship "cost"?

◆ To which of your possessions are you overly attached? Why does this possession mean so much to you? What if you were called to detach yourself from it?

READING I   Exodus 32:7—11, 13—14

The LORD said to Moses, "Go down at once to your people, whom you brought out of the land of Egypt, for they have become depraved. They have soon turned aside from the way I pointed out to them, making for themselves a molten calf and worshiping it, sacrificing to it and crying out, 'This is your God, O Israel, who brought you out of the land of Egypt!' "I see how stiff-necked this people is," continued the LORD to Moses. "Let me alone, then, that my wrath may blaze up against them to consume them. Then I will make of you a great nation."

But Moses implored the LORD, his God, saying, "Why, O LORD, should your wrath blaze up against your own people, whom you brought out of the land of Egypt with such great power and with so strong a hand? Remember your servants Abraham, Isaac, and Israel, and how you swore to them by your own self, saying, 'I will make your descendants as numerous as the stars in the sky; and all this land that I promised, I will give your descendants as their perpetual heritage.'" So the LORD relented in the punishment he had threatened to inflict on his people.

READING II   1 Timothy 1:12—17

Beloved: I am grateful to him who has strengthened me, Christ Jesus our Lord, because he considered me trustworthy in appointing me to the ministry. I was once a blasphemer and a persecutor and arrogant, but I have been mercifully treated because I acted out of ignorance in my unbelief. Indeed, the grace of our Lord has been abundant, along with the faith and love that are in Christ Jesus. This saying is trustworthy and deserves full acceptance: Christ Jesus came into the world to save sinners. Of these I am the foremost. But for that reason I was mercifully treated, so that in me, as the foremost, Christ Jesus might display all his patience as an example for those who would come to believe in him for everlasting life. To the king of ages, incorruptible, invisible, the only God, honor and glory forever and ever. Amen.

GOSPEL   Luke 15:1—32

Shorter: Luke 15:1–10

Tax collectors and sinners were all drawing near to listen to Jesus, but the Pharisees and scribes began to complain, saying, "This man welcomes sinners and eats with them." So to them he addressed this parable. "What man among you having a hundred sheep and losing one of them would not leave the ninety-nine in the desert and go after the lost one until he finds it? And when he does find it, he sets it on his shoulders with great joy and, upon his arrival home, he calls together his friends and neighbors and says to them, 'Rejoice with me because I have found my lost sheep.' I tell you, in just the same way there will be more joy in heaven over one sinner who repents than over ninety-nine righteous people who have no need of repentance.

"Or what woman having ten coins and losing one would not light a lamp and sweep the house, searching carefully until she finds it? And when she does find it, she calls together her friends and neighbors and says to them, 'Rejoice with me because I have found the coin that I lost.' In just the same way, I tell you, there will be rejoicing among the angels of God over one sinner who repents."

Then he said, "A man had two sons, and the younger son said to his father, 'Father give me the share of your estate that should come to me.' So the father divided the property between them. After a few days, the younger son collected all his belongings and set off to a distant country where he squandered his inheritance on a life of dissipation. When he had freely spent everything, a severe famine struck that country, and he found himself in dire need. So he hired himself out to one of the local citizens who sent him to his farm to tend the swine. And he longed to eat his fill of the pods on which the swine fed, but nobody gave him any. Coming to his senses he thought, 'How many of my father's hired workers have more than enough food to eat, but here am I, dying from hunger. I shall get up and go to my father and I shall say to him, "Father, I have sinned against heaven and against you. I no longer deserve to be called your son; treat me as you would treat one of your hired workers.'" So he got up and went back to his father. While he was still a long way off, his father caught sight of him, and was filled with compassion. He ran to his son, embraced him and kissed him. His son said to him, 'Father, I have sinned against heaven and against you; I no longer deserve to be called your son.' But his father ordered his servants, 'Quickly bring the finest robe and put it on him; put a ring on his finger and sandals on his feet. Take the fattened calf and slaughter it. Then let us celebrate with a feast, because this son of mine was dead, and has come to life again; he was lost, and has been found.' Then the celebration began. Now the older son had been out in the field and, on his way back, as he neared the house, he heard the sound of music and dancing. He called one of the servants and asked what this might mean. The servant said to him, 'Your brother has returned and your father has slaughtered the fattened calf because he has him back safe and sound.' He became angry, and when he refused to enter the house, his father came out and pleaded with him. He said to his father in reply, 'Look, all these years I served you and not once did I disobey your orders; yet you never gave me even a young goat to feast on with my friends. But when your son returns, who swallowed up your property with prostitutes, for him you slaughter the fattened calf.' He said to him, 'My son, you are here with me always; everything I have is yours. But now we must celebrate and rejoice, because your brother was dead and has come to life again; he was lost and has been found.'"

Practice of Hope

The father in today's Gospel searches for his son. Even though his youngest son is "dead" to his family, the father never stops looking for him, or hoping that his beloved child will return to life among them. When the son returns, his father runs to embrace him. What gives us hope is that God never stops looking for us. We, too, are greeted with open arms and a royal banquet each time we gather for Mass.

Scripture Insights

"This man welcomes sinners and eats with them." At first reading, this verse can seem to be merely a part of the narrative introduction, setting the stage for the three parables in today's Gospel. Closer examination reveals that it is the key to today's Gospel—the point which the parables serve to illustrate.

Two weeks ago, we spoke of the significance of table fellowship in Jesus' day. The sharing of a meal signified a bond of relationship. For this, and for his "welcoming" sinners, the religious "officials" of Judaism criticized Jesus. Yet, it is for sinners that Jesus has come.

The Pharisees prided themselves on their strict observance of the Law, which they believed made them "righteous" in the eyes of God. The scribes, as their name implies, were those "professional" scholars of the Scriptures. The Pharisees' and scribes' criticism of Jesus reveals their thoughts.

Luke speaks of them as "murmuring"—a word that evokes Israel's rebellious crime in the desert. Although the scribes and Pharisees do not realize it, they are sinners, too. They are likewise among the sinners for whom Jesus came and whom he calls to repentance. We see this particularly in the parables and teachings he spoke while at table with them.

Jesus "welcomed" anyone who invited him, who reached out to him, whether Pharisee, tax-collector or sinner, friend, or disciple. While sharing a meal, he demonstrated the message of reconciliation. Teaching them the ways of the kingdom, he invited them—and us—to receive and to live what God was bringing about in Him.

◆ What qualities of God are emphasized in today's Scriptures?

◆ What "Pharisaical attitudes" do you detect in yourself? When? Why?

◆ Most of us are more receptive to those we consider "saints" than "sinners." How might we become better at welcoming all?

Autumn Ordinary Time

Prayer before
Reading the Word

God of the covenant,
whose promises can never fail,
in every age you place your words
on the lips of the prophets.
We children of this age come to you in faith,
longing to be transformed in Christ
as children of the resurrection.

Give us humility of heart.
Let us cling to your word
in Moses, the prophets and the gospels.
Let each new day be for us
a time to testify to the gospel.

We ask this through our Lord
       Jesus Christ, your Son,
who lives and reigns with you
in the unity of the Holy Spirit,
God for ever and ever. Amen.

Prayer after
Reading the Word

O God, author of life and resurrection,
before whom even the dead are alive,
grant that the word of your Son,
sown in our hearts,
may blossom and bear fruit in every good work,
so that both in life and in death
our hearts may be strengthened
by eternal comfort and good hope.

We ask this through our Lord
       Jesus Christ, your Son,
who lives and reigns with you
in the unity of the Holy Spirit,
God for ever and ever. Amen.

Weekday Readings

September 17: *1 Timothy 2:1–8; Luke 7:1–10*
September 18: *1 Timothy 3:1–13; Luke 7:11–17*
September 19: *1 Timothy 3:14–16; Luke 7:31–35*
September 20: *1 Timothy 4:12–16; Luke 7:36–50*
September 21: Feast of Saint Matthew
   Ephesians 4:1–7, 11–13; Matthew 9:9–13
September 22: *1 Timothy 6:13–16; Luke 8:4–15*

September 24: *Ezra 1:1–6; Luke 8:16–18*
September 25: *Ezra 6:7–8, 12b, 14–20; Luke 8:19–21*
September 26: *Ezra 9:5–9; Luke 9:1–6*
September 27: *Haggai 1:1–8; Luke 9:7–9*
September 28: *Haggai 2:1–9; Luke 9:18–22*
September 29: Feast of Saints Michael,
   Gabriel, and Raphael
   Daniel 7:9–10, 13–14; John 1:47–51

October 1: *Zechariah 8:1–8; Luke 9:46–50*
October 2: *Zechariah 8:20–23; Matthew 18:1–5, 10*
October 3: *Nehemiah 2:1–8; Luke 9:57–62*
October 4: *Nehemiah 8:1–4a, 5–6, 7b–12; Luke 10:1–12*
October 5: *Baruch 1:15–22; Luke 10:13–16*
October 6: *Baruch 4:5–12, 27–29; Luke 10:17–24*

October 8: *Jonah 1:1–2:2, 11; Luke 10:25–37*
October 9: *Jonah 3:1–10; Luke 1:38–42*
October 10: *Johan 4:1–11; Luke 11:1–4*
October 11: *Malachi 3:13–20b; Luke 11:5–13*
October 12: *Joel 1:13–15; 2:1–2; Luke 11:15–26*
October 13: *Joel 4:12–21; Luke 11:27–28*

October 15: *Romans 1:1–7; Luke 11:29–32*
October 16: *Romans 1:16–25; Luke 11:37–41*
October 17: *Romans 2:1- 11; Luke 11:42–46*
October 18: Feast of Saint Luke
   2 Timothy 4:10–17b; Luke 10:1–9
October 19: *Romans 4:1–8; Luke 12:1–7*
October 20: *Romans 4:13, 16–18; Luke 12:8–12*

October 22: *Romans 4:20–25; Luke 12:13–21*
October 23: *Romans 5:12, 15b, 17–19, 20b–21; Luke 12:35–38*
October 24: *Romans 6:12–18; Luke 12:39–48*
October 25: *Romans 6:19–23; Luke 12:49–53*
October 26: *Romans 7:18–25a; Luke 12:54–59*
October 27: *Romans 8:1–11; Luke 13:1–9*

October 29: *Romans 8:12–17; Luke 13:10–17*
October 30: *Romans 8:18–25; Luke 13:18–21*
October 31: *Romans 8:26–30; Luke 13:22–30*
November 1: Solemnity of All Saints
   Revelation 7:2–4, 9–14; 1 John 3:1–3; Matthew 5:1–12a
November 2: *Wisdom 3:1–9; Romans 5:5-11; John 6:37–40*
November 3: *Romans 11:1–2a, 11–12, 25–29; Luke 14:1, 7–11*

November 5: *Romans 11:29–36; Luke 14:12–14*
November 6: *Romans 12:5–16b; Luke 14:15–24*
November 7: *Romans 13:8–10; Luke 14:25–33*
November 8: *Romans 14:7–12; Luke 15:1–10*
November 9: Feast of the Dedication of
   the Lateran Basilica
   Ezekiel 47:1–2, 8–9, 12; 1 Corinthians
   3:9c–11, 16–17; John 2:13–22
November 10: *Romans 16:3–9, 16, 22–27; Luke 16:9–15*

November 12: *Wisdom 1:1–7; Luke 17:1–6*
November 13: *Wisdom 2:23–3:9; Luke 17:7–10;*
November 14: *Wisdom 6: 1–11; Luke 17:11–19*
November 15: *Wisdom 7:22b–8:1; Luke 17:20–25*
November 16: *Wisdom 13:1–9; Luke 17:26–37*
November 17: *Wisdom 18:14–16; 19:6–9; Luke 18:1–8*

November 19: *1 Macabees 1:10–15; 41–43, 54–57, 62–63; Luke 18:35–43*
November 20: *2 Macabees 6:18–31; Luke 19:1–10*
November 21: *2 Macabees 7:1, 20–31; Luke 19:11–28*
November 22: *1 Macabees 2:15–29; Luke 19:41–44*
November 23: *1 Macabees 4:36–37, 52–59; Luke 19:45–48*
November 24: *1 Macabees 6:1–13; Luke 20:27–40*

November 26: *Daniel 1:1–6, 8–20; Luke 21:1–4*
November 27: *Daniel 2:31–45; Luke 21:5–11*
November 28: *Daniel 5:1–6, 13–14, 16–17, 23–28; Luke 21:12–19*
November 29: *Daniel 6:12–28; Luke 21:20–28*
November 30: *Romans 10:9–18; Matthew 4:18–22*
December 1: *Daniel 7:15–27; Luke 21:34–36*

September 23, 2007

TWENTY-FIFTH SUNDAY IN ORDINARY TIME

READING I   Amos 8:4—7

Hear this, you who trample upon the needy
    and destroy the poor of the land!
"When will the new moon be over," you ask,
    "that we may sell our grain,
    and the sabbath, that we may display
        the wheat?
We will diminish the ephah,
    add to the shekel,
    and fix our scales for cheating!
We will buy the lowly for silver,
    and the poor for a pair of sandals;
    even the refuse of the wheat we will sell!"
The LORD has sworn by the pride of Jacob:
    Never will I forget a thing they
        have done!

READING II   1 Timothy 2:1—8

Beloved: First of all, I ask that supplications, prayers, petitions and thanksgivings be offered for everyone, for kings and for all in authority, that we may lead a quiet and tranquil life in all devotion and dignity. This is good and pleasing to God our savior, who wills everyone to be saved and to come to knowledge of the truth.

For there is one God.
There is also one mediator between God
    and men,
the man Christ Jesus,
who gave himself as ransom for all.

This was the testimony at the proper time. For this I was appointed preacher and apostle —I am speaking the truth, I am not lying—, teacher of the Gentiles in faith and truth.

It is my wish, then, that in every place the men should pray, lifting up holy hands, without anger or argument.

GOSPEL   Luke 16:1—13

Shorter: Luke 16:10–13

Jesus said to his disciples, "A rich man had a steward who was reported to him for squandering his property. He summoned him and said, 'What is this I hear about you? Prepare a full account of your stewardship, because you can no longer be my steward.' The steward said to himself, 'What shall I do, now that my master is taking the position of steward away from me? I am not strong enough to dig and I am ashamed to beg. I know what I shall do so that, when I am removed from the stewardship, they may welcome me into their homes.' He called in his master's debtors one by one. To the first he said, 'How much do you owe my master?' He replied, 'One hundred measures of olive oil.' He said to him, 'Here is your promissory note. Sit down and quickly write one for fifty.' Then to another the steward said, 'And you, how much do you owe?' He replied, 'One hundred kors of wheat.' The steward said to him, 'Here is your promissory note; write one for eighty.' And the master commended that dishonest steward for acting prudently.

"For the children of this world are more prudent in dealing with their own generation than are the children of light. I tell you, make friends for yourselves with dishonest wealth, so that when it fails, you will be welcomed into eternal dwellings. The person who is trustworthy in very small matters is also trustworthy in great ones; and the person who is dishonest in very small matters is also dishonest in great ones. If, therefore, you are not trustworthy with dishonest wealth, who will trust you with true wealth? If you are not trustworthy with what belongs to another, who will give you what is yours? No servant can serve two masters. He will either hate one and love the other, or be devoted to one and despise the other. You cannot serve both God and mammon."

Practice of Prayer

Psalm 113:1–2, 4–6, 7–8 (see 1a, 7b)

R. Praise the Lord who lifts up the poor.
or: Alleluia.

Praise, you servants of the LORD,
    praise the name of the LORD.
Blessed be the name of the LORD
    both now and forever. R.

High above all nations is the LORD;
    above the heavens is his glory.
Who is like the LORD, our God,
        who is enthroned on high
    and looks upon the heavens
        and the earth below? R.

He raises up the lowly from the dust;
    from the dunghill he lifts up the poor
to seat them with princes,
    with the princes of his own people. R.

Practice of Charity

Autumn has begun, and many farmers are preparing for harvest. Whether it has been a good growing season or bad, this is a time of settling accounts and planning for the future.

For many reasons, it has been increasingly difficult for the family farm to survive. The National Catholic Rural Life Conference seeks to help others understand the plight of the small farmer. Visit its website, www.ncrlc.com to discover how you and your parish may be able to aid the family farmer. Reflections from the late Pope John Paul II on respect for rural life and statements from a variety of U.S. bishops may be found at the site. Also available there is the book *Agriculture with a Human Face,* by the late Bishop George H. Speltz, who grew up on a farm in southeastern Minnesota. NCRLC members receive the Catholic Rural Life Magazine and the Catholic Rural Life Newsletter.

Scripture Insights

What a contrast there is between the "quiet and tranquil" life for which Paul (or a later disciple) prays in today's second reading and the agitation and anxiety in our first reading and Gospel! What is this "quiet and tranquil" life? And why the agitation and anxiety?

On the one hand, we have the example of a pastor writing to a co-worker, giving directives for the well-being of the Church. On the other, there are the concerns of merchants and stewards seeking only gain. On the one hand, is the desire to "lead a quiet and tranquil life in all devotion and dignity"; on the other hand, one centered on self-preservation and accumulation of wealth. Today's scriptures calls us to see where we are on this continuum.

Initially, we may be somewhat confused by today's Gospel. The parable is among the most enigmatic in the Gospels. Is the "dishonest steward" (literally, "steward of injustice") really to be commended? Those who study the customs of the times have suggested that what the steward was cutting from the promissory notes was his commission. Thus, without shorting his master even more, he takes a loss that he might gain favor in the eyes of the debtors. A most prudent move, indeed! The last verses consist of various interpretations of the parable and independent sayings of Jesus pertaining to wealth that Luke has placed here.

Today's scriptures pointedly ask about our loyalties, particularly with regard to wealth. In this regard—as in any other—we can have no other master than Jesus.

◆ What do you think Jesus means by making "friends" with wealth?

◆ What does my own use of wealth tell me about my values?

◆ How have you struggled with praying for a leader that you do dislike?

September 30, 2007

TWENTY-SIXTH SUNDAY
IN ORDINARY TIME

READING I   Amos 6:1a, 4—7

Thus says the LORD the God of hosts:
> Woe to the complacent in Zion!
> Lying upon beds of ivory,
>> stretched comfortably on their couches,
> they eat lambs taken from the flock,
>> and calves from the stall!
> Improvising to the music of the harp,
>> like David, they devise their own
>>> accompaniment.
> They drink wine from bowls
>> and anoint themselves with the best oils;
>> yet they are not made ill
>>> by the collapse of Joseph!
> Therefore, now they shall be
>> the first to go into exile,
> and their wanton revelry shall be done
>> away with.

READING II   1 Timothy 6:11—16

But you, man of God, pursue righteousness, devotion, faith, love, patience and gentleness. Compete well for the faith. Lay hold of eternal life, to which you were called when you made the noble confession in the presence of many witnesses. I charge you before God, who gives life to all things, and before Christ Jesus, who gave testimony under Pontius Pilate for the noble confession, to keep the commandment without stain or reproach until the appearance of our Lord Jesus Christ that the blessed and only ruler will make manifest at the proper time, the King of kings and Lord of lords, who alone has immortality, who dwells in unapproachable light, and whom no human being has seen or can see. To him be honor and eternal power. Amen.

GOSPEL   Luke 16:19—31

Jesus said to the Pharisees: "There was a rich man who dressed in purple garments and fine linen and dined sumptuously each day. And lying at his door was a poor man named Lazarus, covered with sores, who would gladly have eaten his fill of the scraps that fell from the rich man's table. Dogs even used to come and lick his sores. When the poor man died, he was carried away by angels to the bosom of Abraham. The rich man also died and was buried, and from the netherworld, where he was in torment, he raised his eyes and saw Abraham far off and Lazarus at his side. And he cried out, 'Father Abraham, have pity on me. Send Lazarus to dip the tip of his finger in water and cool my tongue, for I am suffering torment in these flames.' Abraham replied, 'My child, remember that you received what was good during your lifetime while Lazarus likewise received what was bad; but now he is comforted here, whereas you are tormented. Moreover, between us and you a great chasm is established to prevent anyone from crossing who might wish to go from our side to yours or from your side to ours.' He said, 'Then I beg you, father, send him to my father's house, for I have five brothers, so that he may warn them, lest they too come to this place of torment.' But Abraham replied, 'They have Moses and the prophets. Let them listen to them.' He said, 'Oh no, father Abraham, but if someone from the dead goes to them, they will repent.' Then Abraham said, 'If they will not listen to Moses and the prophets, neither will they be persuaded if someone should rise from the dead.'"

Practice of Prayer

Psalm 146:6 — 7, 8 — 9, 9 — 10
  (see Isaiah 35:4)

R. Praise the Lord, my soul!
or: Alleluia.

Blessed is he who keeps faith forever,
    secures justice for the oppressed,
    gives food to the hungry.
The LORD sets captives free. R.

The LORD gives sight to the blind;
    the LORD raises up those who were
      bowed down.
The LORD loves the just;
    the LORD protects strangers. R.

The fatherless and the widow he sustains,
    but the way of the wicked he thwarts.
The LORD shall reign forever;
    your God, O Zion, through all generations.
      Alleluia. R.

Practice of Charity

The peak season for hurricanes in the Atlantic Ocean is August to October. That has played out powerfully in recent years with hurricanes Katrina, Rita, and Wilma bringing destruction and death to our shores. Take a good look at those hardest hit by the storms, and you'll see the faces of the poor. Without the means to seek shelter beforehand, they continue to suffer afterward. In biblical terms, the very existence of the poor was considered proof that God's people were not keeping faith. But Psalm 146 reminds us that the Lord *does* keep faith and continually calls us to care for each other. So does Catholic Charities USA. The agency works to alleviate suffering on a daily basis and offers long-term assistance in the wake of disaster. Go to www.catholiccharitiesusa.org to discover how you can join in "providing help and creating hope."

Scripture Insights

"Woe to the complacent . . . . they are not made ill by the collapse of Joseph!" Today's scriptures, pointed at those who live "comfortably" (Amos 6:4), receiving much that is "good," can easily trigger unease as we reflect on the comfort of our lifestyles, particularly as contrasted with that of many people in the world. What will be the Lord's words to us when we die?

Neither Amos nor Jesus fault the level of comfort the rich enjoyed but, rather, their lack of awareness of the suffering of those closest to them. Joseph was the son of Jacob, and in the book of Amos, a metaphor for Israel. Did Zion really not care about the afflictions of their neighbors in the northern part of the country? Lazarus literally *lies at the door* of the rich man. Did the rich man never look out? Go out? Did he just ignore him? Whatever the reason, he just never bothered, and for this reason he is judged.

The rich man had not taken to heart God's love and constant concern for the poor manifest throughout scripture, that concern for those with no one to care for them. As the prophets repeatedly reminded, one aspect of fidelity to God's law is the demonstration of this concern. The rich man has failed doing this.

In other respects, the rich man may have been a devoted descendant of Abraham — note the tenor of their conversation. He certainly was a man who demonstrates much love and concern for his family. He just failed to see beyond his door. May we learn from his mistakes.

♦ How does the first reading relate to the Gospel?

♦ Why do you think a righteous person would come to the aid of Lazarus?

♦ Which mandates from scripture do you have a hard time following?

October 7, 2007

READING I   *Habakkuk 1:2—3, 2:2—4*

How long, O LORD? I cry for help
    but you do not listen!
I cry out to you, "Violence!"
    but you do not intervene.
Why do you let me see ruin;
    why must I look at misery?
Destruction and violence are before me;
    there is strife, and clamorous discord.
Then the LORD answered me and said:
    Write down the vision clearly upon
        the tablets,
    so that one can read it readily.
For the vision still has its time,
    presses on to fulfillment,
        and will not disappoint;
if it delays, wait for it,
    it will surely come, it will not be late.
The rash one has no integrity;
    but the just one, because of
        his faith, shall live.

READING II   *2 Timothy 1:6—8, 13—14*

Beloved: I remind you, to stir into flame the gift of God that you have through the imposition of my hands. For God did not give us a spirit of cowardice but rather of power and love and self-control. So do not be ashamed of your testimony to our Lord, nor of me, a prisoner for his sake; but bear your share of hardship for the gospel with the strength that comes from God.

Take as your norm the sound words that you heard from me, in the faith and love that are in Christ Jesus. Guard this rich trust with the help of the Holy Spirit that dwells within us.

GOSPEL   *Luke 17:5—10*

The apostles said to the Lord, "Increase our faith." The Lord replied, "If you have faith the size of a mustard seed, you would say to this mulberry tree, 'Be uprooted and planted in the sea,' and it would obey you.

"Who among you would say to your servant who has just come in from plowing or tending sheep in the field, 'Come here immediately and take your place at table'? Would he not rather say to him, 'Prepare something for me to eat. Put on your apron and wait on me while I eat and drink. You may eat and drink when I am finished'? Is he grateful to that servant because he did what was commanded? So should it be with you. When you have done all you have been commanded, say, 'We are unprofitable servants; we have done what we were obliged to do.'"

Practice of Prayer

Psalm 95:1—2, 6—7, 8—9 (8)

R. If today you hear his voice, harden not
    your hearts.

Come, let us sing joyfully to the LORD;
    let us acclaim the Rock of our salvation.
Let us come into his presence with thanksgiving;
    let us joyfully sing psalms to him. R.

Come, let us bow down and worship;
    let us kneel before the LORD who made us.
For he is our God,
    and we are the people he shepherds, the flock
      he guides. R.

Oh, that today you would hear his voice:
    "Harden not your hearts as at Meribah,
      as in the day of Massah in the desert."
Where your fathers tempted me;
    they tested me though they had seen my
      works. R.

Practice of Hope

Less than a year after the Sept. 11, 2001, terrorist attacks that caused so much death, destruction, and despair, the late Pope John Paul II convened an ecumenical peace gathering in Assisi, Italy. Surrounded by the hills and valleys that formed one of our greatest advocates of peace, Saint Francis, they prayed for reconciliation and a world renewed. That was five years ago. John Paul is gone now and wars persist. As the prophet Habakkuk did, we are tempted to look around and cry, "How long, O Lord?" Just as God consoled Habakkuk, we are encouraged to be patient, "for the vision still has its time." The United States Conference of Catholic Bishops spoke prophetically in their pastoral letter, *The Challenge of Peace: God's Promise and Our Response."* Studying that letter, written in 1983, will give Catholics an understanding of what their faith teaches about peace. Copies of the pastoral letter may be ordered from the USCCB website, www.usccb.org or by calling 1-800-235-8722.

Scripture Insights

"How long, O Lord? I cry for help but you do not listen!" Haven't we all felt this way at one time or another? Maybe many times? The cry of lament is one that resonates deep in our hearts—and, most significantly, in the prayers of all of scripture. It was precisely in the experience of helplessness and powerlessness in Egypt that the Chosen People of God came to know God as redeemer. It is precisely in the midst of deep suffering and affliction that the psalmist experiences the saving power of God. But how long the "long" seems to be when one is in the midst of it.

For the prophet Habakkuk, writing shortly before the Babylonian invasion, things would get worse. The experiences of affliction and exile recorded in the scriptures are replayed in our lives. These are times when faith is not only tested, but has the potential to grow stronger. These are times that call us, as Habakkuk, to "keep watch to see what God will say."

God's response to Habukkuk are marvelous words of hope for anyone facing loss and destruction. God's revelation has its time. The fulfillment of God's plan—though seemingly thwarted or delayed—*will* come to pass. The just person, standing in the right relationship with God through faith, will live.

"Lord, increase our faith"—especially when it is tested and we are tempted to give way to despair. Help us to wait, grounded in ever-increasing faith, for the fulfillment of your plan.

◆ Read today's second reading as addressed to you. When was your imposition of hands? What gift(s) did you receive?

◆ How can you be more attentive to scripture daily?

◆ In today's gospel, humility seems to be required to grow in faith. Why?

October, 14, 2007

READING I   2 Kings 5:14—17

Naaman went down and plunged into the Jordan seven times at the word of Elisha, the man of God. His flesh became again like the flesh of a little child, and he was clean of his leprosy.

Naaman returned with his whole retinue to the man of God. On his arrival he stood before Elisha and said, "Now I know that there is no God in all the earth, except in Israel. Please accept a gift from your servant."

Elisha replied, "As the LORD lives whom I serve, I will not take it," and despite Naaman's urging, he still refused. Naaman said: "If you will not accept, please let me, your servant, have two mule-loads of earth, for I will no longer offer holocaust or sacrifice to any other god except to the LORD."

READING II   2 Timothy 2:8—13

Beloved: Remember Jesus Christ, raised from the dead, a descendant of David: such is my gospel, for which I am suffering, even to the point of chains, like a criminal. But the word of God is not chained. Therefore, I bear with everything for the sake of those who are chosen, so that they too may obtain the salvation that is in Christ Jesus, together with eternal glory. This saying is trustworthy:

If we have died with him
    we shall also live with him;
if we persevere
    we shall also reign with him.
But if we deny him
    he will deny us.
If we are unfaithful
    he remains faithful,
    for he cannot deny himself.

GOSPEL   Luke 17:11—19

As Jesus continued his journey to Jerusalem, he traveled through Samaria and Galilee. As he was entering a village, ten lepers met him. They stood at a distance from him and raised their voices, saying, "Jesus, Master! Have pity on us!" And when he saw them, he said, "Go show yourselves to the priests." As they were going they were cleansed. And one of them, realizing he had been healed, returned, glorifying God in a loud voice; and he fell at the feet of Jesus and thanked him. He was a Samaritan. Jesus said in reply, "Ten were cleansed, were they not? Where are the other nine? Has none but this foreigner returned to give thanks to God?" Then he said to him, "Stand up and go; your faith has saved you."

Practice of Prayer

Psalm 98:1, 2—3, 3—4 (see 2b)

R. The Lord has revealed to the nations his
saving power.

Sing to the LORD a new song,
for he has done wondrous deeds;
His right hand has won victory for him,
his holy arm. R.

The LORD has made his salvation known:
in the sight of the nations he has revealed
his justice.
He has remembered his kindness and
his faithfulness
toward the house of Israel. R.

All the ends of the earth have seen
the salvation by our God.
Sing joyfully to the LORD, all you lands;
break into song; sing praise. R.

Practice of Charity

In Jesus' time, Samaritans were outsiders. Since
their religious practices were not in keeping with
the law, they were not accepted in Jewish society.
Can you imagine the plight of a Samaritan plagued
with leprosy? Twice condemned, he would be
ostracized, even if cured of his disease. Fortunately
for the leper, Jesus does not see as we see. While
others looked with disdain, Jesus saw a faith-filled
heart. It was then that this man was healed. There
are "lepers" among us today. Homeless, hopeless,
and in need, they long to be seen. They long for
dignity and healing. We may not be able to cure
their every ill, but not looking away from them is
a good place to start. This week, make a conscious
effort to look into the face of someone who makes
you uncomfortable. If we look closely enough, we
might even see Jesus' face.

Scripture Insights

"Where are the other nine?" That is a haunting
question, since each of us knows of times when
that could be said of us. Why do those for whom
the Lord has done such wondrous things not
always return to give thanks?

Although thanksgiving is a prominent theme
of today's readings, there is more to be gleaned
from Luke's description of the encounter between
Jesus and the lepers. While scholars generally
accept that the leprosy of the scriptures is not the
same as Hansen's disease, the condition was considered highly contagious. Lepers were deemed
unfit for association with people or with things
consecrated to God.

Notice how the ten keep their distance from
Jesus, aware of their own state and out of respect
for his. It is they who initiate the contact with
Jesus, crying out for his mercy.

Jesus' response is to give them a command.
There is no physical touch, no word of healing.
Simply: "Go, show yourselves to the priests." It is
they who could declare them clean and restore
them to the larger community. And so they went.

What faith they had in Jesus' word! How obedient to his command! On their way, in this way,
it happened: they were cleansed—by God. What
must the realization of their healing have been
like! Their response? One immediately returned
to Jesus with shouts of praise. Falling at Jesus' feet,
he gave thanks (eucharisté).

May we so learn from his faith and the gratitude that he promptly expresses to God, that this
becomes our response as well. May it never be said
of us: "Where are they?"

◆ What elements of today's first reading and
Gospel are found in Psalm 98?

◆ How is the spirit—and practice—of gratitude
cultivated?

◆ In what ways have you taken God's generosity
for granted?

October 21, 2007

READING I   *Exodus 17:8 — 13*

In those days, Amalek came and waged war against Israel. Moses, therefore, said to Joshua, "Pick out certain men, and tomorrow go out and engage Amalek in battle. I will be standing on top of the hill with the staff of God in my hand." So Joshua did as Moses told him: he engaged Amalek in battle after Moses had climbed to the top of the hill with Aaron and Hur. As long as Moses kept his hands raised up, Israel had the better of the fight, but when he let his hands rest, Amalek had the better of the fight. Moses' hands, however, grew tired; so they put a rock in place for him to sit on. Meanwhile Aaron and Hur supported his hands, one on one side and one on the other, so that his hands remained steady till sunset. And Joshua mowed down Amalek and his people with the edge of the sword.

READING II   *2 Timothy 3:14 — 4:2*

Beloved: Remain faithful to what you have learned and believed, because you know from whom you learned it, and that from infancy you have known the sacred Scriptures, which are capable of giving you wisdom for salvation through faith in Christ Jesus. All Scripture is inspired by God and is useful for teaching, for refutation, for correction, and for training in righteousness, so that one who belongs to God may be competent, equipped for every good work.

   I charge you in the presence of God and of Christ Jesus, who will judge the living and the dead, and by his appearing and his kingly power: proclaim the word; be persistent whether it is convenient or inconvenient; convince, reprimand, encourage through all patience and teaching.

GOSPEL   *Luke 18:1 — 8*

Jesus told his disciples a parable about the necessity for them to pray always without becoming weary. He said, "There was a judge in a certain town who neither feared God nor respected any human being. And a widow in that town used to come to him and say, 'Render a just decision for me against my adversary.' For a long time the judge was unwilling, but eventually he thought, 'While it is true that I neither fear God nor respect any human being, because this widow keeps bothering me I shall deliver a just decision for her lest she finally come and strike me.'" The Lord said, "Pay attention to what the dishonest judge says. Will not God then secure the rights of his chosen ones who call out to him day and night? Will he be slow to answer them? I tell you, he will see to it that justice is done for them speedily. But when the Son of Man comes, will he find faith on earth?"

Practice of Prayer

Psalm 121:1 — 2, 3 — 4, 5 — 6, 7 — 8 (see 2)

R. Our help is from the Lord, who made heaven
and earth.

I lift up my eyes toward the mountains;
whence shall help come to me?
My help is from the LORD,
who made heaven and earth. R.

May he not suffer your foot to slip;
may he slumber not who guards you:
indeed he neither slumbers nor sleeps,
the guardian of Israel. R.

The LORD is your guardian;
the LORD is your shade;
he is beside you at your right hand.
The sun shall not harm you by day,
nor the moon by night. R.

The LORD will guard you from all evil;
he will guard your life.
The LORD will guard your coming and your going,
both now and forever. R.

Practice of Faith

Persistence, prayer, and the Word of God are
linked in the readings for this weekend, which
seems only natural since they are also linked
in the life of a disciple. Unlike the widow in Luke's
Gospel, however, the Word of God doesn't have to
go to extremes to be effective. A good example of
this gentle persuasion is Taizé prayer. Developed
by an ecumenical community in France devoted
to peace and reconciliation, Taizé prayer has
Scripture at its core. What sets it apart are the
chants that are sung throughout, many of them
taken from the Word of God. As these chants are
repeated, they give the Word a chance to creep
into our hearts and make its home there. Churches
of all denominations offer this kind of prayer
experience. If it isn't available in your area, you
can still visit Taizé by going to www.taize.fr.

Scripture Insights

"Remain faithful to what you have learned . . .
because you know from whom you learned it, and
that from infancy you have known the sacred
Scriptures." What perfect illustration of attending
to the Word at home! Although Timothy's teachers are not named in today's text, they are identified earlier in the letter as his mother Eunice and
his grandmother Lois. Theirs was a faith that was
"caught" as well as "taught."

Today's reading focuses on the Old Testament
as the foundation of the dynamic faith of these
women and the subject of their teaching. Eunice
and Lois saw Jesus as the fulfillment of these
Scriptures and recognized in them, the wisdom
that leads to salvation. Such insight can be attained
only by prayerful reading and reflection on the
sacred words.

In today's reading, Saint Paul emphasizes that
all Scripture deserves such attention, for every
page, every text, even a single word—as God's
word and divinely inspired—is "useful," indeed,
indispensable for those "who belong to God."
These are words that teach, that refute error or
false doctrine, that correct faults, and that train
one in the right relationship with God and others.
Through these words, believers are equipped for
every good work.

Through their faith-filled sharing of the
Word, Lois and Eunice prepared Timothy for the
ministry that was to be his in the Church. They
treasured God's word, knowing, like the psalmist
before them, that God's Word "is a lamp to my
feet and a light to my path" (Psalm 119:105). So
may it be for us.

◆ What is the message of salvation in Exodus 17
and Psalm 121? How is Jesus the "fulfillment" of
these texts?

◆ How can you share God's Word with others?

◆ Were there people besides your parents who
were important to your knowledge of your faith?

READING I *Sirach 35:12—14, 16—18*

The LORD is a God of justice,
    who knows no favorites.
Though not unduly partial toward the weak,
    yet he hears the cry of the oppressed.
The Lord is not deaf to the wail of
        the orphan,
    nor to the widow when she pours out
        her complaint.
The one who serves God willingly is heard;
    his petition reaches the heavens.
The prayer of the lowly pierces the clouds;
    it does not rest till it reaches its goal,
nor will it withdraw till the Most
        High responds,
    judges justly and affirms the right,
and the Lord will not delay.

READING II *2 Timothy 4:6—8, 16—18*

Beloved: I am already being poured out like a libation, and the time of my departure is at hand. I have competed well; I have finished the race; I have kept the faith. From now on the crown of righteousness awaits me, which the Lord, the just judge, will award to me on that day, and not only to me, but to all who have longed for his appearance.

At my first defense no one appeared on my behalf, but everyone deserted me. May it not be held against them! But the Lord stood by me and gave me strength, so that through me the proclamation might be completed and all the Gentiles might hear it. And I was rescued from the lion's mouth. The Lord will rescue me from every evil threat and will bring me safe to his heavenly kingdom. To him be glory forever and ever. Amen.

GOSPEL *Luke 18:9—14*

Jesus addressed this parable to those who were convinced of their own righteousness and despised everyone else. "Two people went up to the temple area to pray; one was a Pharisee and the other was a tax collector. The Pharisee took up his position and spoke this prayer to himself, 'O God, I thank you that I am not like the rest of humanity— greedy, dishonest, adulterous—or even like this tax collector. I fast twice a week, and I pay tithes on my whole income.' But the tax collector stood off at a distance and would not even raise his eyes to heaven but beat his breast and prayed, 'O God, be merciful to me a sinner.' I tell you, the latter went home justified, not the former; for whoever exalts himself will be humbled, and the one who humbles himself will be exalted."

Practice of Prayer

R. The Lord hears the cry of the poor.

I will bless the LORD at all times;
    his praise shall be ever in my mouth.
Let my soul glory in the Lord;
    the lowly will hear me and be glad. R.

The LORD confronts the evildoers,
    to destroy remembrance of them from
        the earth.
When the just cry out, the Lord hears them,
    and from all their distress
        he rescues them. R.

The LORD is close to the brokenhearted;
    and those who are crushed in spirit he saves.
The LORD redeems the lives of his servants;
    no one incurs guilt who takes refuge
        in him. R.

Practice of Faith

This week the liturgical calendar is full of reasons to reflect on what we're doing in this world and consider what awaits us in the next. The Feast of All Saints on November 1 provides an opportunity to consider the examples of people who have been models of faith. The Gospel, always taken from Matthew, focuses on the Beatitudes or blessings that flow from living a life in Christ. Some have called them a "blueprint" for discipleship. This should sound familiar to fans of motivational authors who advocate having a personal mission statement as a key to success in business and life. It's just as important to have a personal spiritual mission statement. The saints had a clear vision of what they were about and what their goal was. Do you? If not, how will you know if you can join Paul in saying, "I have competed well; I have finished the race; I have kept the faith"?

Scripture Insights

The juxtaposition of Sirach 35 and Psalm 34 with their focus on the poor offers an interesting lens with which to view today's Gospel. Normally, the first reading and the Gospel complement each other. However, in no sense would the tax collector have been economically poor. As an "agent" of the Roman government, the tax collector would have added a surcharge to cover his salary. In what does his "poverty" consist?

Unlike the Pharisee, the "professional religious," the tax collector knew his poverty of spirit. He knew that there was nothing in him with which he could make a claim on God. On the contrary, the Pharisee parades his self-proclaimed virtue, a judgment arrived at by comparison with others.

The tax collector stands back, with lowered eyes, acknowledging his unworthiness to enter into the sacred presence and begging for God's mercy. He knows he is entitled to nothing. He knows his need for God. In this, does his poverty consist.

The tax collector begs for God's mercy. The Greek verb used, *hiláskomai,* occurs only one other time in the New Testament. It means to atone, to reconcile, and is sometimes translated as "forgive." The tax collector was asking God to do for him what he could not do *for* himself or *of* himself.

By virtue of his standing in this truth, which is genuine humility, and in the full awareness of his poverty before God, he is "justified"—set in right relationship with God. "Those who humble themselves shall be exalted"—lifted up, not because of their own merits, but by God who knows their poverty.

• What other things in today's first reading are applicable to the tax collector?

• How do I experience my poverty before God?

• Have you ever become self-righteous about how well you follow some of the Ten Commandments?

November 4, 2007

THIRTY-FIRST SUNDAY
IN ORDINARY TIME

READING I   *Wisdom 11:22—12:2*

Before the LORD the whole universe is as
      a grain from a balance
   or a drop of morning dew come down
      upon the earth.
But you have mercy on all, because you can
      do all things;
   and you overlook people's sins that they
      may repent.
For you love all things that are
   and loathe nothing that you have made;
      for what you hated, you would not
         have fashioned.
And how could a thing remain, unless you
      willed it;
   or be preserved, had it not been called
      forth by you?
But you spare all things, because they
      are yours,
   O LORD and lover of souls,
      for your imperishable spirit is in
         all things!
Therefore you rebuke offenders little by little,
   warn them and remind them of the
      sins they are committing,
   that they may abandon their wickedness
      and believe in you, O LORD!

READING II   *2 Thessalonians 1:11—2:2*

Brothers and sisters: We always pray for you, that
our God may make you worthy of his calling and
powerfully bring to fulfillment every good purpose and every effort of faith, that the name of
our Lord Jesus may be glorified in you, and you in
him, in accord with the grace of our God and
Lord Jesus Christ.

We ask you, brothers and sisters, with regard
to the coming of our Lord Jesus Christ and
our assembling with him, not to be shaken out of
your minds suddenly, or to be alarmed either by
a "spirit," or by an oral statement, or by a letter
allegedly from us to the effect that the day of the
Lord is at hand.

GOSPEL   *Luke 19:1—10*

At that time, Jesus came to Jericho and intended
to pass through the town. Now a man there
named Zacchaeus, who was a chief tax collector
and also a wealthy man, was seeking to see who
Jesus was; but he could not see him because of the
crowd, for he was short in stature. So he ran ahead
and climbed a sycamore tree in order to see Jesus,
who was about to pass that way. When he reached
the place, Jesus looked up and said, "Zacchaeus,
come down quickly, for today I must stay at your
house." And he came down quickly and received
him with joy. When they all saw this, they began
to grumble, saying, "He has gone to stay at the
house of a sinner." But Zacchaeus stood there and
said to the Lord, "Behold, half of my possessions,
Lord, I shall give to the poor, and if I have extorted
anything from anyone I shall repay it four times
over." And Jesus said to him, "Today salvation has
come to this house because this man too is a
descendant of Abraham. For the Son of Man has
come to seek and to save what was lost."

Practice of Prayer

Psalm 145:1—2, 8—9, 10—11, 13, 14 (see 1)

R. I will praise your name for ever, my king and
   my God.

I will extol you, O my God and king;
   and I will bless your name forever and ever.
Every day I will bless you;
   and I will praise your name forever
      and ever.   R.

The LORD is gracious and merciful,
   slow to anger and of great kindness.
The LORD is good to all,
   and compassionate toward all his works.   R.

Let all your works give you thanks, O LORD,
   and let your faithful ones bless you.
Let them discourse of the glory of your kingdom
   and speak of your might.   R.

The LORD is faithful in all his words
   and holy in all his works.
The LORD lifts up all who are falling
   and raises up all who are bowed down.   R.

Practice of Hope

For 15 years, members of church groups and congregations in Omaha, Nebraska, have been joining hands across racial, economic, and religious lines to tackle the city's tough issues. This community organizing effort is known as Omaha Together One Community (OTOC). A unique aspect of OTOC is that it does not rely on polls or surveys for information. To learn about what needs to be addressed and how, leaders hold regular house meeting campaigns. In a world that runs on e-mail and text messaging, it seems the most effective way to reach people is still face-to-face, home to home. As he did with Zacchaeus, Jesus asks us for a "house meeting" every day. It is in these intimate, face-to-face encounters that we can share the tough issues of our lives and find solutions. Are we willing to come down out of the tree and take the meeting?

Scripture Insights

Today's Gospel leaves us breathless—especially if we try to put ourselves in Zaccheus' shoes. You've stretched and stood on tiptoe, you've even tried to elbow your way through the crowd. All you want is to see Jesus. But nothing has worked! And then you get an idea!!! You take off running, determined to get situated in a position where at last you will be able to see—even if it is up in a tree.

What prompted Zaccheus to go to such lengths—or heights, as the case may be? What had he heard about Jesus? Earlier in the Gospel, Luke tells us that "tax collectors and sinners were all drawing near to listen to him (Jesus)." Word had no doubt spread among them, that this man, unlike most everyone else, "welcomed" them. Jesus had even called one of them to be his disciple. Jesus sat at table with them and entered into fellowship with them.

As the narrative continues, it is clear that Jesus is looking for Zaccheus as well. What joy did Zaccheus experience when Jesus found and welcomed him!

As usual, Jesus' gesture met with criticism. But Zaccheus firmly stood his ground, giving evidence of his repentance. How Jesus' presence and acceptance—and his own welcoming *of* Jesus—changed his life! That day was a day of release from his past. That day of welcoming Jesus was a day of salvation. Let us welcome Jesus into our homes, our workplaces, and our lives, that each day might be such a day for us.

• How does Jesus' dealings with Zaccheus exemplify the teaching in today's first reading?

• What difference would an awareness of Jesus' presence with me make in my life?

• In the first reading, we find that God loathes no one. What does that mean for how we are to act?

READING I   2 Maccabees 7:1—2, 9—14

It happened that seven brothers with their mother were arrested and tortured with whips and scourges by the king, to force them to eat pork in violation of God's law. One of the brothers, speaking for the others, said: "What do you expect to achieve by questioning us? We are ready to die rather than transgress the laws of our ancestors."

At the point of death he said: "You accursed fiend, you are depriving us of this present life, but the King of the world will raise us up to live again forever. It is for his laws that we are dying."

After him the third suffered their cruel sport. He put out his tongue at once when told to do so, and bravely held out his hands, as he spoke these noble words: "It was from Heaven that I received these; for the sake of his laws I disdain them; from him I hope to receive them again." Even the king and his attendants marveled at the young man's courage, because he regarded his sufferings as nothing.

After he had died, they tortured and maltreated the fourth brother in the same way. When he was near death, he said, "It is my choice to die at the hands of men with the hope God gives of being raised up by him; but for you, there will be no resurrection to life."

READING II   2 Thessalonians 2:16—3:5

Brothers and sisters: May our Lord Jesus Christ himself and God our Father, who has loved us and given us everlasting encouragement and good hope through his grace, encourage your hearts and strengthen them in every good deed and word.

Finally, brothers and sisters, pray for us, so that the word of the Lord may speed forward and be glorified, as it did among you, and that we may be delivered from perverse and wicked people, for not all have faith. But the Lord is faithful; he will strengthen you and guard you from the evil one. We are confident of you in the Lord that what we instruct you, you are doing and will continue to do. May the Lord direct your hearts to the love of God and to the endurance of Christ.

GOSPEL   Luke 20:27—38

Shorter: Luke 20:27, 34—38

Some Sadducees, those who deny that there is a resurrection, came forward and put this question to Jesus, saying, "Teacher, Moses wrote for us, *If someone's brother dies leaving a wife but no child, his brother must take the wife and raise up descendants for his brother.* Now there were seven brothers; the first married a woman but died childless. Then the second and the third married her, and likewise all the seven died childless. Finally the woman also died. Now at the resurrection whose wife will that woman be? For all seven had been married to her." Jesus said to them, "The children of this age marry and remarry; but those who are deemed worthy to attain to the coming age and to the resurrection of the dead neither marry nor are given in marriage. They can no longer die, for they are like angels; and they are the children of God because they are the ones who will rise. That the dead will rise even Moses made known in the passage about the bush, when he called out 'Lord,' the God of Abraham, the God of Isaac, and the God of Jacob; and he is not God of the dead, but of the living, for to him all are alive."

Practice of Prayer

Psalm 17:1, 5 – 6, 8, 15 (15b)

R. Lord, when your glory appears, my joy will
    be full.

Hear, O LORD, a just suit;
    attend to my outcry;
    hearken to my prayer from lips without
        deceit. R.

My steps have been steadfast in your paths,
    my feet have not faltered.
I call upon you, for you will answer me, O God;
    incline your ear to me; hear my word. R.

Keep me as the apple of your eye,
    hide me in the shadow of your wings.
But I in justice shall behold your face;
    on waking I shall be content
        in your presence. R.

Practice of Hope

Standing in the chapel of the mausoleum, I couldn't help but notice that some of the crypts had names on them but no dates. This seemed to be carrying preparedness too far. "Who would want to stake a claim on death?" I thought. But as the choir sang words of comfort and trust in the love of God, I realized that I was standing in a place of hope. Death may be inevitable, but it doesn't have the final word for the children of God. "They are the ones who will rise," Jesus assures us. Our God is the God of the living. In two weeks, we will all stake a claim on death by acknowledging that our destiny is the same as that of Christ the King. The final word we will hear in Luke's Gospel that day is "paradise." That's our final word—and hope—too.

Scripture Insights

". . . for they are like angels." What images come to mind when we hear Jesus' description of resurrected life? Chubby little cherubs? The glorious, winged creatures that adorn Christmas cards? Something else? Is the idea even appealing? Or, is the image meaningless? Perhaps a look at descriptions of angels in biblical tradition will help us grasp what Jesus is saying.

Although angels appear throughout Scripture as God's messengers, later writings depict them as gloriously luminous, heavenly creatures. Significantly, these descriptions are similar to that of the transfigured Jesus in Matthew 17:2—an event associated with the resurrection of the dead.

Some groups within the Judaism of Jesus' day, notably the Pharisees but not the Sadducees (see Acts 23:8), believed that this was the destiny of all the just (see Daniel 12:2–3). We hear it in today's Gospel, and we see it in the writings of Saint Paul. In chapter 15 of First Corinthians, Paul describes at length what this new glorified existence will be like (1 Corinthians 15:35–56). In Philippians, he says more succinctly: "He (Jesus) will change our lowly body to conform with his glorified body . . . ." (Philippians 3:21; see also 2 Corinthians 5:1–2).

What a glorious destiny awaits us in the age to come when we, too, shall be among the multitude gathered before God's throne! (Revelation 7:9–17). May the promise fill us with excitement and joy!

◆ What image of resurrected life is projected in today's scriptures?

◆ How can this sustain me at the death of a loved one?

◆ Do you ever pray that God will help you reveal himself to others?

November 18, 2007

READING I   *Malachi 3:19 — 20a*

Lo, the day is coming, blazing like an oven,
> when all the proud and all evildoers will
> > be stubble,
and the day that is coming will set them
> on fire,
> > leaving them neither root nor branch,
> > says the LORD of hosts.
But for you who fear my name, there will arise
> the sun of justice with its healing rays.

READING II   *2 Thessalonians 3:7 — 12*

Brothers and sisters: You know how one must imitate us. For we did not act in a disorderly way among you, nor did we eat food received free from anyone. On the contrary, in toil and drudgery, night and day we worked, so as not to burden any of you. Not that we do not have the right. Rather, we wanted to present ourselves as a model for you, so that you might imitate us. In fact, when we were with you, we instructed you that if anyone was unwilling to work, neither should that one eat. We hear that some are conducting themselves among you in a disorderly way, by not keeping busy but minding the business of others. Such people we instruct and urge in the Lord Jesus Christ to work quietly and to eat their own food.

GOSPEL   *Luke 21:5 — 19*

While some people were speaking about how the temple was adorned with costly stones and votive offerings, Jesus said, "All that you see here—the days will come when there will not be left a stone upon another stone that will not be thrown down."

Then they asked him, "Teacher, when will this happen? And what sign will there be when all these things are about to happen?" He answered, "See that you not be deceived, for many will come in my name, saying, 'I am he,' and 'The time has come.' Do not follow them! When you hear of wars and insurrections, do not be terrified; for such things must happen first, but it will not immediately be the end." Then he said to them, "Nation will rise against nation, and kingdom against kingdom. There will be powerful earthquakes, famines and plagues from place to place; and awesome sights and mighty signs will come from the sky.

"Before all this happens, however, they will seize and persecute you, they will hand you over to the synagogues and to prisons, and they will have you led before kings and governors because of my name. It will lead to your giving testimony. Remember, you are not to prepare your defense beforehand, for I myself shall give you a wisdom in speaking that all your adversaries will be powerless to resist or refute. You will even be handed over by parents, brothers, relatives and friends, and they will put some of you to death. You will be hated by all because of my name, but not a hair on your head will be destroyed. By your perseverance you will secure your lives."

Practice of Prayer

Psalm 98:5 — 6, 7 — 8, 9 (see 9)

R. The Lord comes to rule the earth with justice.

Sing praise to the LORD with the harp,
    with the harp and melodious song.
With trumpets and the sound of the horn
    sing joyfully before the King, the LORD.   R.

Let the sea and what fills it resound,
    the world and those who dwell in it;
let the rivers clap their hands,
    the mountains shout with them for joy.   R.

Before the LORD, for he comes,
    for he comes to rule the earth,
He will rule the world with justice
    and the peoples with equity.   R.

Practice of Hope

Sometimes the harmony in a choir loft results in more than beautiful music. In the right circumstances, the blending of voices and lives may provide a counterpoint to the discord of a hurting world. That's what happened when a downtown parish in Peoria, Ill., invited guests in its meal program to be part of a festival choir for the feast of Saint Francis of Assisi. Not only did this give the men a chance to feed the souls of those who feed them with food and love, it also enabled them to praise the God who provides for them daily. As they sang, wars, hurricanes, and unemployment were forgotten, and we received a glimpse of the kingdom of heaven. On November 22, we honor Saint Cecilia and the power of music to make God present in our lives. Find a way to add your voice to the song.

Scripture Insights

As we move toward the end of the Church year, our thoughts are directed to the end of time. We look to that day of punishment and retribution, when the just will be rewarded and the wicked doomed to destruction. As we hear in Malachi, that "day" was of special interest to the prophets, commissioned as they were to speak a word of hope to a suffering people. The New Testament seems particularly interested in the timing of this day and on the signs that precede it, as in today's Gospel. Repeatedly, God's people are called to watchfulness, readiness, and a willingness to suffer.

The scriptures portray such suffering as inevitable — and indeed, paradoxical. Note the seeming contradiction between Luke 21:18 and verses 12–17. In verse 19 is the key, "by your endurance you will secure ('acquire') your lives." God's people must never forget that the day when the blazing fire of his anger destroys all wickedness will also be the day when the healing rays of his light and love will restore the righteous.

It is this promise of vindication that leads believers to pray for the hastening of the day of the Lord's coming, and indeed to celebrate it, as in today's Psalm 98. For those who are faithful, the day of the Lord will indeed be a day of redemption. Sustained by this hope, may we, too, long for the day of his coming.

• Much of the Second Letter to the Thessalonians is concerned with the delay of the Lord's coming. What advice does Saint Paul give to the hessalonians in today's reading in view of this delay?

• When we proclaim the mystery of faith at Eucharist, we pray for Christ's coming in glory. What does this mean to you?

• Who has shown you a way to live as though imitating Christ?

READING I *2 Samuel 5:1–3*

In those days, all the tribes of Israel came to David in Hebron and said: "Here we are, your bone and your flesh. In days past, when Saul was our king, it was you who led the Israelites out and brought them back. And the LORD said to you, 'You shall shepherd my people Israel and shall be commander of Israel.'" When all the elders of Israel came to David in Hebron, King David made an agreement with them there before the LORD, and they anointed him king of Israel.

READING II *Colossians 1:12–20*

Brothers and sisters: Let us give thanks to the Father, who has made you fit to share in the inheritance of the holy ones in light. He delivered us from the power of darkness and transferred us to the kingdom of his beloved Son, in whom we have redemption, the forgiveness of sins.

He is the image of the invisible God,/the first-born of all creation./ For in him were created all things in heaven and on earth,/the visible and the invisible,/whether thrones or dominions or principalities or powers;/all things were created through him and for him./He is before all things,/and in him all things hold together./He is the head of the body, the church./He is the beginning, the first-born from the dead,/that in all things he himself might be preeminent./For in him all the fullness was pleased to dwell,/and through him to reconcile all things for him,/making peace by the blood of his cross/through him, whether those on earth or those in heaven.

GOSPEL *Luke 23:35–43*

The rulers sneered at Jesus and said, "He saved others, let him save himself if he is the chosen one, the Christ of God." Even the soldiers jeered at him. As they approached to offer him wine they called out, "If you are King of the Jews, save yourself." Above him there was an inscription that read, "This is the King of the Jews."

Now one of the criminals hanging there reviled Jesus, saying, "Are you not the Christ? Save yourself and us." The other, however, rebuking him, said in reply, "Have you no fear of God, for you are subject to the same condemnation? And indeed, we have been condemned justly, for the sentence we received corresponds to our crimes, but this man has done nothing criminal." Then he said, "Jesus, remember me when you come into your kingdom." He replied to him, "Amen, I say to you, today you will be with me in Paradise."

Practice of Prayer

Psalm 122:1—2, 3—4, 4—5 (see 1)

R. Let us go rejoicing to the house of the Lord.

I rejoiced because they said to me,
　　"We will go up to the house of the LORD."
And now we have set foot
　　within your gates, O Jerusalem.　R.

Jerusalem, built as a city
　　with compact unity.
To it the tribes go up,
　　the tribes of the LORD.　R.

According to the decree for Israel,
　　to give thanks to the name of the LORD.
In it are set up judgment seats,
　　seats for the house of David.　R.

Practice of Faith

Our calendar year usually doesn't end quietly. We throw parties, set off firecrackers, and ring bells to send the old year forth and welcome the new year, with its opportunities for growth. Do we feel a sense of celebration and anticipation as our church year comes to an end this weekend? Perhaps we should. The opportunity for new life that comes with the end of one church year and the beginning of another holds more promise than a resolution to quit smoking or lose twenty-five pounds. Through his death and resurrection, Christ the King offers us the same hope he offered to the repentant thief—endless joy with him in Paradise. The new church year will offer us countless opportunities to grow in faith, hope, and charity. In what ways will we resolve to live as the people of God in the coming year?

Scripture Insights

What an inglorious Gospel is set before us on this Feast of Christ the King. Jesus, executed as a criminal, sneered, jeered, and reviled by those around him. A man accursed, mockingly called "The King of the Jews" as he dies upon the cross.

Luke is the lone evangelist recording the dialogue between Jesus and the "repentant" criminal. Acknowledging Jesus' kingship, the criminal begged to be remembered in the kingdom. The parallel between kingdom and Paradise is important. Jesus' kingdom *is* Paradise.

The Greek word used in Luke's text (*paradeisos*), meaning an enclosed garden, is the same word used of the Garden of Eden. In some Jewish religious writings not found in the canon of scripture, Paradise is where the righteous dwell after death. The criminal who acknowledged his wrongdoing and professed Jesus' kingship was reckoned as righteous—by Jesus.

We find that Jesus and the repentant criminal entered into the kingdom—and Paradise—on the day of their deaths. "Today, you will be with me in Paradise." The cross, though a hideous and shameful death, was the means of Jesus' passing over into the full realization of his kingdom.

Through his death, Jesus has delivered us from the powers of darkness and brought about our reconciliation, restoring to wholeness all that had ruptured. This is the reality into which we have been initiated through our baptismal anointing. Let us never lose sight of the inheritance that is ours even now, that one day, we too, may be with him in Paradise.

◆ What connections can you find between today's responsorial Psalm 122 and the other readings?

◆ How can an experience of failure or loss in our lives become an occasion of transformation?

◆ Do you think it took courage for the repentant thief to rebuke the others? Or do you see another virtue in that criminal?

Information on the License to Reprint from At Home with the Word 2007

The low bulk rate prices of *At Home with the Word 2007* are intended to make quantities of the book affordable. Single copies are $8.00 each; 5–99 copies, $7.00 each; 100 or more copies, $6.00. We encourage parishes to buy quantities of this book.

However, Liturgy Training Publications makes a simple reprint license available to parishes that would find it more practical to reproduce some parts of this book. Scripture Insights, Practice of Faith, Hope, or Charity, prayers titled Preparation for the Word and Thanksgiving for the Word, and lists of Weekday Readings may be duplicated for the parish bulletin or reproduced in other formats. These may be used every week or as often as the license-holder chooses.

The license granted is for the period beginning with the First Sunday of Advent—December 3, 2006—through the solemnity of Christ the King—November 25, 2007.

Please note that the license does *not* cover scripture readings or psalms (Practice of Prayer) from the Lectionary. See the acknowledgments page at the beginning of this book for the name of that copyright owner.

The materials reprinted under license from LTP may not be sold, may not be used in connection with any program or event for which a fee is charged, and may be used only among the members of the community obtaining the license. The license may not be purchased by a diocese for use in its parishes.

No reprinting may be done by the parish until the license is signed by both parties and the fee is paid. Copies of the license agreement will be sent on request. The fee varies with the number of copies to be reproduced on a regular basis:

Up to 100 copies: $100
101 to 500 copies: $300
501 to 1000 copies: $500
More than 1000 copies: $800

For further information, call the reprint permissions department at 773-486-8970, ext. 261, or fax your request to 773-486-7094, att: reprint permissions.